Napoleon III
and the Stoffel Affair

Roger L. Williams

Napoleon III and the Stoeffel Affair

High Plains Publishing Company

Copyright ©1993 by
Roger L. Williams
All rights reserved. No part of this book may be reproduced in any form
without permission in writing from the publisher.

Library of Congress Catalog Card Number 93-77109
ISBN 1-881019-03-9 (cloth)

Frontispiece. From the portrait of the aging Napoleon III by an unknown photographer. The author bought this photograph more than thirty-five years ago as a curiosity in Bairritz and only later discovered the same pose had served as the model for a painting in the possession of Dr. Mercier des Rochettes entitled *Napoleon III on the Terrace of the Villa Eugénie*. This villa was the imperial residence at Bairritz, usually in the month of September, where Captain Stoffel first met the emperor.

High Plains Publishing Company, Inc.
Post Office Box 1860
Worland, Wyoming 82401

Contents

Preface	vii
List of Personages	xi
I. The Swiss Connection	1
The Caesarian Connection	5
The Prussian Connection	11
II. Maneuvering for Military Reform	33
III. The Gadfly: Stoffel's Final Two Years in Berlin	59
IV. The Outbreak of War	81
V. The Defense of Paris	99
VI. The Bazaine Trial	121
Testimony by Witnesses at the Court-Martial	137
VII. Judicial Equivocation	165
VIII. Active Retirement	185
Sources	205
Index	215
The Author	219

Preface

Colonel Stoffel has never been entirely lost to history. One would be hard pressed to find a book on the Franco-Prussian War, or on the diplomatic origins of that war, which does not give him a sentence. He was the man who had issued *warnings* from Berlin, as military attaché, about Prussian military preparations. The failure to heed his opinions, it is said, accounted in large measure for the French defeat in 1870. Such judgments embodied truth, but were far from the whole truth.

This study began as an inquiry into the nature and quality of Stoffel's reports from Berlin. The reader will find that, in scope, they went far beyond those technical considerations one might have expected from a military attaché. Therein were sown seeds that finally flowered as the Stoffel Affair in November of 1873 when the colonel was called to testify at the court-martial of Marshal Bazaine. Stoffel would find *himself* charged with a deliberate suppression of military intelligence meant for Marshal de MacMahon in August of 1870, thereby abetting the strategy that ended in catastrophe at Sedan.

If that charge against Stoffel were to be verified, two causes would have been served. The army would have destroyed the reputation of the man who had been its critic before 1870 by sending him to prison. And, as Marshal de MacMahon had recently assumed the presidency of the Third French Republic, Stoffel's alleged treachery could serve to muffle lingering doubts about the marshal's military capacity on the route from Châlons to Sedan. Not everyone, after all, was comfortable with the idea that the capitulation of Metz had led to a trial for treason, while the capitulation of Sedan had led to the presidency of the Republic. Stoffel's guilt, if it could be proved, would cleanse MacMahon's record.

The Stoffel Affair, therefore, was never merely a military matter, but was, in that respect, a variation on those political themes that complicated the case of Marshal Bazaine, whose Bonapartist sympathies were also put on trial. The duc d'Aumale, as president of the court-martial, although generally regarded to be an honorable man, could not escape the suspicion that the interests of his family, the Orleans dynasty, could be served in the trial. And we come full circle by noting that Colonel Stoffel had been an associate of Napoleon III long before his appointment to the embassy in Berlin, remaining loyal to the imperial cause even after the emperor's death in January of 1873.

In the search for scapegoats after 1870, and in the scramble for political ascendency after the collapse of the imperial regime, Colonel Stoffel may well have become a more palatable target than Bazaine himself. Whatever one may have thought of Bazaine's conduct, only the most pathologically partisan could relish the idea of a marshal of France being capable of treason. Whereas to strike at Colonel Stoffel was close to striking at the fallen emperor himself. That Stoffel had escaped from Sedan to serve again, and with distinction in the defense of Paris, was necessarily overlooked when his day of reckoning came.

The title of this book indicates its primary focus upon Stoffel's career and its consequences. But Napoleon III will always be found in the background: from 1861 when Stoffel began to collaborate on the Emperor's *Histoire de Jules César*, until Stoffel's decision, when in retirement, to complete the historical project left unfinished in 1866. His reassignment to Berlin that year redirected their collaboration toward obtaining military reforms in France, and they were both with Marshal de MacMahon at Sedan in 1870.

Despite the warnings he issued from Berlin between 1866 and 1870, Stoffel was never anti-German. He belonged to that pre-war generation including Ernest Renan, Edgar Quinet, and Emile Ollivier, which had been impressed favorably by the surge in educational development and intellectual activity in the German world. Therein lay their hope for a more liberal civilization in the West: the idea that France, Britain and Germany would soon overcome ancient enmities and, in concert, assume the leadership of the world. Because Napoleon III had been predisposed, by his Germanic education, to such views, he became vulnerable to later and bitter charges that they had blinded him to the Prussian military menace.

The war and the Treaty of Frankfurt doomed such aspirations. Yet, in 1890, when it appeared that France and Russia might be driven into alliance to cope with events in Central Europe, Colonel Stoffel sought to revive the ideal of Franco-German unity. Settle all disputes, including the territorial, through negotiation, he recommended, and cap the settlement with a treaty of alliance. No other alliance, he believed, could give Europe stability and peace. He suspected he would not be heard on either side of the Rhine. Stoffel had had the misfortune to see his earlier prophecy confirmed. Dying in 1907, he was spared the spectacle of the outcome he feared for the twentieth century.

Let me thank the Bibliothèque du service historique du ministère de la guerre, Vincennes, most sincerely for access to critical documents bearing upon the Stoffel affair; and also gratefully acknowledge the invaluable assistance of Liliane Ziegel in obtaining that access.

A List of Personages

This list does not include every person whose name will be found on the pages of this book. There is no need to identify such major figures as Napoleon III or Bismarck. And there are lesser figures who appear only once, and who are identified then and there. The list is meant to include names that appear here and there, many of them obscure even for specialists on the Second Empire or the early Third Republic, providing an easy reference for the reader.

Abzac, marquis d', colonel: aide-de-camp to Marshal de MacMahon in 1870 and when MacMahon was President of the Republic.
Amiot, Jules-Armand-Gustave, telegrapher: supervised the telegraphic service for the Army of Châlons.
Andlau, Gaston, comte d', lieutenant-colonel: an officer in the Army of Metz who became a major critic of Bazaine.
Baraguay-d'Hilliers, Achille, comte, marshal of France: chaired the commission on capitulations beginning 1871.
Bazaine, François-Achille, marshal of France: commanded the Army of the Rhine, later the Army of Metz in 1870.
Bazelaire, student at the Ecole polytechnique: carried duplicates of dispatches from Bazaine for Colonel Turnier to Paris.
Benedek, Ludwig, Ritter von, field marshal: commander of the Austrian Army of the North in 1866.
Benedetti, Vincent, comte, career foreign service officer: ambassador to Prussia, 1864–1870.
Berthaut, Jean-Auguste, colonel, later general: early proponent of military reform; associated with the formation of the garde mobile.

Bertrand, Alexandre-Louis-Joseph archaeologist: member of the Commission de la topographie de la Gaule.

Bleichröder, Gerson, Berlin banker: managed Bismarck's personal finances.

Bourbaki (Charles-Denis Sauter), general: aide-de-camp to Napoleon III in 1869; commander of the Imperial Guard in 1870.

Broyé, Louis de, colonel: aide-de-camp to MacMahon on the Sedan campaign.

Caignart de Saulcy, Louis-Félicien-Joseph, senator: president of the Commission de la topographie de la Gaule.

Canrobert François-Certain, marshal of France: favorable to military reform after 1866.

Castelnau, Henri, general: aide-de-camp to Napoleon III; favored military reform after 1866.

Cavaignac, Louis-Eugène, general: minister of war in 1848; unsuccessful candidate for the presidency of the Second Republic, also 1848.

Chabaud-Latour, François-Henri-Ernest, baron de, general: a reservist called to active duty during the siege of Paris, where he commanded the engineering service; served on the Bazaine court-martial.

Challemel-Lacour, Paul-Armand, philosopher: collaborator with Gambetta in the campaign to found the republic.

Changarnier, Nicolas-Anne-Théodule, general: an officer of Orleanist sympathies; an opponent of military reform.

Chassepot, Antoine-Alphonse, gunsmith: developer of the French breech-loading rifle.

Chuquet, Arthur-Maxime, historian: author of *La Guerre 1870–1871*, one of the polemical postwar treatments of the subject.

Cissey, Ernest-Louis-Octave Courtot de, general: participated under MacMahon's command in the suppression of the Commune in 1871; minister of war, 1871–1873; premier and minister of war, 1874–1875.

Clappier, Alexandre-Victor-Edmond, colonel: prosecutor charged with the Stoffel court-martial, 1873–1874.

Clermont-Tonnerre, Aynard-François-Antoine-Aymé, comte de: French military attaché in Berlin, 1863–1866, replaced by Stoffel; called attention to Prussian military preparations.

Coffinières de Nordeck, Grégoire-Gaspard-Félix, general: commander of the place de Metz in 1870.

Delacroix, Alphonse, architect: in the Department of Le Doubs.

Desjardins, Ernest, classical historian: specialist in Roman antiquities.

Dollfus, Charles, Alsatian industrialist: co-founder of the *Revue germanique*.

Du Barail, François-Charles, general: minister of war, 1873–1874.

Ducrot, Auguste-Alexandre, general: critic of prewar army; assumed command of the Army of Châlons at Sedan in 1870; commanded the ill-fated sortie from Paris on 30 November 1870.

Duquet, Alfred, attorney: author of the polemical history *Froeschiller, Châlons, Sedan*, in 1880.

Failly, Pierre-Louis-Charles, general: defeated Garabaldi at Mentana in 1867; the disgraced commander of V Corps in the Army of Châlons, replaced by General Wimpffen.

Favre, Jules, Republican attorney: foreign minister in the Government of National Defense.

Fleury, Emile-Félix, general: favored military reform after 1866; ambassador to Russia 1867–1870.

Fould, Achille, financier: minister of finance 1861–1869; an opponent of military reform after 1866.

Froehner, Wilhelm, classicist: research assistant to Napoleon III.

Gambetta, Léon, attorney: Republican political leader; minister of the interior in the Government of National Defense, 1870–1871, and its most vigorous member as head of the Tours Delegation.

Gouvion-Saint-Cyr, Laurent, marshal of France: minister of war 1817–1819; responsible for revising the army from a revolutionary to a conservative force.

Gramont, Antoine-Alfred-Agénor, duc de, diplomat: ambassador to Austria 1861 1869; minister of foreign affairs 1870.

Guiod, Adolphe-Simon, general: favored military reform after 1866; commanded the artillery during the siege of Paris; a substitute judge for the court-martial of Bazaine.

Guyard, Augustin, commissaire de police: stationed in Longwy in 1870.

Heuzey, Léon, historian: contributed material for the work on Caesar.

Hohenlohe-Ingelfingen, Kraft Karl, Prince zu, artillery expert: commanded Prussian artillery during the siege of Paris.

Hulme, deputy-mayor of Mouzon (near Sedan): interviewed by both Napoleon III and MacMahon shortly before the battle of Sedan; testified at the court-martial of Bazaine.

Janicot, Paul-Joseph-Louis, captain: conducted the *instruction* for the Stoffel court-martial.

Krupp, Friedrich, Rhenish Prussian industrialist: advocate of the steel guns developed at his foundry in Essen.

Lachaud, Charles-Alexandre, Bonapartist defense attorney: engaged for both the defense of Bazaine and Stoffel.

Ladmirault, Paul de, general: governor of Paris commanding the First Military Division in 1874 when the Stoffel case was dismissed.

Lamoricière, Louis-Christophe-Léon Juchault de, general: minister of war in 1848; active opponent of Louis-Napoleon Bonaparte.

La Motte-Rouge, Joseph-Edouard, comte de, general: summoned from retirement by the Tours Delegation to command XV Corps at Orléans, a brief and unhappy tenure; member of the Bazaine court-martial.

Leboeuf, Edmond, marshal of France: minister of war 1869–1870; briefly major general of the Army of the Rhine 1870 before giving way to Bazaine.

Lebrun, Barthélemy-Louis-Joseph, general: favorable to military reform after 1866; aide-de-camp to Napoleon III 1869; commander of XII Corps at Sedan.

MacMahon, Marie-Edme-Patrice-Maurice de, duc de Magenta, marshal of France: commander of the Army of Châlons 1870; President of the Republic 1873–1879.

Marescalchi, lieutenant: the missing witness at the Bazaine court-martial.
Martineau-Deschenez, Gaston-Philippe-Augustin, baron, general: commanded a division in the Army of the Loire; member of the Bazaine court-martial.
Massaroli, colonel: commander of the post at Longwy 1870.
Maury, Louis-Ferdinand-Alfred, classicist and academician: librarian of the Tuileries; research assistant to Napoleon III.
Mérimée, Prosper, writer and academician: an intimate of the imperial family.
Miès, Frédéric, police agent: employed by Stoffel to obtain intelligence from Bazaine.
Moltke, Helmuth Carl Bernhard, Graf von, field marshal: chief of the general staff of the Prussian Army beginning in 1858; chief of the general staff of the army at the headquarters of His Majesty the King 1870; resigned as German chief of staff in 1888.
Nefftzer, Auguste, Protestant journalist: editor of *Revue germanique* and of *Le Temps*.
Niel, Adolphe, marshal of France: military reformer after 1866; minister of war 1867–1869.
Ollivier, Emile, attorney: liberal Republican converted to liberal Bonapartist; chief minister in the Government of 2 January 1870; author of the monumental *L'Empire libéral*.
Oppermann, Auguste, retired military: research assistant to Napoleon III with the title maréchal des logis de l'empereur.
Orléans, Henri-Eugène-Philippe-Louis d', duc d'Aumale, general: president of the court-martial that tried Bazaine.
Pajol, Eugène, general: aide-de-camp to Napoléon III 1870.
Palikao, Charles Cousin de Montauban, comte de, general: conservative Bonapartist; minister of war for 24 days 1870.
Passy, Frédéric, liberal political economist; founder of the Ligue de la paix.
Pernet, Victor, archaeologist: first director of the dig at Alise-Sainte Reine 1861.
Perrot, Georges, historian: contributed material for the work on Caesar.
Picquart, Georges, general: minister of war 1906–1909.
Piétri, Franceschini: personal secretary to Napoleon III, and to the Empress Eugènie after the emperor's death in 1873.
Pourcet, Joseph-Auguste-Jean-Marie, general: prosecutor (commissaire du gouvernement) in the Bazaine trial.
Quicherat, Jules, archaeologist: professor at the Ecole des chartes.
Quinet, Edgar, philosopher, historian, and poet: a liberal with pro-German views.
Rabasse, Achille-Napoléon, police agent: employed by Stoffel to obtain intelligence from Bazaine.
Randon, Jacques-Louis-César-Alexandre, marshal of France: minister of war 1859–1867; removed as an opponent of military reform.
Reinach, Joseph, attorney and political writer: an associate of Gambetta; a leading Dreyfusard; brother of Salomon and Théodore.
Reinach, Salomon, classicist: reviewed Stoffel's historical volumes.
Renan, Ernest, philologist and historian: a liberal with pro-German views.
Renson, General: a close associate of General de Cissey; head of the personnel division in the ministry of war; enjoyed the confidence of President MacMahon.

Rivières, Raymond-Adolphe Séré de, brigadier-general: In charge of the *instruction* for the court-martial of Bazaine 1872–1873.

Robert, Pierre-Joseph, colonel, later general: published anonymously *La Second Campagne de 1870* jusqu'au ler septembre, par un officier de l'armée du Rhin; a severe critic of MacMahon.

Rossignol, Jean-Pierre, classicist: at the Collège de France.

Rouher, Eugène, attorney: conservative Bonapartist; minister of state 1863–1869; opposed military reform after 1866; mission to Châlons 1870.

Rousset, Léonce, lieutenant-colonel: author of the first substantial history of the Franco-Prussian War in French, *La Second Campagne de France*, in six volumes.

Saisset, Théodore, admiral: commander of the naval personnel in Paris during the siege.

Schmitz, Isidore-Pierre, general: a close associate of Trochu both before and during the siege of Paris.

Sheridan, Philip Henry, American general: a witness to the Franco-Prussian War from the German side; present at Sedan.

Thiers, Louis-Adolphe, historian: Orleanist statesman; chief of the executive power 1870–1873.

Tissot, Charles-Joseph, historian: contributed material for the work on Caesar.

Tripier, Emile-Jules-Gustave, general: an engineering officer brought out of retirement for duty on the defense works of Paris; member of the Bazaine court-martial.

Trochu, Louis-Jules, general: *author of L'Armée française en 1867*; governor of Paris 1870 and head of the Government of National Defense.

Turnier, colonel: commander of the post at Thionville 1870.

Vaillant, Jean-Baptiste-Philibert, marshal of France: minister of war 1854–1859.

Vaulgrenant, commandant, later general: testified during *instruction* for the Stoffel court-martial.

Vuitry, Adolphe, attorney: minister-president of the council of state 1864–1870.

Waru, Paul Laurens de, lieutenant, later general: assistant to Stoffel at the Camp de Châlons 1870.

Welschinger, Henri, archivist: author of *La Guerre de 1870, causes et* responsabilités, 1910.

Wimpffen, Emanuel-Félix de, general: employed by General Palikao to interfere with the direction of the Army of Châlons 1870; became responsible for signing the terms for the surrender of Sedan.

Zurlinden, Emile-Auguste, general: minister of war 1895; author of *La Guerre de 1870–1871, réflexions et souvenirs*, 1904.

Part I

The Swiss Connection

Our subject, Eugène-Georges-Henri-Céleste Stoffel, was born in Paris on 14 March 1821, the first member of his family to be a native-born Frenchman. The family home was Arbon, in the canton of Thurgau on Lake Constance, a small community where three-quarters of the population was Protestant. The Stoffels had long been the leading Catholic family within the minority. Military service had become a family tradition, often in foreign armies. In the cosmopolitan climate of a Europe before the French Revolution, such foreign service aroused little prejudice. Swiss soldiers employed abroad retained their Swiss identity and preserved their native language, expecting to return home eventually. Such an arrangement could not long survive the arousal of nationalism by the end of the eighteenth century. Henceforth, one could only legitimately serve one's own nationality.

Eugène Stoffel's grandfather, Jacob, was an officer in the Spanish Army at the time his two sons were born in Madrid. The elder, *Christoph*-Anton-Jacob, was born 19 July 1780; the younger, *Augustin*-Eugen, was born 15 November 1781. Both brothers were commissioned as lieutenants in the Spanish Army on 17 March 1798. After the death of Jacob Stoffel in 1806, Christoph resigned from the Spanish service and sought military employment in France, finally obtaining a captaincy in 1807. Augustin passed into French service in May of 1808, serving the French cause in Spain until 1813. The brothers' two service records, the skeletal remains of their professional careers, suggest that Christoph was the more fortunate of the two under Napoleon. And it may be that Spain, given the long agony of the French campaign, was an inauspicious place to win recognition.

Christoph, in contrast, was quickly rewarded. We find him, as a battalion commander, named a chevalier in the Légion d'honneur on 15 January 1809; then raised to the lowest rank in the nobility, chevalier de l'Empire, on 18 August 1810.[1] The following year, he was advanced to be officier de la Légion d'honneur, 6 April 1811. It is known that he participated in the Russian campaign and was in Moscow. Following the Battle of Leipzig, by which time he was a colonel, he was created baron de l'Empire, 20 September 1813.[2]

Both brothers remained in the army during the First Restoration of the Bourbons in 1814. Christoph was named a chevalier de St. Louis by Louis XVIII, the highest distinction traditionally conferred upon Swiss officers by the kings of France. And Augustin finally reached the Légion d'honneur on 27 December 1814 as a chevalier. It appears that both brothers were in the military escort that protected Louis XVIII during his flight from Paris after Napoleon's escape from Elba in 1815. Whether they subsequently obtained official leaves, as the records claim, may be open to doubt; for they were soon again under Napoleon's command and took part in the Waterloo campaign.

The easy reconciliation of 1814 was no longer acceptable to the Bourbon regime after the Second Restoration in 1815. The royal regiment of Swiss Guards, suppressed after their slaughter on 10 August 1792, was now reconstituted, but without those Swiss who had rallied to Napoleon. Christoph was one of the officers chosen for punishment for his collaboration. He accepted banishment and lived thereafter in Poland for several years. Others had to choose between returning to their ancestral cantons or applying for French citizenship. Some discovered, as did Augustin, that they were no longer welcome in Switzerland. He had been put on inactive duty at half-pay as a lieutenant-colonel, meanwhile, as the restored regime did not recognize his promotion to colonel during the Hundred Days. He met his dilemma by applying for French citizenship. Naturalization was granted him by royal ordinance on 11 March 1818, but he remained on inactive duty for the duration of the Bourbon regime.

Christoph Stoffel had better luck. His appeal from exile was favorably heard, and he was granted citizenship on 23 December 1817. On 27 May 1818, he was restored to active military service as a colonel, his prior rank, but never again promoted. (The spelling of his name was also Gallicized as Christophe.)

The July Revolution in 1830 led to the second suppression of the Swiss Guards and also meant the Bonapartist officers were no longer suspect. The creation of the Foreign Legion on 9 March 1831, meant for service in Algeria, provided a place for any foreigner who sought French employment. The new unit was initially stationed at Bar-le-Duc, and Colonel Christophe Stoffel took command of it in May of 1831. His knowledge of several languages other than French must have been a critical factor in the appointment. The few inspection reports that remain on the quality of his service indicate that he was a brave and capable officer, but a man not distinguished by an extensive education. His command of languages, however, was always noted as exceptional and useful. He had had two daughters by his first marriage. A second marriage in 1834 was childless. It meant that the barony would not be passed on. He retired in 1841 with a pension of 3,600 francs, but with no other private means. He died shortly thereafter, 4 July 1842, at Passy.

Augustin Stoffel, meanwhile, had been restored to active service by the July Monarchy and promoted to the rank of colonel in order to assume command of the 21st Light Infantry Regiment in 1831. He was also named officier de la Légion d'honneur on 20 April 1831. It appears that he had remained unmarried for many years while on active service, but that the leisure imposed upon him by the Bourbons had domesticated him. He took up residence with Georgette-Victoire-Elisabeth Gelinek, the widow Simon; and our subject, Eugène Stoffel, was born to them on 14 March 1821. She had been French born (5 September 1793), her father a musician of Bohemian origin. The couple did not marry until 9 October 1823.[3]

At the time of his promotion to the rank of colonel by the July Monarchy, Augustin Stoffel had petitioned to have his date of grade antedated to 28 April 1815, the moment of his promotion by Napoleon. While the appeal was granted, giving him considerable seniority in rank, he would never again be promoted. Inspection reports indicated that he served honorably and well in grade, but that he had reached his capacity. In 1833, he was given command of the place de Lille, and he was still there in 1842 when the inspector-general recommended him for the cross of commander in the Légion d'honneur. His retirement, at the age of 62, became effective on 24 December 1843.

After the death of his brother the previous year, Augustin Stoffel asserted that it had been his brother's intention to ask the king to arrange the transfer of the baronial title to his nephew, young Eugène, newly embarked upon his own military career. His brother's intentions could now be carried out, Augustin argued, by having the title conferred upon himself—to be passed on to his son. In his petition to that effect, he also asked to be recognized as the dean of the colonels in active French service.

Louis-Philippe did not act upon the petition until after Augustin's retirement; but he acted favorably, probably encouraged by reports that the son was immensely gifted and seemingly destined for great distinction. Augustin was named commandeur de la Légion d'honneur, the necessary third step before the transfer of the barony (chevalier, 27 October 1814, and officier, 20 April 1831); and by letters patents, 24 January 1844, Louis-Philippe conferred the title of *baron héréditaire* on Augustin Stoffel.[4] He survived for another ten years, dying at his residence in Versailles in 1854.[5]

Eugène Stoffel had entered the military service at the age of eighteen as a student at the Ecole polytechnique on 1 November 1839. He emerged two years later commissioned as a second lieutenant and was enrolled in the Ecole d'application de Metz on 1 October 1841 for specialized training in artillery. Upon completion of the course a year later, he was advanced in grade to lieutenant second class and assigned to his first regiment of artillery (17 January 1844). What remains of his service record suggests the slow, methodical routine of promotions and reassignments characteristic of peacetime service, until the War of 1859; and were it not for the favorable report on his qualities given to the king relative to the transfer of the barony to his father in 1844, we would have no early evidence that his was to be an exceptional career.[6] The barony passed to him after his father's death in 1854, about six months before he was promoted to the rank of captain first class (29 December 1854).

On 21 April 1859, two days before the Austrian ultimatum to Piedmont, Captain Stoffel was detached from his regiment and put at the disposition of Marshal Randon, the major general of the Army of Italy. Early in May, Stoffel was assigned to General Niel, commander of IV Corps, as an ordnance officer. The IV Corps was partially employed at Magenta, but fully and valiantly engaged at Solferino on 24 June 1859. The victory won a marshal's baton for Niel, and Captain Stoffel was made a chevalier in the Légion d'honneur the following day. (Somewhat later, 23 March 1860, he received the Medal of Military Valor from Sardinia-Piedmont.) The conflict came to an end on 12 July 1859, and Captain Stoffel was reassigned to his regiment in mid-August.[7]

One of the few surviving reports on Stoffel's professional conduct dates from August of 1860, the rating having been made by the colonel commanding the 15th Regiment of Artillery at Auxonne and by an officer from the inspector-general's department. The rating was superior in every possible respect: in health, appearance, and moral conduct; in the breadth of his general education; in his aptitude for continuing study and learning, and his knowledge of spoken German. He was said to be at once an energetic and excellent subordinate, and a very good battery commander, effective with his own subordinates. His decorations were noted, as was the fact that, at thirty-nine, he was still unmarried,[8] his status for the remainder of his life.

The Caesarian Connection

The reference to Stoffel's continuing scholarship by the inspector-general indicated knowledge of an historical article which Stoffel had published that very month. He had, in effect, thrust himself into an academic controversy of several years duration concerning Julius Caesar's conquest of Gaul. This called him inadvertently to the attention of Napoleon III, who, by 1860, had plans of his own to write something major on that topic: a history of Julius Caesar. At some point before that date, the emperor had read the *Précis des guerres de César*, as dictated by Napoleon I to his valet, Louis Marchand, on St. Helena, and first published by Marchand in 1836. Having always been driven to develop the written rationale for a Napoleonic empire, Napoleon III was moved to complete the fragment left by the revered uncle. As one of his research assistants would later explain, "One must always seek out the great Emperor as the hidden motor behind his nephew's initiatives."[9]

As for the scholarly dispute of that moment, it concerned the correct location of Alesia, the battleground where Caesar had defeated the Gauls under Vercingetorix in 52 B.C. Until 1855, no one had doubted that the site was on Mont-Auxois in old Burgundy, near the town of Alise-Sainte-Reine, now in the department of Côte-d'Or. This consensus was shattered on 10 November 1855 when Alphonse Delacroix, an architect and a member of the Société d'émulation du Doubs, declared the site to have been near the village of Alaise in old Franche-Comté, twenty-five kilometres south of Besançon in the department of le Doubs. His assertion was based upon his study of Caesar's *Commentaries*. Several eminent scholars rallied to his view, notably Ernest Desjardins, the historian of antiquity; and Jules Quicherat, a professor at the Ecole des chartes and one of the important archaeologists of that day. The latter's publications in 1856 and 1857, in fact, made him the chief defender of what came to be called the Comtoise thesis.

The traditional site had its defenders, too, notably Jean-Pierre Rossignol, a classical scholar at the Collège de France; but the scholars were soon eclipsed by the intrusion of notables whose motives transcended scholarship. Writing anonymously in the *Revue des deux mondes* of 1 May 1858, Henri d'Orléans, the duc d'Aumale, not only disputed the recent interpretation but took the opportunity, with all due respect to Caesar, to express his preference for

Vercingetorix as a fighter for Gallic liberties against Caesar. The author's identity was quickly and widely known.

Napoleon III's only public response was a decree of 17 July 1858, which created the Commission de la topographie de la Gaule. He put ten men on the commission, but only four of them ever took an active part in its work: its president, Senator Louis-Félicien-Joseph Caignart de Saulcy; Major Raymond Coynart; Alexandre-Louis-Joseph Bertrand; and General Casimir Creuly. The question about Alesia became the most important problem among those the commission undertook to resolve. The accidental uncovering of some bronze artifacts by a landowner near Alise-Sainte-Reine in the autumn of 1860 helped to convince the commission that the traditional site was the proper place to begin excavations. Only later was it recognized that the objects did not date from Caesar's period; so that the excavations were, in fact, pursued on the basis of false evidence, yet were ultimately successful.[10]

The active members of the commission, all of whom had had archaeological training, reached Alise-Sainte-Reine on 20 April 1861. They hired a team of workers and gave the direction of the dig to Victor Pernet. The project clearly required active professional supervision from the archaeologists on the commission, from Alexandre Bertrand in particular, the most eminent among them; but the commissioners all had duties elsewhere and visited the site with increasing irregularity. In later years, Bertrand would assert that the emperor had abruptly, and without reason, discharged the commission in 1862. It has since become evident that the commission members, with the possible exception of Saulcy, had abandoned their task by that date. The emperor soon reached the not unreasonable conclusion that he would have to put an individual in charge in whom he had full confidence.

He had visited the site unannounced on 19 June 1861, coming by train. His small party included Saulcy, Prosper Mérimée, and the historian Alfred Maury, one of the scholars chosen to assist His Majesty for a history of Julius Caesar. Mérimée, long an intimate of the imperial family, had already provided the emperor with an extensive outline for that project. The visit gave the local villagers immense satisfaction, but in their excitement they did not forget to voice local hopes that the artifacts recovered from the site would be housed in Alise, not sent off to Paris as they feared. The plea forced the emperor for a time to consider establishing a museum at Alise; but the national importance of the material led him, ultimately, to found the Musée gallo-romain by decree on 8 November 1862, the establishment later known as the Musée des Antiquités Nationales, located in the château de Saint-Germain-en-Laye.

The citizens of Alise were compensated with a heroic statue of Vercingetorix commissioned by the emperor and executed by the now-forgotten Burgundian sculpter, Aimé Millet, which was placed on Mont-Auxois. Its pedestal was designed by Viollet-le-Duc, another imperial intimate. The emperor declined to inaugurate the monument, saying that the ceremony should be postponed until the archaeological work had been completed and the site restored to a proper state. In fact, he never again visited the site, and the circumstances he anticipated never came to pass in his lifetime.[11]

Shortly after his visit in June of 1861, however, the emperor and his court took up residence in Biarritz for the annual autumn sojourn. He had noticed—as had members of the commission—Captain Stoffel's clear and concise article in the *Moniteur* of 6-7 August 1860 favoring the traditional Alise site. On 7 September 1861, the colonel commanding the 15th Regiment of Artillery stationed at Auxonne received orders from the ministry of war to detach Stoffel immediately and send him at once to Biarritz. He would take orders directly from His Majesty, who meant to assign him research on certain aspects of Caesar's campaigns.[12] For the courtiers, accustomed to a jolly September in Biarritz, life became boring and sad, with the emperor and Captain Stoffel continually occupied with the life of Julius Caesar.[13]

As Stoffel himself later explained, Caesar, if appreciated for the clarity of his style, usually omitted the manner of detail that the modern mind requires, a factor which Napoleon III had recognized at the outset of his own work, especially when the military campaigns were concerned. Events were usually undated, as were the dispatch or the reception of his orders and the movement of troops. He frequently omitted place names, and his battles were not given a name. Historians, subsequently, had not always agreed on the modern equivalents for ancient sites, as in the recent dispute over Alesia. Stoffel, who had been a student of classical warfare, also brought to that dispute the expertise of an artillery officer on terrain and sites. Napoleon III saw him as an ideal research assistant on geographical matters in particular. The field research would occupy Stoffel from 1862 into 1866. When actual publication began, the emperor included a resumé of Stoffel's inspection of battle sites.[14]

Stoffel was quite aware that the circumstances under which he engaged in research were enviable. He was promoted to the grade of major early in 1862, and his official capacity was described as ordnance officer to His Majesty.[15] The material resources available to him were unlimited, and his titles made him welcome everywhere. He had, in short, the means to undertake excavations of numerous battlefields, sometimes employing several hundreds of workers; and his discoveries were put in the form of reports to the emperor.[16] Stoffel took charge of the site at Alise in August of 1862 and was, thus, in charge when the controversial silver vase of Alise was uncovered in September. He took the still uncleaned vase to Biarritz, giving it to the emperor in the presence of Prosper Mérimée.

As Stoffel was an improvised archaeologist, he was vulnerable to the charge that he was a fraud; and as the find seemed to honor his archaeological flair, it aroused a flood of malicious rumors, among them the story that Stoffel had bought the vase in Paris. As Stoffel did not publish anything relating to the actual dig at Alise, such stories were not at once refuted and probably contributed to those suspicions about his character that would be revived in 1873. The story of the excavation at Alise only reached print through articles by Victor Pernet in 1906 and 1907 (the original director of the dig), when work on the site had been resumed. A worker known to us as Gros-Lapipe, who had been reengaged for the revival, recalled being present when the vase had been removed from the soil in 1862. The piece was eventually displayed at the museum in Saint-Germain-en-Laye and is still regarded to be authentic.[17]

Senator Saulcy, the president of the original commission, was not among the jealous rumormongers. Salomon Reinach, when preparing an obituary on Stoffel in 1907, discovered correspondence between Saulcy and Stoffel in 1864 that reflected a friendly collaboration in regard to the excavation.[18] Aside from the fact that Saulcy was fourteen years older than Stoffel, the two had much in common that set them apart from the professional scholars who invented the spiteful gossip. Both had passed through the same military schools; both had been commissioned as artillery officers; both had devoted leisure time to classical studies; and both, as amateurs, had ventured to publish in that field. Saulcy's appointment to the Senate in 1854 was public acknowledgment of his loyalty to Napoleon III; whereas the academic world, in general, remained unreconciled to the restoration of Empire. Intellectual discourse, in other words, infrequently escaped the intrusion of academic politics.

Once Major Stoffel undertook supervision of the site at Alise, a military tone and a greater rigor were immediately evident. He could not be present at the site at all times, but his visits were considerably more frequent than those of the commissioners he had replaced. And even the emperor on occasion sent down instructions in the hand of his secretary, Franceschini Piétri, to Millot, the engineer on the project. The modern verdict has been that Stoffel and his staff did their work well so far as it went, but the project was not completed. By 1865, Stoffel was largely occupied with the preparation of plates for the emperor's book. Before the end of that year, Pernet and Millot paid off all the workers as well as the final indemnities owed to property owners for damages to cultivated lands. The operation was closed down, not to be reopened until after the turn of the century. After the publication of the *Histoire de Jules César* (1865–66), the emperor had copies sent to both Pernet and Millot. Both men retained a great pride in their work for the rest of their lives as Pernet would attest forty years later.[19]

As for the preparation of the life of Caesar, Major Stoffel's contribution was chiefly geographical information based upon fieldwork. In Paris, especially during the first several years of research and composition, the emperor's principal assistant was Louis-Ferdinand-Alfred Maury, who carried the title librarian of the Tuileries. Maury was a very learned man, especially in ancient religions, and he had already been elected to the Académie des Inscriptions et Belles-lettres. In 1863, when a vacancy existed in the Académie française, and when the first volume of the book was in proof, the emperor thought the moment had come to advance his own candidacy for the seat. Perhaps he thought to seek reconciliation with the academics; probably he sought recognition for his *Histoire de Jules César*. Maury pursuaded him to wait until the work was entirely finished, assuring him of an election which, in fact, never came.[20]

Even though Maury was the specialist most frequently consulted, he was supremely long-winded, a defect that could vex the emperor. That may account for the employment of an additional assistant, Wilhelm Froehner, at the beginning of 1863. Froehner was told, at the time of his appointment, that the emperor required a Latin scholar who could read treatises in German, somewhat surprising in that Napoleon III knew German perfectly well. Froehner, born in Karlsruhe and trained at the University of Bonn, had come to Paris in 1859 at the age of twenty-five to find work in libraries and museums, his ultimate aspiration being a position at the Louvre. Such employment was still possible for a foreigner as the Louvre was then a crown property, not yet administered by the state, but supported from the civil list through the Maison de l'Empereur. Froehner, who was really a classicist, finally reached the Louvre early in 1862. His employer, comte de Nieuwerkerke, holder of the unfortunate title superintendent of fine arts, recommended him to the emperor when the need for a German reader became known. The emperor offered him 500 francs a month beyond the salary he drew at the Louvre.

At the time that Froehner was summoned for assistance, the material for the first volume of the work had already been printed in proof so that corrections did not have to be made from manuscript, a luxury perhaps available only to sovereigns. It would appear that Froehner's primary task was to help the emperor with the correction of proof. He routinely went to the Tuileries every evening, even on Sundays; and they began work after dinner about nine o'clock, often working past midnight. It quickly became clear to Froehner that most of the necessary corrections derived from the limitations of the emperor's schoolboy Latin. While he read the language, he did not have the scholar's more sophisticated knowledge of it. Even when the court moved to

Fontainebleau for a few weeks in June, the emperor continued work there on his corrections, bombarding Froehner with questions by official telegraph at least once a day.

An ex-cavalryman named Auguste Oppermann, about whom little is known, was also counted within the coterie of the emperor's assistants. An Alsatian, born in 1808, he became known to the emperor as a passionate collector of ancient coins and art objects. In 1859 he was made maréchal des logis de l'empereur, a post he held until 1870. Stoffel, Froehner, and Oppermann became—and would remain—firm friends and colleagues, held together by mutual regard and personal devotion to the emperor. They also enjoyed the confidence of Piétri, the emperor's personal secretary, who could therefore serve them as a transmitter of unofficial information. Alfred Maury, the librarian, while he gave faithful service on the project, apparently kept some distance between the others and himself, perhaps conscious of his distinction as an academician. The emperor, always a man of great reserve, could be highly congenial without becoming intimate. He was well-known to be an enthusiastic handshaker, a habit he had formed during his exile in England. But he came to a point with Froehner of extending only his index finger, a deliberate but tacit sign of favor. Stoffel, of them all, was the least reserved: bluff and outspoken, described by Froehner as a bit *gascon*, meaning inclined to boast, qualities that would not always serve him well in later years.

The first two volumes of the *Histoire de Jules César*, published in 1865 and 1866 respectively, ended with the crossing of the Rubicon. The results of the battle of Sadowa, 3 July 1866, brought work on the third volume to a virtual halt. His Majesty no longer studied the campaigns of Caesar, but rather the means of assuring, like Caesar before him, the frontier of the Rhine. Froehner discovered that the maps of Gaul, which had covered the walls of the emperor's office, had been replaced with maps of Germany. The nightly routine had to be terminated, and he saw the emperor infrequently henceforth. Knowing that the two volumes had been based upon much research and enormous documentation, Froehner was distressed by the indifference or disdain displayed by most French writers, Mérimée being a notable exception. But Froehner may not have entirely understood that the rejection was a matter of politics.[21]

The Prussian Connection

It has long since been established that the swift victory of Prussia over Austria in 1866 upset the general expectation of a lengthy, and perhaps inconclusive, war. The French military, in particular, had emerged from the War of 1859 with a pronounced respect for the skill and tenacity of the Austrians, so that the relative ineffectuality of the Austrians in 1866 was quite unanticipated. By the great majority, that is, for an occasional officer had already warned that the development of the Prussian military system was impressive; and others had perceived that the inadequacies of the French system in 1859 had greatly contributed to the appearance of Austrian strength. The French military attaché in Berlin from 1863 to 1866, Major Aynard-François-Antoine-Aymé, comte de Clermont-Tonnerre, clearly advised his government on Prussian progress. As for the War of 1859, the shortages of essential materiel, the reliance upon improvisation, and the mediocrity of the senior French officers was apparent to at least a few of the participants. The official histories of the campaign concealed the facts by focusing on French courage and élan; much documentary evidence of the deficiencies was deliberately destroyed, evidently on the order of the minister of war, Marshal Jacques-Louis-César-Alexandre Randon (1859-67); while the victory itself argued for the adequacy of the French system.[22]

When the deficiencies were fatally exposed in the Franco-Prussian War of 1870, questions about responsibility were raised within a climate that was anything but dispassionate. Whatever may have been the evidence brought to light through official inquiries or by independent writers, the immediate popular verdict, which was sustained well into the twentieth century, was that Napoleon III had wanted the war that he had done nothing to prepare for.[23] His defeat in battle and consequent political downfall were seen as proper retribution, but there remained scores to be settled with his associates.

The contemporary French military system had been founded by Marshal Laurent Gouvion-Saint-Cyr as minister of war in 1818 when the army was fixed at 240,000 men. That figure was to be attained through the annual conscription of 40,000 men for six-year terms. The reserve was to comprise men belonging to the levies of the ten preceding years. The Guard was preserved as the nucleus of the army, a privileged unit numbering 30,000. To become an officer, a man had to have served in the ranks and then gone through one of the military schools. Gouvion-Saint-Cyr sought a truly national army, meaning to eliminate the local character of particular units which had been a feature of the pre-revolutionary royal army. Whereas in Prussia, the system had become founded upon local military institutions: soldiers were drafted into the same units as their neighbors; quartered in the locality of their origin; and rarely moved in peacetime. Each military unit, in consequence, retained a pronounced provincial color.[24]

The basic French system was altered in 1832 when the period of service was fixed at seven years, the last two of which were on reserve. The intended five years of active service never really amounted to a full five years in practice, first of all because there was a several-months delay between conscription and actual induction into the service. Six-month furloughs were available, moreover, for soldiers able to support themselves financially and who were not committed to reenlistment as professionals. In individual cases, this could mean as little as three years of actual duty. Within the annual contingent reaching military age, those men drawing a "good number" were exonerated forever from military service, said to be the most popular feature of the Law of 1832. While that law did not provide for an official replacement system, an unofficial replacement practice was tolerated. An individual drawing a "bad number" could find and pay a substitute for his military obligation.

After the February Revolution of 1848, it was anticipated that the proclamation of universal suffrage would be logically supplemented by the democratization of the military establishment. And, on 9 June 1848, the minister of war, General Louis-Eugène Cavaignac, did announce that a new army law would include the principle of universal military obligation and elimination of the practice of replacement. When Cavaignac formed his cabinet after the June Days, he took General Louis-Christophe-Léon Juchault de Lamoricière as his minister of war, an officer also committed to the principle of universal service. His plan, as first presented to the Assembly on 8 November 1848, implemented that principle by providing for a large number of citizen reservists. Cadres from the regular army were to be detached to provide training in all of the departments. The reservists were to be called up for training for forty days during the initial year of service, but only for ten days a year during the six succeeding years of obligatory service. Meanwhile, within the parliamentary commission preparing the constitutional laws, the practice of replacement was abolished in the name of equality.

When the measure reached the Assembly in final form, Lamoricière spoke eloquently to the effect that the army, under a Republic in particular, must be the image of the nation; that it must reflect the national spirit and thought. As we know today, the great majority in the Assembly was only nominally

Republican; so that Lamoricière's appeal for a Repubican measure was ill-chosen. Adolphe Thiers led the opposition to the principle of universal military service. Obligations must be equal, he argued; but if you mean to impose the same conditions and mode of life upon people who are, in fact, quite different, you will do damage to the principle of equality. The peasant brought into the ranks of the army finds there conditions superior to what he had at home. Whereas military service is an intolerable tyranny for those destined for civilian careers. Those bourgeois who may have a taste for military life can go to military schools, become officers, and become the backbone of the army: brave, enlightened, and ambitious.

But Thiers also gave voice to an anxiety widespread among the educated in France since the days of the *levée en masse*, and which accounted for the decision in 1818 to limit the size of the army: "The society where everyone is a soldier is a barbaric society. . . . In a country where everyone is a soldier, everyone turns out badly. . . . Without specialization, the army cannot be."[25] He was interrupted at that point by Jean-Baptiste Payer from the Left who remarked that the right to die for the rich was about to become the specialty of the poor. Be that as it may, the idea of arming the nation by mobilizing the entire virile population for the field was disquieting; and Lamoricière's measure lost 663 votes to 140.

The well-to-do, therefore, could only regret that they had lost the possibility of legal replacement. While Napoleon III did not want to allow the former replacement practice, his Law of 28 April 1855, formalized replacement through official exoneration. Individuals drawing "bad numbers" could buy exemption from military service through the payment of money, usually between 2,000 and 2,500 francs. Such payments provided the state the funds for paying premiums to soldiers who agreed to reenlist for an additional seven-year term of service. The initial assumption was that the number buying exoneration would roughly equal the number of reenlistments.

The new system never worked as anticipated by the emperor. By 1855, the annual contingents available for service had been raised in steps by legislative action from 40,000 men to 100,000. During the next decade, the average number of exonerations exceeded 20,000 a year, one-fifth the annual conscription. To put the army on a war footing in 1859, the conscription was raised temporarily to 140,000 men. The exonerations that year exceeded 44,000, nearly one-third of the contingent. Reenlistments, especially during wartime, fell far short of expectations, on an average of little more than one-third the number of exonerations for that period. The army soon made it known that the older system of informal replacement was preferable, as the army wanted men, not income for the state.[26] Meanwhile, the moral objections to any or all methods of replacement were never overlooked by the political enemies of the regime.

It seems curious that a system of conscription, which exempted in perpetuity a large portion of the males reaching military age for simply drawing a "good number," did not provoke greater moral criticism on that score. The convinced democrats aside, opinion seemed to accept this apparent injustice out of the general desire to maintain the smallest and least costly army possible. It also may be that fewer males benefited from the injustice than we would be led to believe if consulting only the census figures. Pierre-André Cochut, a contemporary public administrator and a specialist on economic issues, put together a demographic profile of the military class of 1864 that he published in the *Revue des deux mondes*. This referred to male children born in France in 1843, in round numbers a total of 530,000. Even when subtracting from that number the 16,000 of them who were still-born, one might suppose that at least 80% of the class would become exempt from military service in 1864, as the annual contingent was 100,000.

The awful truth of the matter is that only 325,000, or 60% of them, were still alive in 1864. Roughly one-third of the survivors did not meet the physical requirements for active service; that is, either they were found to be of weak constitution, incapacitated, lame, deaf or blind, or they did not reach the minimum height of 1 metre 560 millimetres (5' 1-1/2"). In addition, 57,000 were exempted as the sons of widows or aged men, as only children, or on moral grounds. Cochut showed only 159,000 of the surviving 325,000 actually available for conscription, from which number had to be deducted the draft for maritime service. As Cochut also found that a number of conscripted men later broke down during their basic training, he calculated that only about 132,000 men of the class of 1864 were really fit to bear arms. The bleak demographic implications of such figures were compounded by conscripting the most vital segment of the male population at an age when it would normally be marrying.[27]

Thus, while one might argue against the development of a larger national defense, suspecting that a militarized society was incompatible with the libertarian aspirations of the French in the nineteenth century, the demographic truth of the matter was that the nation could not have then expanded the army substantially without a dramatic reduction in the physical qualifications for service (which was infeasible) and the elimination of exemptions for family reasons (which was socially and politically intolerable). Even conscripting those able-bodied who drew "good numbers" would have provided only limited improvement; but that was the only viable option should greater numbers be needed, and it implied accepting the principle of universal obligation.

Thus, until such time as the mortality rate could be immensely lowered and the state of the public health vastly improved, the issue of universal obligation was an unavoidable moral and political matter, something that the military reformers after 1866 would understand.

Not every military notable believed that greater numbers were desirable or would be needed in the future. It is not the number of men you have, the old adage went, but the number of good men, which gives the advantage in war. General Nicolas-Anne-Théodule Changarnier, the Orleanist loyalist, was known to believe that three or four corps of 60,000 men each, well-trained and well-led, could be successful against far greater numbers. The opinion was founded upon his assumption that very few generals are competent to command much larger bodies of troops efficiently. The British experience in the Iberian peninsula, a sobering episode for the French military, was the case in point most frequently cited.[28]

Napoleon III called a halt to the work on Caesar after the battle of Sadowa in 1866 to devote his attention to military reform, but the subject was not new to him. Most of his earlier recommendations had been made in the knowledge of Prussian reforms and innovations, and he had long since experienced the resistance of officers and politicians ostensibly loyal to him when urged to accept changes. He may be criticized, therefore, not for having been blind to military reality, but for failure to exercise his authority more decisively when confronted with intransigence. His decision to send Major Stoffel to Prague to gather technical information in the aftermath of Sadowa surely suggests, besides his confidence in Stoffel, reservations about the integrity of information routinely provided through regular military channels. Napoleon III had shown himself to be a shrewd politician (Bismarck would call him "an old fox") and he had to know by then that loyalty to his regime and loyalty to his person were not the same thing.

The long debate over the adoption of a breech-loading rifle for infantry provides a striking example of the emperor's readiness to temporize when meeting opposition within his entourage. The example also illustrates his persistence, no matter the opposition, when a principle or an objective had won his support. In retrospect, it is difficult to fathom the opposition of any professional soldier to the development of a breech-loading rifle. For breech-loading made rapid fire a reality for the first time; it brought to an end the era of very large calibres for portable weapons, meaning that infantrymen could henceforth carry much larger supplies of smaller-calibre rounds; and they could fire with a range and an accuracy unknown with smooth-bore muskets. In 1855, when Napoleon III lent his support to the adoption of such a weapon, it was well-known that the Prussians had been perfecting such an instrument since 1841, the Dreyse rifle or "needle-gun" (a reference to the firing-pin). The model ready by 1855 would become the rifle issued to the Prussian infantry.

That was the year a worker named Antoine-Alphonse Chassepot, an employee of the artillery shops of Saint-Thomas d'Aquin, wrote to Napoleon III to say that he had invented and built a breech-loading rifle during his spare time and wished to present it to His Majesty. Only twenty-two at the time, Chassepot had been trained at the Manufacture d'armes de Châtellerault to be a specialist in precision arms. Once he had examined the rifle, the emperor ordered one hundred more to be built for distribution to three infantry regiments for experimental use.

The early models were not perfect in operation. The combustible cartridges burned only partially; and, following the build-up of substantial débris in the chamber, jammings were frequent after thirty rounds had been fired. The story of troopers urinating in the barrels to clear them out is no myth, evidently a frequent practice no matter that steel cleaning rods (*baguettes*) had been provided by the manufacturer. As the defect was remediable through the improvement of the cartridge, the emperor pressed the army for adoption of the rifle. The Committee on Artillery, chaired by General Ducos de la Hitte, rejected the innovation on 12 January 1858, and again on 8 June 1858, as "quite unsuitable for the service." The verdict was approved by the minister of war, Marshal Jean-Baptiste-Philibert Vaillant (1854-59), on 6 July 1858.

Recognizing the conservatism of the committee and the minister, the emperor gave orders to have the weapon studied and improved. But not until 3 September 1865, when the Committee on Artillery had a new chairman, General Edmond Leboeuf, was the earlier decision reversed with an order to manufacture 1,500 pieces for experimental use. The minister of war, Marshal Randon at that moment, disallowed the order.[29] Consequently, the French did not have the Chassepot rifle at the time of the Austro-Prussian War, and got it two months after Sadowa when the emperor overrode the objections of technical committees and ministers through the decree of 30 August 1866. Known officially as the Infantry Rifle Model 1866 at the moment of its adoption, the weapon was baptized the *chassepot* in common parlance.

The Model 1866 was revolutionary for French arms beyond its introduction of a breech-loading rifle. It broke the traditional dependence upon brazed iron in favor of cast steel, made possible by the Bessemer process. It went beyond the traditional dependence upon wood and metal by utilizing a plastic part for the first time. The breech was sealed, and made gas-tight, with a ring made of vulcanized rubber. This made the *chassepot* safer and easier to fire than the Dreyse needle-gun, and gave it a longer effective range. Finally, the mass production required by the emperor's order to have 400,000 rifles available by 1 January 1868 brought an end to the day of artisanal methods for providing military armament and opened the era of industrial manufacture of arms. Neither the works at Châtellerault nor at St.-Etienne, despite immediate efforts to retool, could produce such quantities in the time given; so that subcontracts were let to a number of foreign firms. Probably as many as 50,000 of the required number were manufactured abroad. In any case, the Manufacture Nationale d'Armes de Saint-Etienne, as it functions today, can be said to have emerged from the Model 1866. The distribution of the *chassepot* to infantry regiments began in 1867, and the troops led against the Garibaldians at Mentana that November were the first to try the rifle in battle. General Charles de Failly's report to the emperor, "Sire, the *chassepots* have worked wonders," was a gratifying, if impolitic, assessment.[30]

The matter of universal military obligation was another issue on which Napoleon III had long temporized, aware that a strong majority of his senior officers favored an army of professionals. Among the papers written at Ham between 1840 and 1846, "De l'organisation militaire en France" was a clear statement favoring a military system modeled upon that of Prussia, where, in his words, the army was a great school for all citizens to learn the vocation of arms. A system, in short, which did not distinguish between the soldier and the citizen. The clinching argument, at least for Prince Louis-Napoleon Bonaparte, was that the Prussian system had been the development of a Napoleonic idea.[31]

He revived this theme in 1843, while still imprisoned at Ham, through four short articles under the heading "Projet de loi sur la recrutement de l'armée," which appeared in *Le Progrès du Pas-de-Calais*. As in the earlier piece, these articles exposed his knowledge of the contemporary Prussian Landwehr and its use, and he charged the July Monarchy with a failure to provide adequate trained reserves. The official French view of the Prussian system was that it amounted to an iron yoke imposed upon the population, a system contrary to French liberal institutions and standards. In response, he held that the Prussian system rested upon a conception of complete equality, even upon democratic principles, that belonged to France more than any other nation.

He called the contemporary French system morally deficient by comparing the Landwehr with the Garde nationale. In the former, every citizen was a soldier and armed for the defense of his country; and he characterized the Garde nationale as the middle class alone armed for the defense of private interests. The Prussian system, moreover, did not allow replacements: "You cannot buy a man if you are rich in order to avoid military service, or send out a humble man to be killed in your place." He called the replacement system, in fact, "the white slave trade." In sum, he found the Prussian organization as the only one suitable "to our democratic nature, to our egalitarian principles, and to our political situation." But he also saw the mission of the Prussian system to be the preservation of independence, not conquest.[32]

Early in his reign, the emperor moved to implement his views by drafting a decree on obligatory military service. The plan provided for regional recruitment, that is to say, for assigning recruits to regiments stationed in their native regions to facilitate rapid mobilization. He met a wall of resistance from advisers and ministers, and from the army which then assigned recruits to regiments without regard to place of origin. The military committee which reviewed and rejected the plan in May of 1853 expressed unmistakable hostility to the idea of a nation-in-arms. Colonel Louis-Jules Trochu, the committee secretary who wrote the report, put the issue succinctly: "Such an army would be a national army, and that is what it must not be. . . . The most perfect military constitution is that which creates an army whose instincts, beliefs, and customs make it a corporation distinct from the rest of the population." His report concluded with a thinly-veiled suggestion that only such an army could have been relied upon to back the coup d'état of 1851.[33]

As there could be no question of alienating the army, the emperor necessarily backed away. In late August of 1866, several weeks after he had dispatched Stoffel to Prague, His Majesty told military luncheon guests at Saint-Cloud that he had never abandoned his earlier views; and the implication was that the outcome of Sadowa would enable him to resume the offensive for universal conscription, just as it had enabled him to force the issue on the *chassepot*. His guests that day, Marshal Francois-Certain Canrobert and General Barthélemy-Louis-Joseph Lebrun, had apparently been invited in the knowledge that they had rallied to the emperor's ideas.

The two returned for lunch at Saint-Cloud on 11 September 1866 to find a slightly larger group of military guests: Marshal Adolphe Niel, General Adolphe-Simon Guiod, the Intendent-General Robert, and the emperor's aide-de-camp, General Henri Castelnau. After coffee, Castelnau read a short paper the emperor had asked him to prepare. It contained the flat prediction that, if France should find herself in the recent position of Austria, either in 1867 or in 1868, she would share Austria's recent fate. As against the 1,200,000 experienced men then available to Prussia, the French forces amounted to 288,000 men, the figure including those stationed in Algeria, Rome, and Mexico. The only feasible response to the situation, in Castelnau's opinion, was to inaugurate universal military obligation between the ages of 20 and 50. General Lebrun concurred, adding that replacement in any form should be eliminated. Marshal Canrobert also agreed, but Marshal Niel gave no indication of approval or disapproval. Before dispersing, the emperor asked each of the generals present to prepare, in writing, a recommendation for the most practical way to obtain the necessary manpower in preparation for a third meeting in Saint-Cloud he would arrange for November.

In the aftermath, the emperor had it announced that a special commission would be convoked at Saint-Cloud on 6 November 1866: all the marshals and admirals; three members of the cabinet (Rouher, Vuitry, and Fould); and Generals Trochu, Frossard, Palikao, and Lebrun. In advance of the meeting, each member of the commission was given copies of six projected plans. Two had been signed by the emperor himself, one by Marshal Vaillant, one by Marshal Niel, one by General Lebrun, and the sixth by General Guiod (who was also a councillor of state). The projects from Lebrun, Guiod, and the emperor all recommended adopting short-term obligatory service. Niel took a middle ground, proposing to double the size of the active army through the formation of a *garde nationale mobile*, which could be employed either for service on the home front or against an enemy. Marshal Vaillant, no longer on active military service but head of the Maison de l'Empereur, argued for preserving the existing system, but augmenting the annual contingents conscripted.[34]

During the interim, the court moved to Biarritz for the usual sojourn in September; there Napoleon III would receive Major Stoffel's assessment of the Austro-Prussian War. For the purposes of his mission, Stoffel had been formally attached to the French Embassy in Berlin as of 2 August 1866. Ten days later, 12 August 1866, the emperor nominated him to be officier de la Légion d'honneur,[35] either a gesture of thanks or an expression of confidence.

Stoffel had gone directly to the headquarters of Prince Frederick Charles at Prague, where he was given, for a period of three weeks, free rein to observe and to interview. He talked to officers of every rank, as well as to non-commissioned officers, privates, prisoners, and the wounded. While forthrightly admitting in his report that a three-week sojourn in Bohemia had not provided him a thorough knowledge of the Prussian army, he remained confident that he had at least detected the reasons why it had been incontestably superior to the Austrian army. Beyond his general conclusions, Stoffel focused in particular on the two matters which preoccupied Napoleon III at that moment: the merits of universal military obligation, and the utility of breech-loading rifles.

General conclusions: On the Austrian side, a mediocre instrument had been put at the disposition of a chief incapable of handling it. On the Prussian side, an instrument superior in organization and prepared long in advance, had been put in the hands of skillful commanders. Because he knew that, in France, the Prussian success was being attributed solely to the needle-gun,

Stoffel dwelt upon the superficiality of that view. He did not deny that a rifle capable of rapid fire had given the Prussians an advantage, but argued that the Austrian army would have been beaten if both armies had had the same rifle.

Stoffel's assessment of the incapacity of the Austrian commander, Ludwig, Ritter von Benedek, has since been confirmed by military historians. What has also since become clear is that Benedek had attempted to decline the command of an army new to him and on a terrain unfamiliar to him. His pessimism was reinforced by the hostility of his staff officers, who resented taking orders from a commander of middle class origin. Early in the campaign, he notified his government of the unlikelihood of victory, but was advised that a decisive battle must be fought. Therefore, instead of retreating across the Elbe, he concentrated his entire strength near Königgrätz (Sadowa) with the unfordable Elbe at his rear. Every ingredient likely to guarantee defeat, in short, contributed to the Austrian disaster on 3 July 1866.

In Stoffel's view, the differences between the contending armies reflected the differences in their political and social institutions, the character of the two peoples, their moral state, not to speak of differences in military organization. As for personnel, he found a Prussian superiority at every level in the military hierarchy, most notably in the field grade officers and the company commanders. He was surprised by their high level of instruction, not simply in military matters, but in their general education. He found them to be true professionals in the sense that they revealed a real taste for their métier and had a genuine interest in the developments within armies elsewhere. The non-commissioned officers were satisfactorily trained and, in Stoffel's opinion, superior to their French counterparts because of a better education.

As for the soldiers, the privates, what Stoffel saw only confirmed his opinion that the principle of obligatory military service was incontestably beneficial. Introducing men of background and instruction into the ranks, men from well-to-do families, had obviously augmented the intelligence and the moral worth of the fighting forces; and such men had exercised a positive influence upon soldiers coming from inferior social origins. Stoffel had no doubt that the system gave the Prussian army an element of superiority over *all* other European armies. He also recognized that the Prussians, with a more homogenous population than Austria, had derived an advantage from the unquestionable loyalty of all groups within the state; and it is true that the Austrian command had doubted the reliability of some regiments drawn from the multinational empire.

While Stoffel's task was to provide a technical explanation for the Prussian victory in 1866, one must deduce from this, and subsequent reports, that the emperor had made him understand the need for any particular information that would fortify His Majesty's campaign for military reform at home. Thus, during Stoffel's evaluation of the Prussian rank-and-file, he remarked that, whatever might be said about the qualities which distinguished the French army, it was not the best army the French could field because of the social factor that only universal obligatory service could provide. He added that a system which provided for replacements, no matter the form, violated the principle of equality, not to speak of elementary justice. "Finally, it draws the poorest and the most ignorant into the French Army, who, in times of internal troubles, as in June of 1848, are asked to fight against their own kind."[36]

The portion of the report devoted to the influence of the needle-gun went considerably beyond a technical assessment of its performance in battle. While not denying that the Prussian infantry drew notable advantages from its superior armament, Stoffel asserted that the mere possession of such a rifle was a manifestation of Prussian intellectual superiority; and therein lay the primary Prussian advantage. As for the conventional assumption after Sadowa that the rapidity of fire was the needle-gun's critical superiority, Stoffel argued that its superiority had been founded primarily upon the success that army instructors had had in convincing the soldiers that they possessed a rifle without equal. That assertion, drilled into them for more than a decade, had been supplemented with instruction on the firing range, each foot soldier being required annually to fire more than 100 cartridges. Young soldiers with no prior battle experience were given a thorough knowledge of, and confidence in, their weapons. It enabled them to perform with the coolness of battle-hardened veterans. Their courage and firmness derived from their confidence, not from the fact of rapid fire itself.

Furthermore, the Prussians recognized two modes of infantry fire: salvos, that is to say, simultaneous fire by platoons, companies, or even by battalions; and free fire, which they called rapid fire (*Schnellfeuer*). An enemy attack had generally been met with salvos, followed by free fire. But the salvos had been the more fearful and effective form of fire. Stoffel knew of no engagement where the Austrians had been able to overrun Prussian infantry at bayonet point, the tactics recommended by Benedek. The first Prussian volley would shatter the Austrian charge and produce a disorderly retreat. Only then did the rapid-fire advantage of the needle-gun, with free fire, convert the retreat into a rout, explaining the heavy losses the Austrians suffered in all engagements.

The Prussian infantry demonstrated, finally, that it could repulse Austrian cavalry without having to form into squares, a further indication of the infantryman's confidence in his weapon. Major Stoffel learned that the Prussian infantry had been taught in peacetime not to fear cavalry attacks, but to meet them in lines rather than forming into the traditional squares. The instructions had recommended allowing the enemy cavalry to approach within 200 steps; then to deliver salvo fire, followed by free fire. The tactics had worked.[37]

Stoffel sent his report of 8 September 1866 to the ministry of war as was required by his appointment as military attaché to the French embassy in Berlin. That appointment also required him to proceed to Berlin once he had completed his inquiry in Prague. He knew, to be sure, that his appointment had been arranged by Napoleon III; and that the emperor expected to read his report once it had been examined at the ministry. Aware that not everything in his report would be welcomed at the ministry of war, Stoffel had the wit to notify the emperor's secretary by personal letter that the report had been submitted. The court was by then at Biarritz, which offered the ministry a plausible explanation for failure to forward the report. "You did well to tell me about it," Piétri, the emperor's secretary, replied. After learning of the report, the emperor had waited with increasing annoyance for a number of days until finally obliged to send to Paris for it. Piétri suspected that the obligation to forward the report to His Majesty had been "overlooked" in Paris.[38]

Stoffel, apparently anticipated his mission to be a short assignment, asked for orders to return to Paris. The circumstances surrounding the reception of his report dictated otherwise. You will likely be told to stay on for some time, Piétri warned Stoffel; and in addition to the official reports you will be sending the ministry of war, political and military information will be sent *unofficially* to His Majesty. Piétri included a list of nine short questions about the Prussian Landwehr, explaining that the emperor was greatly occupied at that moment with the problem of increasing the military strength through the formation in France of a Landwehr system.

Thus it was that Stoffel would find himself unexpectedly attached to Berlin until the outbreak of war in 1870. Of the 45 reports he would send home, 39 of them would be addressed to the ministry of war, 6 of them to the emperor. But most of his unofficial letters, written to Piétri for the emperor's use, have been lost. We know of them through Piétri's letters in response, and one was found among the papers in the Tuileries after the fall of the regime.[39] Piétri eventually published his own letters (1911) as evidence of the emperor's preoccupation with military reform by 1866.

Major Stoffel meanwhile, awaiting orders to return home, had filled his time by preparing a supplementary report, which he divided into four sections: 1) "On Railroads from the Point of View of Operations." Rumors to the effect that the Prussians had employed entirely new principles in the strategic use of railroads he called much exaggerated. They had simply taken advantage of the circumstances offered them. When the First Army under Prince Frederick Charles was in Saxony, and the Second Army under the Prince Royal (Frederick) was in Silesia, they had the use of the Prussian railways as well as the line between Dresden and Breslau without any impediments. Even though Saxony had declared her neutrality at the outset of the war, the Prussians had violated that neutrality in order to use the critical rail line between Dresden and Breslau. Critical because the Prussians had no transverse line between the lines connecting Berlin-Dresden and Berlin-Breslau. By using the Dresden-Breslau rail line, troops could be shifted between Saxony and Silesia without having to make a long detour through Berlin. But from 23 June, when the First Army crossed the Saxon frontier into Bohemia and bore down upon Reichenberg, until 3 July, the beginning of the battle of Sadowa, the railroad did not play any significant role. The advancing Prussians, however, did repair the line between Reichenberg and Zittau which the retreating Austrians had cut.

In Stoffel's opinion, the most notable use of the railroad during the war had been made by the Austrians after Sadowa. Benedek has hastily gathered the remnants of his army by transporting every corps successively by train from Pardutitz to Olmutz, a movement completed by 9 July. The railroad and the bridges were then cut to facilitate a further retreat upon Vienna. The line between Olmutz and Vienna was used successfully in that retirement; but nothing unusual or unexpected occurred during the war, in his opinion, because of rail transport.[40]

2) "On Railroad Companies:" Even so, Stoffel found the Prussians to be keenly aware of the importance of rail transport. They had formed special military units called railroad companies and had trained them to repair and restore railroads to service quickly. One such company was attached to every Army Corps and put at the disposition of the Corps' chief engineering officer. The units were also responsible for the destruction of rail lines should that be necessary. Each unit numbered 71 men, drawn from engineering personnel in the army as well as from the civilian employees of the companies owning railroads. The units had proved to be efficient during the recent war, which Stoffel attributed to the quality of instruction they had received during peacetime.[41]

This led him back to the matter of education. 3) "The Advantages of Elementary Instruction in an Army:" As a consequence of the obligatory primary education in Prussia, virtually all the soldiers know how to read and write. This makes the instruction of troops easier. They come to the army susceptible to more sophisticated instructional methods than can be used in any other European army. They can be shown models, drawings, and maps. The widespread resistance to arming troops [in France] with rapid-fire rifles, he added, stems from the belief that troops would quickly exhaust their supply of cartridges, and that the rifle would soon wear out and not provide long service. Stoffel agreed that it would be wrong to arm a troop of savages with the needle-gun; but the Prussian experience had proved that the weapon can be given to troops capable of absorbing instruction. The more the soldier is enlightened, the more the rifle given to him can be used effectively.[42]

Finally, and at considerable length, Stoffel turned away from Austrian deficiencies to focus more directly upon Franco-Prussian comparisons. 4) "Lessons to be Drawn from the Study of the Prussian Army:" *Material conditions*: French soldiers are better off than the Prussian soldiers, being better housed, fed, and paid. *Disciplinary system*: The French disciplinary practices need to be reviewed for possible modification, as punishments are handed out too freely in the French army. Stoffel believed that the key was to find ways to develop a deeper sense of duty among the privates and the non-commissioned officers, thus lessening the need for so much punishment. He had found punishments to be far fewer in the Prussian army; yet, no one could accuse it of being undisciplined.

Administrative services: Stoffel believed that the French intendance (Quartermaster Corps) was better organized than the Prussian, whose performance in the recent campaign had been vastly overrated. He had learned in Bohemia that neither food supplies nor forage had kept up with the troops during the first week of the campaign, forcing them to live off the country; and he subsequently learned in Berlin that the distribution of supplies had been inadequate for the remainder of the campaign.

Medical service: Stoffel recommended an immediate study of the Prussian system, as it had evidently functioned very well. The numbers of physicians may have been insufficient, but only because the Austrians had abandoned their wounded to the enemy. The sites for field hospitals, whether at the front or at the rear, had been chosen as accessible both to running water and to railroad service. Prompt evacuation of the more advanced hospitals, always a difficult operation, had been well managed. A company of 180 stretcher-bearers had been routinely attached to each army corps to provide first aid and to transport the wounded to field hospitals. Such men were drawn entirely from the Landwehr and had been chosen because of a prior reputation for good conduct. Each medical company was divided into three sections, two of which served the two divisions in the corps, the third serving the vanguard. Each section included one officer and one physician. The men wore infantry uniforms and were armed with carbines. The French entrusted such duties in combat to their bandsmen, who had always proved to be inadequate to the task in Stoffel's view. Not infrequently, therefore, when a man had been wounded, three or four of his neighbors left ranks with the pretext of carrying him to the rear, a very undesirable procedure!

On the Intellectual Quality of the Army: Stoffel called this topic the first of the two principal keys to the organization of the Prussian army. He claimed that the intellectual quality of the army derived not merely from the advanced educational development in Prussia, but from the principle of obligatory military service which brought all the country's intellectual skills into the army without exception.

> The Prussians are notable neither for the loftiness nor the nobility of their sentiments. Greatness of soul, generosity, and engaging gifts of wit are not their property. But they possess to a very high degree solid qualities: a dedication to work, a sense of duty, perseverance, order, thrift, and obedience. Their rulers have nearly always been the incarnation of the national character. Deficient in nobility and grandeur, this people will never have a Louis XIV. Neither, it may be added, will they have a Louis XV. The Prussian army reflects the national virtues more than is the case in France or any other country.[43]

Instruction within the Prussian army, moreover, was better than that given within the French army, and he found Prussian officers generally better educated than their French counterparts. He denied the Prussians to be of superior intelligence, but emphasized the instructional opportunities in Prussia and a more serious commitment to duty. While French officers were held to be professionals, Stoffel had found most of them content to live on the knowledge they had acquired at school. Most Prussian officers continued to study long after their formal schooling. The typical Prussian garrison contained a military society, a circle where officers frequently gathered for lectures. He had learned that even the king and the royal princes participated occasionally at the meetings of the Military Society of Berlin. Stoffel was particularly sensitive to the competence in military history exhibited by officers attached to headquarters units, especially to a widespread knowledge of the memoirs of Napoleon. Even high-ranking French officers were generally unaware of their existence in Stoffel's experience.

The second of the principal keys to the organization of the Prussian army he called *The Principle of Justice and Morality*: He meant by that title the strict application of the principle of obligatory service for all citizens as the foundation of justice and morality, a contrast to the French system which permitted, upon the payment of money, "the hideous stain of replacement." Does that practice not contribute to the demoralization of the army as well as the nation itself?

> Much has been said on the subject in France by people well aware that such a traffic is morally intolerable: that nothing demoralizes a society more than to

allow the wealthy to buy their way out of civic obligations. It implies that the nation has reached a point where all duty, every obligation, is up for sale or can be bought. Must that not inevitably open a gulf between the well-to-do and the disinherited? And can an army founded upon such lack of principle be expected to enjoy the respect and esteem that is indispensable to its very existence? It is hard to describe the degree of respect that the army enjoys in Prussia; and it can only be explained by the fact that universal military service has, in effect, merged the army with the nation.[44]

Once these criticisms had been dispatched to the ministry of war, Major Stoffel devoted his next report to those questions about the Landwehr directed to him by order of the emperor. His Majesty wished to know how Landwehr officers were chosen and appointed. They come from two sources, Stoffel replied, the major source being from men called Annual Volunteers. In the Prussian system of universal military obligation, any man wishing to serve only one year of active service (instead of the normal three-year term) must appear before his regional examination committee. He must prove, either by producing a certificate of competence or by submitting to an examination, that he possesses a particular skill needed by an established service in the army. Those most apt to qualify are young men who have specialized in a science or an art, or who have been practicing their métier in a shop or factory where their skills are essential to its operation. The local committee may issue a certificate of eligibility for one-year service, whether as a line soldier, an army doctor, as a veterinarian, or as a pharmacist, several examples of desirable vocations.

Such an individual will enjoy considerable freedom in his choice of military career and regiment, even being free to choose which year (between the ages of 21 and 24) he will serve. But he will also have the obligation to clothe, equip, feed, and lodge himself, at his own expense, for that year. Weapons are furnished him by the unit he enters. No company or squadron may accept more than 4 one-year volunteers, and an officer in every battalion is responsible for their training. Stoffel was told that there had been about 2,000 such volunteers annually before 1866. [But the number would rise to 12,000 by 1868 in the army of the North German Confederation.][45]

After the first six months of training, those volunteers who have shown particular dedication or intelligence are marked for commendation. But all volunteers, at the end of the year, are tested on their practical and theoretical knowledge. Those judged to be capable of exercising a lieutenant's duties are so certified, and they are further tested during several weeks of exercises with either Landwehr or regular troops. Those still found to be meritorious are promoted to be non-commissioned officers, and they may then be nominated by their battalion to a lieutenancy, subject to approval by the king. Roughly one-third of the Annual Volunteers survived all tests to become officers in the Landwehr.

Stoffel added that it was possible for regular army officers to request transfer in grade to the Landwehr. The option applied to lieutenants and captains who had reached the age of 27. In practice, most applications came from cavalry officers who were landed and well-to-do and who were anxious to manage their estates themselves.

Major Stoffel found that military opinion in Prussia was divided as to the merits of those officers produced by the annual volunteer system. The dilemma was caused in part by the need for strict economy within the entire military system. As a matter of policy, a deliberate shortage of officers in the regular army had been maintained. It could mean, for example, the assignment of four officers to a company instead of five. The circumstances obviously required that an additional supply of company-grade officers be found for the Landwehr. The shortages had not been critical in peacetime, but became so with the formal mobilization in 1866. Not only were field-grade officers transferred to command the Landwehr battalions, but a substantial number of regular lieutenants were transferred to the Landwehr companies to guarantee greater stability and firmness.

The debate after Sadowa revealed a difference of opinion as to whether the dislocation within the regular officer ranks had been offset by the contributions of the Landwehr to the victory. Stoffel had met several officers who had commanded battalions of Landwehr in the late war, and who said that the one-year volunteer officers, with a few exceptions, had shown themselves not well qualified for an officer's duties. Most Prussian officers to whom Stoffel talked argued that the presence of regular line officers within the Landwehr had provided a firmness equal to that of the regular companies. Stoffel implied in his report that the economy to be derived from maintaining reservists such as the Landwehr need not compromise military effectiveness.[46]

Napoleon III had also asked how non-commissioned officers were recruited for the Landwehr. From three sources Stoffel replied: Non-commissioned officers leaving the regular forces sometimes chose to continue service in the Landwehr. But every company within the regular army selected two privates during their third year of obligatory service for special training to become non-commissioned officers in the Landwehr at the end of their term in the army. Privates within the Landwehr, finally, who demonstrate particular aptitude, can be promoted.

In responding to a question about how cadres were provided for the Landwehr, Stoffel again illustrated the economy of the Prussian system. In 1866, the Landwehr had comprised 32 infantry regiments, 4 regiments of guards, and 12 squadrons of cavalry. None of them possessed permanent cadres or headquarters troops, the rationale being that such units are really on leave. Each battalion was provided with an armory administered by a regular army officer with a very small staff during peacetime. In wartime, regimental cadres, identical to what one would find in the regular army, had been detached for service with the Landwehr. Even in uniform the two services would be indistinguishable in wartime were it not for the difference in headdress.[47]

As the emperor prepared for the convocation of 6 November at Saint-Cloud, he received one additional report from Major Stoffel, the first part of which he entitled "The Advantages in Having a Permanent Chief of the General Staff in a Major Military Country," written in late October. By then, Stoffel had met General Helmuth von Moltke, chief of the Prussian general staff since 1858. A single discussion with Moltke was sufficient to reveal his sound judgment, his rare common sense, and his extensive military knowledge; for one first-rate mind will recognize another one almost immediately. Stoffel had already learned of Moltke's reputation for integrity and hard work. Beyond his profound knowledge of the Prussian army, he had acquired a familiarity with the composition and the organization of foreign armies: their resources, their spirit, and their military history. And he had a detailed knowledge of European geography.

The most immediate advantage such a talented permanent chief-of-staff offered, Stoffel asserted, derived from the fact that the chief-of-staff supervised the instruction of all staff officers in the Prussian army. Unlike the French army where the general staff was a body unto itself, a distinct headquarters, the Prussian general staff in Berlin functioned as a training center. A lieutenant, after spending three years in the Academy of War, plus three years of active service in his regiment, then went to the General Staff School in Berlin directed by Moltke. The curriculum encompassed the organization of foreign armies, military history, military geography, topography, as well as the study of tactics and strategy. As Moltke both directed the study and examined the results, he obtained first-hand knowledge of the merits and aptitudes of his officers; on the basis of which he nominated them for promotion and assignment to staff positions in army corps and divisions. In its capacity as a school, the Prussian general staff also served as the collection point for those publications, maps, plans, and brochures used for the study of foreign armies and institutions. In Stoffel's opinion, the French had no comparable collection anywhere, giving the Prussian a great advantage in reconnaissance (as they had had over the Austrians).

Nor did the French have a permanent chief of the general staff. If war seemed to be imminent, either the sovereign or the minister of war chose one of the available marshals or generals for the position. Stoffel claimed that, no matter the man's personal merit, he could not be sufficiently prepared to meet all the demands that would suddenly fall upon him: "He will lack those particular knowledges and aptitudes that can only be acquired by extensive study and practice. And he cannot be expected to have the personal knowledge of his generals, and most importantly of those officers who will make up his command staff, that is critical to successful command."[48] The French, in sum, must appoint a permanent chief-of-staff.

By appending to this urgent recommendation an appraisal of Austrian strength and morale, Stoffel inadvertently provided information useful to those in France who resisted the argument that Prussian reforms had led to Prussian effectiveness in 1866. He meant to show that Austria had not been as formidable in 1859 as portrayed in France, nor should she be regarded as a reliable ally for the future. The evidence he supplied attested to an enfeeblement of character and a loss of morale within the Austrian service even before the battle of Sadowa, which had simply deepened into defeatism in its aftermath.

Stoffel had learned that both the Prussians and the Italians had procured, both before and during the late war, a surprising amount of information about the Austrian military establishment through the treason of Austrian officers and civilian employees. The number of Austrian prisoners taken by the Prussians was noticeably high, and they were shocked in particular by the fact that more than 500 of the Austrian officers taken had not been wounded. In the field hospitals, where Austrian officers and men were treated together, the officers usually showed a complete indifference to their men, even when they came from the same battalion. They behaved, in short, as complete strangers, arousing strong disapproval in Prussian observers. Signs of a degeneration of character, Stoffel concluded: a true moral decadence.[49]

Notes

1. Jean Tulard, *Napoléon et la noblesse d'Empire*, p. 351; Willy Schädler, *Les Barons Stoffel* 1: 1–12 (a 2-volume typescript completed in 1979 and deposited in the Bibliothèque du service historique du ministère de la guerre, Vincennes, Cote 66.174). Schädler, of Arbon in the canton of Thurgau, collected biographical data from local sources and during a short visit to Vincennes. I am indebted to him for information on the antecedents of Eugène Stoffel.

2. Albert Révérend, *Armorial du Premier Empire* 2: 267.

3. Schädler, *Les Barons Stoffel* 1: 17–19, 27–28, 37–38, 45–48.

4. Révérend, *Titres et confirmation de titres: Monarchie de Juillet, 2e République, 2e Empire, 3e République 1830–1908*, p. 139.

5. Schädler, Les Barons Stoffel 1: 49–51.
6. Etat des services. Dossiers Stoffel, Cote 76381/2 (lst dossier). Bibliothèque du service historique du ministère de la guerre, Vincennes.
    Lieutenant second class, 7 October 1843
      2nd Regiment of Artillery, 17 January 1844
    Lieutenant first class, 19 July 1845
      15th Regiment of Artillery, 5 August 1845
      12th Regiment of Artillery, 16 January 1848
      10th Regiment of Artillery, 19 March 1848
    Captain second class, 13 January 1850
      Adjutant, Manufacture d'armes de Mutzig (Alsace), 30 January 1850
      7th Regiment of Artillery, 9 January 1852
      4th Regiment of Artillery, 14 May 1853
      12th Regiment of Artillery, 6 March 1854
    Captain first class, 29 December 1854
      15th Regiment of Artillery, 3 February 1855

7. Etat des services. Dossiers Stoffel (lst and 3rd dossiers). Also see César, baron de Bazancourt, La *Campagne d'Italie* 2: 292–93.
8. Inspector-General's Report, Auxonne, 27 August 1860. Dossiers Stoffel (lst dossier).
9. Cécile Aubry-Vitet, *Souvenirs de Froehner*, p. 12.
10. Raymond Cazelles, *Le Duc d'Aumale, prince aux dix visages*, pp. 188–89; Joël Le Gall, *Alésia; archéologie et histoire*, pp. 38–45.
11. Le Gall, *Alésia*, pp. 58–61, 72–75; Salomon Reinach, "Le Colonel Stoffel," *Revue archéologique* 9, sér. 4 (April 1907): 330.
12. Ministry of War to Commanding Colonel, 15th Regiment of Artillery, 7 September 1861. Dossiers Stoffel (lst dossier).
13. Esprit-Victor de Castellane, *Journal du maréchal de Castellane, 1804–1862* 5: 351. Also see Melvin Kranzberg, "An Emperor Writes History," H.S. Hughes, ed., *Teachers of History: Essays in Honor of L. B. Packard*, pp. 79–104.
14. Napoléon III, *Histoire de Jules César* 2: 49n–55n, 299n.
15. Chef d'escadron, 12 March 1862; Ordnance Officer to the Emperor, 23 March 1862. Etat des services. Dossiers Stoffel (lst dossier).
16. Eugène Stoffel, *Histoire de Jules César; guerre civile* 1: i–iii.
17. Reinach, "Le Colonel Stoffel," p. 330; Le Gall, *Alésia*, pp. 64–65.
18. Reinach, "Le Colonel Stoffel," p. 332.
19. Le Gall, *Alésia*, pp. 65–71.
20. Hortense Cornu to Nassau William Senior, "Louis-Napoleon Painted by a Contemporary," *Cornhill Magazine* 27 (January–June 1873): 613–14.
21. Aubry-Vitet, *Souvenirs de Froehner*, pp. 1–4, 11–16, 22, 26; Etat des services. Dossier Auguste Oppermann, No. 383—2e Série.
22. Pierre Lehautcourt, "La Réorganization de l'armee avant 1870," *Revue de Paris* 4 (August 1901): 536; General Guillaume-Auguste-Balthazar-Eugène-Henri Bonnal, *Le Haut Commandement français au début de chacune des guerres de 1859 et 1870*, pp. 7–8.

23. Germain Bapst, *Le Maréchal Canrobert: souvenirs d'un siècle* 4: 47

24. Charles C. Chesney and Henry Reeve, *The Military Resources of Prussia and France, and Recent Changes in the Art of War*, pp. 140–41.

25. Joseph Monteilhet, *Les Institutions militaires de la France 1814–1932*, pp. 21–22, 28–30.

26. Ibid., pp. 33–34 ; Chesney and Reeve, *The Military Resources of Prussia and France*, p. 148; Castellane, *Journal du maréchal de Castellane* 5: 279.

27. Chesney and Reeve, *The Military Resources of Prussia and France*, pp. 144–45.

28. Ibid., p. 139.

29. Bapst, *Le Maréchal Canrobert* 4: 48–49.

30. Robert Marquiset and Pierre Lorain, "Le Système 1866 dit 'Chassepot'," *Armes à feu françaises modèles réglementaires: 1858– 1918, chargement culasse*, pp. 1–2.

31. Napoleon III, *Oeuvres de Napoléon III* 1: 423–28.

32. Ibid. 2: 301–15.

33. Bapst, *Le Maréchal Canrobert* 4: 49–52.

34. Ibid. 4: 52–54.

35. Etat des services. Dossiers Stoffel (lst dossier).

36. Report of 8 September 1866. Eugène Stoffel, *Rapports militaires écrits de Berlin 1866–1870*, pp. 2–8.

37. Ibid., pp. 9–13.

38. Franceschini Piétri to Eugène Stoffel, 27 September 1866. Piétri, "Lettres au colonel Stoffel," *Revue de Paris* 3 (15 June 1911): 719; Edward Legge, *The Comedy and Tragedy of the Second Empire*, pp. 325–26.

39. Stoffel, *Rapports militaires*, p. xxiv.

40. Report of 4 October 1866. Stoffel, *Rapports militaires*, pp. 4–17.

41. Ibid., pp. 17–18.

42. Ibid., pp. 19–21.

43. Ibid., p. 26.

44. Ibid., pp. 21–29.

45. Report of 15 October 1866. Stoffel, *Rapports militaires*, pp. 30–32.

46. Ibid., pp. 32–34.

47. Ibid., pp. 35–36.

48. Report of 25 October 1866. Stoffel, *Rapports militaires*, pp. 39–43.

49. Ibid., pp. 44–47.

Part II

Maneuvering for Military Reform

In August and September of 1866, Napoleon III had offered lunch at Saint-Cloud to a few officers whom he knew to be sympathetic to his desire to enlarge the army substantially. His Majesty had made it known once again that he believed universal military service to be the most politic and practical means to that end. Those supporting the emperor's commitment to reform were given the opportunity to prepare specific recommendations for reform before the military convocation announced for 6 November at Saint-Cloud. But the publicity also gave those opposed to the principle of universal service, or to any costly expansion of the army, time to organize resistance. The emperor's tactics indicated his desire to point the way, to persuade the reluctant, to negotiate an agreement, rather than to use his vast authority arbitrarily. His was the politician's, rather than the soldier's, way; and he may have believed that it was the only possible way in a nation that recognized popular sovereignty, not the sovereignty of the crown.

At the outset of the convocation on 6 November, most everyone present agreed that France needed in the neighborhood of one million soldiers. The question was how, and at what cost, they should be recruited. The emperor, newly armed with Major Stoffel's information, had his own recommendation read to the group: universal military service plus the creation of a French equivalent of the Landwehr. The aged Marshal Vaillant (76) replied that such a plan would generate formidable difficulties, and that the legislative assemblies were bound to reject it. The three civilian cabinet ministers present (Rouher, Fould, and Vuitry) concurred. Marshal Niel presented his favored alternative: the creation of a trained *garde mobile*, which he estimated would provide reserves of 400,000 men. The discussion then got out of hand, everyone talking at once, as the emperor was insufficiently authoritarian to preside effectively. At the end of the session, when the hubbub had subsided, the emperor indicated that he was holding to his idea for short-term obligatory service; and the military present supported him except for Marshals Vaillant and Randon, and General Louis-Jules Trochu. The civilian ministers present favored Marshal Niel's plan.

On the second day of the convocation, each member present was handed a copy of a project explaining how obligatory military service could be implemented, the work of General Emile-Félix Fleury and Colonel Jean-Auguste Berthaut. It eliminated any possibility of exoneration and replacement. General Lebrun backed the plan without a quibble, but the emperor supported it with the hope that exoneration could be retained. Exoneration had been his idea in 1855 as the price for eliminating the unofficial replacement system; he seems to have felt obligated to preserve exoneration as a political commitment despite its demonstrated ineffectuality.

The opposition then raised a new objection. Adolphe Vuitry, the minister-president of the Council of State and an experienced attorney, expressed his belief that obligatory service would be unconstitutional. The Corps législatif, he argued, had the constitutional right to authorize the draft of the annual contingent. Eugène Rouher and Achille Fould at once agreed with that interpretation, with the result that the convocation broke up without any decision having been reached. As the court was on the verge of moving to Compiègne, the emperor ordered the commission to reconvene at Compiègne a week hence.[1]

During the interim, General Fleury was told that he would become the new minister of war in the event that universal military service was adopted. But, during that week, all manner of political pressure was brought to bear upon the emperor, notably through the use of reports from the prefects about the state of public opinion. He was made to understand that, while he had the support of a half-dozen generals, to force the issue of universal military obligation would be to break with his ministers, most of the military, the bulk of the Corps législatif, and the country as a whole.

The commission assembled at Compiègne on the evening of 13 November 1866 and resumed work the following morning.[2] By then, the emperor believed he must adopt the half-measure sponsored by Marshal Niel as the only way to get at least half of what he wanted. During the initial session, however, the commission was treated to an impassioned speech by Prince Napoleon, the emperor's cousin, who reviewed all the arguments in favor of obligatory service, declaring it to be indispensable; that is, personal and equal service for a three-year term. He was seconded by General Trochu, hitherto an opponent of universal service, for reasons that would only become clear later in the debate. As Prince Napoleon had always been outspoken and independent, his intent may have been to dissuade the emperor from accepting the half-measure. It remains possible that he had been inspired by the emperor in a last-ditch attempt to rally support. Whichever the case, the ploy failed in the face of ministerial opposition.

For the remainder of the conference, the wrangling focused exclusively upon the viability of the Niel proposal. It went on behind closed doors, the group sometimes meeting twice a day. While a public announcement had been made of the commission's appointment, the press was thereafter kept in the dark about its proceedings; and the members maintained a prudent silence about the debate. The attack upon the Niel proposal was led by Marshal Randon, the minister of war, who represented the typical military preference for older, veteran soldiers and a serious doubt about the value of young recruits. Randon argued for extending the term of active service from five to eight or even nine years as the best device to obtain a larger army. The political liability in maintaining the larger standing army derived only in part from its cost: Randon's plan implied the retention of a replacement system in some form. Various modifications of Randon's proposal intended to reduce its cost were introduced, but nothing had been resolved by the commission when the sojourn at Compiègne ended on 28 November. A few additional sessions were held in early December, but the differences remained deep.

As a consequence, the emperor opted for the Niel plan, the middle road so to speak between universal military obligation and a professional army of long-term veterans: the only plan for which he had political support. His marshals and generals had remained too divided in support of the other two options to chose one of them without alienating a substantial section of the military. Even in the early years of his regime, when the emperor enjoyed autocratic power, he had retreated from reforms obnoxious to the military. In 1866, when he was bent upon liberalizing the regime, any expectation that he would act arbitrarily on military reform was unfounded. His public announcement on 11 December of an initiative to increase the size of the active army and to provide a reserve of 400,000 men in a *garde mobile* mentioned no one on the commission by name, much less the nature of the disputes.[3]

Had the issues been publicized, or had the degree of the emperor's concern been conveyed, their effect upon public opinion cannot be estimated. The extent of Prussian armament was noted, to be sure; but the fear of probable Prussian attack was necessarily muted, contributing to the postwar assumption that the government had been uninformed or too casual. During the meeting in Compiègne, the emperor had employed "ideas and appreciations upon certain members of the commission" furnished him by Major Stoffel.[4] And, at some point, he was given a copy of an alarming letter written by General Ducrot, commander of the garrison in Strasbourg, predicting an imminent Prussian invasion for the purpose of annexing Alsace. Having heard privately from General Trochu about the discussions in Compiègne, Ducrot replied to the effect: Here we are deliberating "pompously and at length" about what should be done to improve the army while Prussia is very actively preparing to invade France. He cited intense activity of Prussian agents in the border regions, testing the loyalty of the local population between the Moselle and the Vosges, the Protestant element in particular. "While we, with our stupid vanity and silly presumption . . . believe that we can choose the day and the hour to complete military improvements, namely, at the end of the Universal Exposition [1867]. In truth, I share your view; and I am beginning to believe that our government is struck with madness."[5]

The wrangling at Compiègne, and the necessity of compromise, did not deflect the emperor from his determination to seek further information through his trusted channel. Suspecting that the Prussians made more economic use of military funds than was the case in France, he had military budget figures sent to Stoffel in the hope of obtaining recommendations for economic improvements in French military administration. Having heard that a new rifle had been submitted to the King of Prussia for examination, Napoleon III also indicated he would like to see the rifle.[6] As a measure of his satisfaction with Stoffel, the emperor had him promoted to the rank of lieutenant-colonel, which became effective on 21 December 1866.[7]

Stoffel's response was his "Note on the Military Organization of Prussia," not so much a statement of comparative military finances as a report on the economies realized through the development of an efficient Landwehr. The report provided a valuable review of Prussian military organization since 1814 and was meant to explain to the French military that the efficient organization of 1866 had not been molded overnight. Nor had it been founded and repeatedly altered in response to military theory, but rather as a result of actual experience. His story began with the adoption of the principle of obligatory service for all citizens and the institution of the Landwehr as the supplement to the permanent army.

The deficiencies of the Prussian organization had been first revealed during the campaigns of 1848 and 1849 in Schleswig and Baden, and later during the mobilizations of 1850 and 1859. The attempt to eliminate them began, consequently, in 1859, although the reformed system became known as the "Reorganization of 1860." An additional factor had forced the reform: between 1814 and 1860, the Prussian population increased from 10 to 18 million. Yet, the standing army had remained relatively constant (between 130,000 and 140,000 men), as the law permitted an annual recruitment of 40,000 men, as in 1814. As a result, an increasing number of young reaching military age, and suitable for service, were, in effect, becoming exempt despite the principle of universal obligation. By 1859, more than one-third of the annual class eligible for service had had to be exempted. During the mobilization of 1859, the injustice of the situation became transparent. Men between 25 and 32 in the Landwehr, who had previously served their term in the regular army, were called up; while some younger men between 20 and 25 had no obligation. As the reformers were determined above all else to adhere to the principle of universal obligation, they raised the annual contingent to 63,000, retaining the three-year term of active service. This permitted the increase in the standing army to roughly 210,000 men, very affordable in view of the substantial increase in the national budget.

The confusion and the inefficiencies perceived earlier during mobilizations and campaigns had largely derived from the traditional practice of integrating Landwehr units into the standing army. The reformers of 1860 concluded that it would be better henceforth to confine the Landwehr to home defense. In order to bring the active army to a total of 370,000 without recourse to the Landwehr, the active reserve status was extended from 2 to 4 years. The Landwehr was then divided into two bans, based upon age, for a more appropriate mobilization:

Active or standing army (7 years): 3 years actual service
    (Ages 20 to 27) 4 years on reserve
Landwehr (12 years): 5 years in the First Ban
    (Ages 27 to 39) 7 years in the Second Ban

The reforms, in sum, permitted a substantial rise in the standing army without recourse to the older men of the Landwehr. The latter were available for territorial defense, but they knew they would be called on to fight with the regular army in extreme circumstances. As it was known in France that troops of the Landwehr had been employed in both Denmark and Bohemia in 1864 and 1866, Stoffel explained their use as a temporary expedient. Many new cadres had been formed in 1860 in anticipation of the greater numbers of regular troops to become available, but with the knowledge that the full strength of the reserves would not come to pass until the end of 1866. Before that date, it had been necessary to draw from the Landwehr in time of war to bring the new battalions up to strength.

Stoffel, writing in late November of 1866, estimated that Prussia was just then reaching the full complement of men anticipated by the reformers of 1860, meaning that she was stronger than six months earlier at Sadowa:

A. Active Army		370,000 men
Regular or permanent forces	210,000	
Four-year Reservists	160,000	
B. Depot forces, comprising		
Reservists and Recruits		110,000 men
C. Landwehr (First Ban), for		
internal defense		150,000 men
		630,000 total

In the event of a major war or a disaster, the First Ban of the Landwehr was to be used either to fill voids or as a second line. Although Stoffel made no pointed reference to the conventional French preference for seasoned veterans, one can deduce from his discussion of the new Prussian organization and the relegation of the Second Ban strictly to territorial defense that he found the use of young, vigorous troops preferable.[8] Napoleon III, while agreeing with Prussian military theory in general, seems to have had reservations about the wisdom of abandoning efforts to integrate reservists and regulars. How else were the reservists to acquire those qualities they lacked?[9]

The emperor anticipated reception of his military commission's report in early February 1867, in time for the preparation of his speech opening parliament on 14 February. He took the prior step of removing Marshal Randon as minister of war on 19 January 1867, replacing him with Marshal Niel, further admission that he had no hope of obtaining universal military obligation but an indication that he expected implementation of the Niel plan. The final recommendations of the commission reached the emperor on schedule, and he studied the report carefully, annotating it with favorable comments, agreeing with most everything except the recommendation to suppress all units which drew an inordinate amount of support at the expense of the mass of the army.

The report also recommended a better grouping of troops; an increase in the artillery; further study of the use of the telegraph and the railroads; a simplification of complicated maneuvers; and an upgrading of the intellectual level in the military schools. The commission saved to last the following observation: "Recalling the inadequacy of preparation revealed at the outset during the Crimean, Italian, and Mexican expeditions, the Commission notes the necessity to lay down a set of general rules to provide for the quick concentration of an army in the theater of war for the pursuit of operations."[10]

The emperor was displeased not to find any recommendation for restructuring the general staff along the lines that Stoffel had urged. During the Crimean War, the emperor had found the general staff to be defective. In the aftermath, he had recommended that the general staff be converted into a more major organization, bringing in line officers to serve brief terms on rotation. The special commission he had appointed to review the matter thought poorly of his ideas, and its report was written by General Trochu: "The structure of the general staff, having for forty years proved its sufficiency, requires no modification."[11] As the recent discussions at Compiègne had not undermined that satisfaction, Napoleon could only write on the margins of the report his continuing desire to convert the general staff into a chief headquarters where, in peacetime, foreign maps would be available for study to promote a knowledge of roads, invasion routes, and local resources wherever the army might be called upon to campaign. The document remained confidential, and the emperor and Marshal Niel were left with the responsibility of implementing its recommendations.[12]

In his speech opening the legislative session on 14 February 1867, Napoleon III prefaced his military statement with the announcement that, after fifteen years of stability and prosperity, the time had come to introduce legislation to offer new guarantees of political liberty. As for the army, it had already demonstrated its quality, he said; but the conditions of warfare had been changing and would require the augmentation of French defensive forces. The projected law, he assured his audience, had been carefully studied and prepared to lighten the burden of conscription in peacetime, but to provide considerable resources in time of war. "And everyone partakes of the responsibility as befits the principle of equality." He argued that the influence of any nation henceforth would depend upon the number of men it could put under arms. Neighboring states imposed considerably heavier obligations upon their citizens and would be watching to see whether French influence would increase or decline in the world.[13]

His language was coldly received, as had been anticipated,[14] not only in parliament but generally in the press. Only the *Revue des deux mondes*, *Le Constitutionnel*, *Le Temps*, and *Le Siècle* recognized the need to enlarge the army. The speech provoked a rash of publications, of very unequal value; and General Changarnier again manifested his distain for the Prussian army. By July, when the parliamentary session ended, none of the government's three major bills under consideration had yet been adopted: the Niel plan, a new press law, and a law on assemblies.[15]

Two of the publications were of special interest, both appearing in March of 1867. One, an article in the *Revue des deux mondes*, entitled "Les Institutions militaires de la France," was a digest of a forthcoming history by the

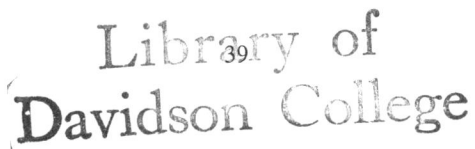

duc d'Aumale. But the article appeared under the name Laugel. While ostensibly a study of those institutions and personalities contributing to French military success in the past, the work had obviously been inspired by the recent success of Prussian military institutions. Aumale used that format, however, to criticize the practice of replacement, arguing that the time had come to treat military service as a duty, not a tax. After reading the article, Marshal Niel had the name of the true author tracked down and brought the matter to the emperor's attention.[16]

The second publication, General Trochu's *L'Armée française en 1867*, became infinitely better known and controversial. The coincidence led some in the imperial government to suspect that Aumale had inspired Trochu's work, others to suppose that Trochu had always been an Orleanist, erroneous assumptions that have not faded with the passage of time. The duc d'Aumale read the work at once and called it the work of a patriot. "I agree with him on many points, but not on all. In particular, I do believe it is high time to abolish both bounties and exoneration."[17]

Louis-Jules Trochu cannot be understood, or his work fairly appraised, without the prior knowledge that he was a tragic figure, in that respect like the emperor himself. Both men were intelligent critics of the army; both were resented as meddlers and treated as outsiders; both resorted to publication to advance unpopular views; both held supreme political power and exercised military command; both revealed a penchant for deliberation when the moment required firm and swift resolve; and both became objects of public contempt when the days of ultimate reckoning came. Greatness brought down, in sum, whether by flaws in judgment or in character, and culminating in exile, whether at home or abroad.

In an army not known for rapid advancement, Trochu's promotion had been spectacular. During his service in Africa as a young officer, all the leading military chiefs vied for his services as an aide-de-camp as he was the most intelligent of collaborators and the most delightful of companions. During the Second Republic, he served as an ordnance officer to the President and reached the rank of lieutenant-colonel in 1851. He was promoted to the rank of colonel in 1853 despite it being known that he had opposed the *coup d'état* of 1851; and, as a brigadier-general, he led a brigade in the Crimea in 1854. His promotion to be division-general coincided with the Italian War in 1859, during which he led the 2nd Division in Marshal Canrobert's III Corps.

While Trochu's memoirs, published immediately after his death in 1896, must be used with considerable caution, he did not evade in those pages those ambiguities in his career that so often had made him an object of suspicion. Prizing both liberty and propriety, he had disapproved both the restoration of an authoritarian empire and the illegal action that had paved its way. Yet, he served the regime and knew that he enjoyed the special confidence of the emperor. Other officers believed him to be inordinately ambitious and in search of acclaim; and surely his excessive intelligence did not endear him to the less gifted. He had too many ideas, and he exposed them too well. From that cerebral activity came his highly-developed critical sense, which made him an adversary of tradition, and which led him to publish *l'Armée française en 1867*.[18]

The book appeared anonymously about six weeks after the reform commission had delivered its confidential report of February, 1867, to the emperor. Trochu would later declare that the book reflected views he had accumulated during thirty years of military service. And it is true that, during the Second Empire, Trochu had refused command positions except in time of war, preferring to work on military committees and as an inspector-general of infantry, positions that gave him unusual insight into technical and personnel deficiencies.[19] He would also claim that the introduction of exoneration in 1855 had offended his military convictions; and that, when a member of the reform commission in 1866-1867, only Prince Napoleon and he had seen the necessity of adopting the principle of obligatory service. Thereafter, he had published his book in good faith "to provoke reflection within the government."[20]

These assertions were made long after the events and in an era when it was conventional to accuse the late emperor of blindness, as Trochu did. As we know, the record shows that Trochu had opposed the emperor's proposal to introduce universal military obligation in 1853; and it remains quite unclear when he reversed himself in order to take the stand he did in 1867. His book gave no indication that the criticisms therein had recently been the topics of debate within the reform commission, but the members of the commission quickly recognized that the book had to have been authored by one of the members. Some of the material in the book had been paraphrased from their confidential report: there was a similarity in organization and chapter-headings, and an occasional sentence or paragraph appeared as in the original report. It became an easy matter to trace Trochu as the author. The publication was as much resented as a breach of confidence as it was as an attack upon the traditions of the army. On the other hand, the political Left fell upon Trochu as a useful critic of the emepror and his regime and leaped to the conclusion that he was a republican. His quick notoriety, and the fact that he *was* a reformer and a man of demonstrated intelligence, moved the emperor to remark that, in the event of war, Trochu ought to become the commander-in-chief. Marshal Niel, reflecting professional resentment, said he would prefer General Lebrun.[21]

To read *l'Armée française en 1867* is to recognize that both Trochu and his detractors were partly right in their assessment of the work. Only a man of long and dedicated experience could have accumulated the variety of perceptive observations he made; and only a man who had served on the reform commission would have organized and presented the material in the manner he did. The timing opened him to the charge of opportunism; he would argue in the opening pages that he had been pondering solutions to the near-disorder he had witnessed on the French side in the Crimean and Italian campaigns, and that the outcome of Sadowa had merely driven him to expose French deficiencies. Prussian officers had studied the French performances and had come to understand the vulnerability of the usual French tactics on the battlefield. "They know us better than we know ourselves!"[22] It may be that the evident resistance to reform from November into January led Trochu to try to force the issue, lacking confidence that the official report alone would suffice to accomplish its mission.

Among his recommendations, we must note not only those that were critical of established practices, but those that ought to have undermined the contemporary notion that Trochu advocated the military philosophy of the Republican opposition. It would appear that more people talked about Trochu than read him. His remarks about the mind of the military administrator have not lost their cogency.

One must find a way, he argued, to reduce drastically the number of army regulations. The administrator tends to forget that simplicity is a fundamental requirement in regulating both the maintenance and the action of troops on campaign. The most brilliant, the most ingenious, inventions of peacetime are attractive because they are workable in garrison. Trochu implied that a certain mold of administrative mind contrives complexities that become worse than useless in the field. The tendency is to seek continual refinement, meaning that there is an endless doing, undoing, and redoing. The regulations, as a result, lack both simplicity and fixity; they provide internal contradictions, promote uncertainty, even paralysis.[23]

He devoted a chapter to recruitment and reserves. He noted correctly that the military laws of 1818 and 1832 had been formulated in peacetime and upon the assumption that warfare on the Revolutionary or Napoleonic scale would never be resumed. When a certain amount of conscription became necessary, that principle could only be reintroduced by providing ample opportunity for replacement or exoneration. As Trochu knew that the exoneration system practiced under the Second Empire had never provided the numbers anticipated, he argued here for a return to the replacement system: "It can provide long-term recruits [or professionals] and avoid the inadequacies of drafting short-term recruits, who return home on reserve and are never adequately militarized."[24]

As such a proposition was evidently at variance with Trochu's recent advocacy of universal military obligation with Prince Napoleon, one must call attention to a passage toward the end of Trochu's book where he sought to resolve the ambiguity. He acknowledged that a system of universal obligation for a short term was more equitable than the actual system which imposed service upon a limited number of men for a proportionately longer term. "In theory, it is the best and would be recommended *if* France had the prospect of many years of certain peace to educate the country for its adoption. Under the current circumstances, it is impossible."[25] That assertion would be more convincing had not Trochu rejected the idea of universal military obligation in 1853 on grounds that revealed his deep conservatism.

That quality was again exposed in *L'Armée française en 1867* when Trochu turned to the relative merits of young soldiers and old soldiers. He was quite aware of the national belief that only old veterans are fit to make war vigorously, a view he did not share; and, as young recruits usually were obliged to serve against their will, the army had come to suspect their value, an attitude he sought to remedy. It was reasonable to expect a recruit to resist the idea of military service for up to a year, Trochu believed. But, during the remaining years of his active service, the recruit could be expected to accustom himself to the idea of professional service and to become attached to his regiment as his "other family." Every effort should be made during those years to develop a maturity which Trochu called the military spirit. "You make an old soldier out of him, a reliable veteran, but artificially; not by aging him. My old soldier is a young man, who has all the elasticity of youth, both physical and moral; and he retains the beliefs and the illusions of youth. He is full of strength and of honor."[26] Trochu would have further emphasized youth by reducing the active service from 5 to 3 years.

The notion of reenlistment at the end of the term was not to be encouraged. Trochu's ideal recruit remained loyal to his prior obligations and family. Upon leaving the service, he would return to his native region, marry, and rear a family imbued with those virtues taught to him during military service: obedience, respect, and personal discipline. He would not, in other words, augment that group of *déclassés* to be found in all large French cities. The army, for Trochu, was to become a powerful instrument for *moralisation publique*.[27] In time of war, such reservists would be patriotic and reliable.

He recognized that permanent military service had always offered some recruits financial advantages beyond what they had known. Such men sought reenlistment rather than a return to family life. Trochu's description of their destiny was meant to shatter the myths about old soldiers, especially those surrounding the *grognards* of the First Empire. At that moment of reenlistment, such a soldier relinquishes his liberty forever and accepts the fact that gradual estrangement from his family will follow. If at first this seems to be a sacrifice, in time he will become coarsened; and he will develop unattractive personal qualities. His sensibilities become dulled, he generates no enthusiasms, but is a skeptic and a scoffer, and ultimately a drunk. Trochu attributed this degeneration of the professional rank-and-file to prolonged life in barracks; to the slackness of garrison life; and to the absence of the humane associations of ordinary life that help to maintain dignity and honorable character. If classified as veterans at the moment of retirement, the old soldiers could be admitted to Les Invalides in Paris. Otherwise, as Trochu put it, they merged with the riffraff of the urban population. Trochu thought that most officers would agree with his characterization of old soldiers,[28] not anticipating that his book would be resented as an attack upon the legends and the traditions of the army.

If younger recruits were to achieve the efficiency and morale to which Trochu aspired, the level of their basic training would have to be substantially raised. What is the unual diet of instruction for soldiers, he asked, when the units of any given regiment are assembled for periodic training? Nothing more than the packing and maintenance of their equipment, the disassembly and reassembly of weapons, plus an occasional reading of pertinent clauses from the military penal code! Nothing of any serious intellectual or moral content which, alone, prepares armies for the great duties and trials which await them in actual war. Their officers, meanwhile, feast on a diet of army regulations: the study of rules governing garrison service, firing practice, service when on campaign or on maneuvers, and on the maintenance of accurate accounts.

Officers, he argued, needed to be subjected to lectures by generals on principles of warfare drawn from actual experience in war: on such matters as the behavior of troops on campaign, either in the midst of many temptations or in the actual crisis of combat. How is morale acquired? How is it lost? What about respect for persons and property, or for the customs and religions of others, which give an army self-respect and promote moral stability? Once officers themselves have been given such instruction, they should be required to see that it penetrates downward into the mass of the army.

What he sought, in a word, was communication from top to bottom, to develop a sense of common standards and purpose; for he believed a sense of purpose to be at the very root of maintaining discipline and order (which had been so often lacking during the Italian campaign). He advocated, in fact, a preoccupation with honor, duty, and dedication. Morale, in his view, can only be built through an educational program which produces dedicated professionals.[29] Trochu's own preoccupation with morale and morality, with propriety and honor, with legality and order, provided the key to his political *character*; for, as a soldier, he never adhered publicly to a political party.

That he had been aware of his political dispositions, however, slipped out later, in 1872, during testimony in a trial. Referring to the widespread assumption that he had been an Orleanist, Trochu remarked: "Evidently they found me too bourgeois to be a Legitimist."[30]

While General Trochu gave substantial space in his book to his views on the best use of infantry, cavalry, and artillery, his own summary remarks gave clear indication that he had been moved to publish primarily to argue that military reorganization did not so much require a new recruitment law or increasing the number of men under arms, but rather the elimination of fundaental errors and the perfection of those methods by which the army was prepared and organized for war. What gave him distinction as a reformer was his preoccupation with moral reform, inspired by his conservative Catholicism. Baron Stoffel's initial reports in 1866 had, as we know, lent support for a new recruitment law based upon universal military obligation. But, in the months to come, Stoffel, too, would expose his own commitment to moral revival as the ultimate key to reform. The duty of intelligent criticism carries with it the risk of unpopularity. By adding moral issues to the criticism in exposing the indifferent professionalism within the army, Trochu and Stoffel converted that risk into a guarantee.

One can find in the concluding pages of Trochu's book a summary of his propositions for reform. Some were strictly practical, such as his recommendation to provide and maintain large stocks of military supplies in arsenals at the army corps level rather than at regimental or divisional levels; or his recommendation to prepare substantial reserves of money such as Prussia had done in preparation for her enterprise of 1866.[31] Once such elementary preparations had been fulfilled, the next step was to implement those principles of moral and technical order outlined in the earlier chapters of his book, in particular: 1) Establish a system of French general education for the army. 2) Eliminate those rules and regulations that currently lead to confusion and disorder; and recodify according to the actual needs of the army to guarantee unity of execution, thus providing regulations that command respect and are binding on everyone. 3) Abandon exoneration as well as those special payments aimed at securing the reenlistment of recruits after their three-year service. Provide no pensions for troopers before the completion of at least thirty years of service, or for company grade officers until the completion of twenty-five years of service. The idea being to encourage an ideal of service rather than a fixation on money. 4) Encourage promotion on the basis of merit rather than routine. 5) Reinforce a respect for hierarchy and discipline by assuring the holder of every military authority both the complete attributions and responsibilities that belong to that position.[32]

Such reforms, he argued, would provide for a reorganization of the army without requiring any new law on recruitment. The basic principles of the Law of 1832 were to remain in force, and the annual contingent to be conscripted would remain at 100,000. As that law required seven years of service, the last two of which were on reserve, Trochu did not press for the three-year term he had advocated in earlier pages, but merely recommended several amendments to the law, another instance in which the urgency of the moment militated against the adoption of the more ideal system. He thought, for example, that the minimum acceptable height for service could be reduced by two centimeters (from 1m.56 to 1m.54), because the muzzle-loaders were being replaced by breech-loading rifles. The difference would allow the retention of several thousand draftees who escaped service every year.

He would also have obtained a few extra months of active service from recruits by dating it from actual induction into the army rather than from the moment of conscription as had been traditional. A more substantial increase could be realized by adding a year of reserve status, but he thought it well to sweeten that eighth year by permitting marriage that final year. Once the system was fully employed, in eight years, Trochu calculated it would provide at least 700,000 men, enough to create five armies of at least 100,000 men each for foreign service, the remainder for service in Algeria and at home. In a crisis, all former soldiers between the ages of 28 and 40 could be recalled in various capacities. While he admitted that France could raise ten such armies for foreign service by adopting universal military obligation, he believed such exactions would provoke intolerable social disorders.[33]

Even though General Trochu's recommendations did not lend support to the principles advocated by Napoleon III a few months earlier, the emperor welcomed them as reformist and well-meant. What he did not find in the book, as he had not in the Commission's report, was any encouragement to create the Prussian-style general staff which he had advocated with Stoffel's support. And that was particularly on his mind by May of 1867 after the recent collapse of his efforts to purchase Luxembourg from William III of the Netherlands thanks to Bismarck's intervention. No matter that France was unready for war, the emperor understood that war might be forced upon him at any time.[34] We know already that he advanced Trochu's name as a possible chief-of-staff to Marshal Niel, who said he would prefer General Lebrun.

It appears that the emperor had already discussed the matter with Lebrun who shared the emperor's reformist views. Lebrun had believed Marshal Niel to be the best choice to command the army. While the emperor did not disagree, he told Lebrun that in case he, the emperor, had to leave Paris to be with the army, he would need Niel at the ministry of war. The discussion is arresting as it suggests that Napoleon III, if constitutionally commander-in-chief, no longer expected to take command in the field, as he had done in 1859. He had not, after all, taken personal command in the Crimea. If he did so in 1859, his motive was to curb the bickering among senior officers that had characterized the Crimean campaign. His experience with the realities of command in battle, not to speak of the unsettling state of his health, made it imperative that he find a chief-of-staff approaching Moltke's stature: a man intelligent, resolute, and reformist in temper.

Lebrun's second recommendation, after Niel, was General Trochu. His book had revealed his capacities and his intelligence; and, above all else, it had amounted to a protest against those ministers of war who had for many years blocked the emperor's progress efforts. His actual experience in combat, especially in the Crimea, was of a quality to inspire confidence. "To be sure," Lebrun added, "Trochu would have done better not to publish his book, simply presenting it as a report to Marshal Niel. Beyond those occasional exaggerations in expressing the deficiencies Trochu enunciated, the minister of war would have found truth as well as information useful for the improvement of the army."[35] The emperor quite concurred with the argument, saying, "General Trochu's great merit is incontestable; but his ideas are so mystical!"[36] This exchange took place on 12 May 1867. Thereafter, as the emperor believed that an international conference would provide for the neutralization of Luxembourg (and the evacuation of the Prussian garrison), the immediacy of war faded; and the nomination of a chief-of-staff was postponed. It says much about Napoleon III's confidence in his senior generals and marshals that none of them had received the nod by the summer of 1870; and the unexpected death of Marshal Niel in 1869 had robbed him of the best he had.

Why, then, had he not moved to bring Trochu to the top command in 1867? Was he put off by Trochu's religious moralizing? Or, given his keen political sense, did he anticipate the anger the appointment would have provoked within the army which believed itself to have been corporately criticized in Trochu's book? As in so many other matters of policy, the emperor kept his reasons to himself. His silence only encouraged the gossip that Trochu was out of favor because of his Orleanism. (Not even the emperor's later appointment of Trochu to a position of critical responsibility has ever been able to dispel the legend of the emperor's distrust of Trochu.)

The emperor, to be sure, had always intruded in military affairs. As a Napoleon, he could not escape an interest in military matters. Beyond that, any chief executive must seek to coordinate his political, foreign, and military policies. But Napoleon III aroused resentment in his own time, and criticism ever after, for his persistent intrusion in all aspects of government. The army regarded him as an outsider. But the interference of the outsider, even when his ideas are sound, can disrupt the routine and threaten the authority of those on the inside.[37] The emperor was equally well-known for his penchant for bypassing ministers to consult directly with ambassadors, officials, and journalists, the results being similar. Stoffel's mission to Berlin obviously fitted the well-known pattern.

Such a governing technique was said, behind Napoleon III's back, to have derived from his many years as a conspirator before he reached power. In truth, it derived from two dilemmas which went without hope of resolution until the first months of 1870. In the first place, the Bonapartist party was split into two factions, authoritarian and liberal, rendering his political base unreliable. Only when the authoritarian faction was ultimately banished from court in January of 1870 did unambiguous policy become attainable. In the second place, the liberalization of the regime held the promise of gradually attracting to government service many able figures who had been alienated by the dictatorship. While it would be a distortion to claim that the Second Empire was only served by mediocrities, it would be correct to argue that much talent was wasted in obstructionism. As for the army, nonpolitical though it may have been, the insiders had been free for many decades from any criticism of military structure or doctrine. When it finally came in the person of Napoleon III, the army gave much energy to its defense of the status quo. Such a climate does not so much produce mediocrities as it discourages innovation.

The apparent reluctance of Napoleon III to impose his views upon the intransigent military, at least until the crisis of 1866, reflected the ambiguity and the vulnerability of his political base. It has been asserted that his regime, as a result of the coup d'état of 1851, was dependent upon the army for internal security to an inordinate degree; meaning that he had to be solicitous of military opinion.[38] The thesis has some merit, but misleads by implying that this condition was particular to the Second Empire. The structure or nature of the army, including its clear obligation to provide internal security, had become a primary political consideration after 1789, if for no other reason than the Revolution introduced the era in which political opposition was not loyal. Changes in regime thereafter were accomplished by coups and revolutions, and occasionally authority was preserved by a timely coup. When Marshal Gouvion-Saint-Cyr reforged the army in 1818, its size and structure were predicated on the assumption that the vast campaigns of the Napoleonic era were over. Revolution was no longer to be exported, but rather to be contained.

The record of the army thereafter in internal security was mixed. In 1831 and 1834, and again during the June Days of 1848, violent insurrections were suppressed with great severity. In 1830 and February of 1848, not all the troops proved to be reliable; and established regimes fell victim to insurrection. The political opposition to Napoleon III, hoping to overthrow his regime, was necessarily sensitive to his proposal in 1867 to increase the size of the army substantially. As his proposal came at a time when he also sought to liberalize the regime, to reduce the components of the police state, the only military device consistent with liberalization was to adopt the principle of universal military obligation. There could have been no better guarantee that the army would have been used primarily against foreign enemies.

As for the matter of disruptive intrusions into military affairs by the outsider, one searches in vain for any evidence that the army chiefs, in their complacence, would have become avid for reform. Even the insider made recommendations for change at his own peril as General Trochu's fate indicated. In 1870, despite his seniority in rank, he would seek nothing higher than a divisional command. In response, the minister of war would offer him command of an army to be formed at Toulouse for the defense of the southern frontier against a Spanish invasion, a threat Trochu knew to be imaginary.[39] Colonel Stoffel's day of reckoning, as the insider become outsider, would yet come.

Marshal Niel does not seem to have resented the emperor's interference, even encouraging it; either because he required the emperor's support in carrying out reforms, or because he was more politic than his predecessors. In the spring of 1867, with Niel's approval, the emperor undertook a study of French military organization that occupied him for eight months. He had the collaboration of General Lebrun, and Lebrun acknowledged the technical assistance of several officers from the intendance. His Majesty's purpose was to ascertain the true state of French military resources by providing detailed tables illustrating all the components necessary for fielding several armies, from which it could be determined what France possessed and what she lacked. The minister of war was to be responsible for filling the gaps as quickly as possible. The manuscript of about twenty-five pages was completed on 20 January 1868, and a hundred copies were printed. Ten of them were sent to the ministry of war and were gratefully acknowledged by Marshal Niel.[40] The work provides further evidence that Napoleon III's military forte was administration.

The emperor's preoccupation with French military structure through much of 1867 brought a temporary end to his bombardment of Colonel Stoffel with questions about Prussian preparations. He used the leisure well to collect valuable information and made several reports on his own initiative during the year. From the fragmentary correspondence remaining, one can deduce that he worried about his neglect, perhaps wondering whether he ought to seek reassignment, perhaps fearing that opponents of his point-of-view in the ministry of war were undermining him successfully.

Somewhat before this uncertainty was resolved, he reported on the new Prussian military law of 9 November 1867, which reduced service in the Landwehr from twelve to five years; and which, therefore, eliminated the distinction between the first and second bans of 1 January 1868. The reduction, as Stoffel demonstrated, was no cause for complacence as it was a consequence of the substantial increase in manpower available to Prussia following the war of 1866. That is to say, made *potentially* available through the extension of the Prussian military system to those states which had formed the North German Confederation.

The first step had been to organize militarily the territory actually annexed by Prussia in 1866: Hanover, Schleswig-Holstein, and Hesse. The division of the new territory into Landwehr battalion districts was carried out even before providing for a new civil administration, a hint of priorities in Prussia that Stoffel did not miss. Once the civil administration had been definitively organized in 1867, the Landwehr districts were modified to coincide with the civil districts. Prussia expected to recruit three new army corps from the annexed territory.

While Prussia could not treat the member states of the North German Confederation as annexed territory, the extension of the Prussian military system into the states of the Confederation was an obvious step in the direction of coordinated military policy. To make that point, Stoffel noted that Prussia had simultaneously undertaken the redistricting of the Landwehr battalions in Prussia proper to reflect recent shifts and increases in the population. His report claimed that Prussia was achieving a high degree of military coordination within the North German Confederation, where there would now be two hundred districts of Landwehr battalions. The reogranization was to become operative on 1 January 1868.[41]

In private letters to the emperor's secretary, Stoffel also warned about the heightened degree of anti-French feeling in Germany in 1867 in the aftermath of the Luxembourg affair. Because the French regarded the failure to complete the purchase of the grand-duchy as a humiliation instigated by Prussia, they tended to be blind to the fact that Prussia, too, emerged from the affair not a little irritated. A Prussian garrison had provided Luxembourg's security during the years that Luxembourg was a member of the Germanic Confederation. As she was not a member of the succeeding North German Confederation, the international conference called to settle the issue ruled that Prussia should remove the garrison. The decision was received in Prussia as another slap from the French. "What you tell me about the state of opinion," Piétri replied, "does not surprise me. Although German pamphlets are little read in

France, we hear a long, dull buzz much resembling hostile clamors. I read to the emperor the greater part of your opinions on the feelings of the Prussians toward us."[42]

In these letters, Stoffel had also mentioned hearing rumors of his pending recall and replacement. As Piétri knew nothing of the matter, he spoke to the emperor and found him to believe that Stoffel wanted to leave Berlin and to return home. "I showed him your letter as proof that you had expressed no such desire, and that you had been surprised at the news that a successor was being contemplated. His Majesty said, that being the case, he would speak to the minister of war."[43] Stoffel was told, meanwhile, that he would remain at his post and not to worry. Piétri was circumspect in his choice of words, but managed to convey the message that the insiders at the ministry of war had been endeavoring to rid themselves of an annoyance.

"As you are accused of negligence within the ministry of war," Piétri added, as a further justification for Stoffel's recall, "you would do well to send the ministry all the information you can procure, significant or otherwise. If nothing is new, repeat old news of value. They want to be supremely informed, or at least to receive communications that prove *they* are busy." Stoffel was subsequently told that Lt. Col. Gaston, comte d'Andlau, had been the officer nominated to succeed him in Berlin; but that Andlau, not wanting the assignment, had been relieved by its cancellation. The letter revealed that Stoffel had been receiving small sums periodically, usually about 1,000 francs, from the emperor personally, enclosed in Piétri's letters for expenses in procuring information. Henceforth, Stoffel was to obtain necessary money directly from the French Embassy in Berlin. "His Majesty would like to have today a complete report upon *a new system of mobilization adopted by Prussia, by which she will be able to put all her troops on a war footing in nine days.* If you have already sent such a report, send another in more detail."[44]

At that moment Stoffel had a backlog of information to be converted into reports (he would submit eighteen in 1868, not all of which have survived); and he was most immediately concerned to transmit a summary of the debate on artillery then occupying the Prussians. Among the documents that would be found in the Tuileries after the overthrow of the régime in 1870 was a group published under the heading "Les canons Krupp." The intent was to prove that the régime had had the opportunity to acquire the superior guns the Prussians had used so effectively against the French, but had failed to recognize their superiority, in part because of Stoffel's report. The issue had, in fact, been considerably more complicated than the published documents could reveal.

Thanks to the emperor's initiative, the French had been equipped with rifled muzzle-loaders in 1858; and they had performed well against the Austrians in 1859. The Prussians, however, had breech-loading guns known to be effective if properly employed. Napoleon was anxious to have the French guns converted to breech-loaders, but the recent great expenditure incurred in adopting the *chassepot* aroused stiff political resistance to major expenditures on artillery. The army itself had no enthusiasm for the reform given the satisfactory performance of its guns in 1859. The argument about artillery was complicated by the fact that the new Prussian breech-loaders were steel rather than the traditional bronze, and the Prussians themselves were not of one mind about the superiority of steel.[45]

Lt. Col. Stoffel obtained a Prussian report of comparative studies made in Berlin using Austrian guns taken in 1866. He sent the report to the ministry of war in Paris with a recommendation that the full German text be translated. His accompanying resumé of it not only indicated that the tests had established the clear superiority of the Prussian field pieces but contained his unequivocal assessment, as an artilleryman, that the Prussian guns were superior to what the French then had.

After the campaign of 1866, Stoffel added, he had been permitted to examine eleven steel guns that had exploded: six of them before the war, five during the war itself. Ten of the eleven had exploded at the breech. In the case of the eleventh, a large piece had broken off the gun just ahead of the trunnions. But there was evidence that the gun had earlier been hit by an enemy projectile. In any case, the explosions had considerably unsettled artillery personnel.

Towards the end of 1866, Prince Charles, then the chief of Prussian artillery, presided over a series of meetings during which the leading artillery generals had debated rather hotly the merits of the two metals. The partisans of steel, Stoffel learned, had argued that the explosions at the breech did not disprove the superiority of steel, but had simply demonstrated the need for a better method of closure to give the breech a greater resistance. Given the large amount of money already invested in steel guns, it made no sense in their view to return to bronze without first endeavoring to correct such defects.

The opponents of steel argued that the defects in steel barrels were internal and could not be perceived: that one would never be able to see from the exterior whether the metal possessed the "homogenous conditions" necessary to provide the essential resistance. They held, moreover, that the widespread knowledge of the explosions had to be taken into account by providing gun crews only those guns which enjoyed their confidence. The lower ranking officers in particular were said to lack faith in the steel guns.

The dispute was unresolved during 1867, although the king did not flag in his support for Krupp's steel guns. Steel was as yet used only for field artillery. The foundary at Spandau continued to pour bronze gun barrels for the navy and for the defense of forts. But, given the clamor, Stoffel suspected that, if Prussia did not already have much steel campaign material on hand, she would probably return to bronze. At Essen, it was known that Friedrich Krupp feared the loss of his market.[46]

In fact, only a month before Stoffel submitted this assessment, Krupp had endeavored to interest Napoleon III in adopting his steel breech-loading guns by sending him two reports on firing tests: a test on a nine-inch gun (228 mm.), and with four-inch guns (101.33 mm.).[47] The brochures were at once forwarded to General Leboeuf, chairman of the Artillery Committee. By the time Leboeuf sent his appraisal of the brochures to the emperor, he had received and read Stoffel's report on the debate in Prussia. While Leboeuf acknowledged that the tests had indicated the viability of steel, he reminded the emperor that experiments on steel guns of various calibres from a variety of manufacturers (including Krupp) had been made in France for the previous ten years. Some guns had withstood a great number of rounds, others had exploded after firing only a few rounds. Having been informed by Stoffel that the Prussians were contemplating a return to bronze, Leboeuf could only believe that the steel guns were as yet unreliable. He anticipated further information from Stoffel when the Prussian decision was made.[48] The dossier on the issue in the emperor's office was consequently closed, 11 March 1868, with the notation, "Nothing to be done."[49]

Somewhat over a year earlier, the emperor had asked Stoffel about rumors the Prussians had a new rifle under consideration. Stoffel had only been able to find evidence that the Prussians were eager to improve their established model, the needle-gun, being aware of the *chassepot*'s superior range. An agent of an American firm had been in Berlin recently attempting to interest the Prussians in a mechanism alleged to extend a rifle's range at a cost of eight francs per rifle, but his proposition had not been accepted. In one respect, Stoffel added, the Prussians regarded the needle-gun to be superior to the *chassepot*: for hand-to-hand combat. As the butt was preferred in close combat to the bayonet, the heavier, stouter rifle was an advantage.[50]

Napoleon III, meanwhile, anxious for legislative action on the delayed military bill, had summoned parliament early for its 1868 session. His speech from the throne, 18 November 1867, opened with the assurance that his government was unchanged in its desire for peace, despite persistent rumors that the interior changes in Germany must be cause for conflict. "We must frankly accept changes worked out across the Rhine; and make it known that, so long as our interests and our position are not threatened, we shall not interfere with those transformations produced by the will of the populations."[51] Even so, he continued, the government has the duty to work for the improvement of all institutions which make the country strong, including the perfection of the military establishment. The military law to be submitted for debate, he claimed, amounted to simple modifications in the Law of 1832. "But it will attain the end I have always pursued: to reduce service in time of peace and augment it in time of war."[52] The bill was introduced on 14 January 1868.

Entitled the Law on Army Recruitment and the Organization of the National Mobile Guard, the measure was soon called simply the Niel Law and with some justice. The idea had originally been his as a politic alternative to universal military obligation, and it was his intention to make the mobile guards a second army to defend the home front in time of war. That would permit the active army to be engaged entirely and immediately against the enemy and beyond the frontiers if required. Territorial troops, in other words, but they could serve as a reserve in case of emergency. As far as the army itself was concerned, the Niel Law amounted to a return to the principles of 1832, eliminating the changes that had been made in 1855. Active service for those drawing "bad numbers" was fixed at five years, after which the men remained in the Reserve for four years. Exoneration was abolished, but the purchase of replacements was again officially condoned.

The creation of the mobile guards was the only novel aspect of the law. This force was to encompass young men who had drawn "good numbers" since the annual contingent of 1864, or who would draw them in the future as well as those who bought replacements. The term of service was to be five years, but the individual was to be subject to no more than fifteen days of training in any given year; and a man could not be removed from his home or job for more than twenty-four hours at a time. The possibility of replacement did not apply to the mobile guards. It could be argued, therefore, that the principle of universal service had been restored, but only to the limited degree that service in the mobile guards required. The drastic restrictions upon training time, imposed by the Corps législatif as the compromise necessary to get any law at all, fell short of imperial expectations for a French Landwehr. As Adrien Dansette put it, the mountain had labored and brought forth a mouse.[53]

Marshal Niel, who had been profoundly committed to the government's project, set himself to organize the mobile guards despite the crippling format. He established a special bureau within the ministry of war, comprising officers from the General Staff, to prepare instructions for the generals who commanded the territorial divisions. The units were to be organized on a departmental basis, their officers to be drawn either from retired officers still capable of active service, or from officers who had resigned from the army, but who wished to take part in these new formations. Anticipating a shortage of such officers, Niel meant to commission young men at the local level who, thanks to their education or their rank in society, showed the necessary aptitudes for command positions. Once cadres of officers could be established, suitable non-commissioned officers were to be located.[54] Niel's death on 13 August 1869, following an operation for a bladder stone, removed the prime mover from the scene; and precious little would come of his project.[55]

Stoffel's dismay over the legislature's gutting of the Niel Bill can be deduced from Piétri's response to his letter: "What you said in your last letter is fair enough. But I, like you, do not expect to see the emperor reconcile himself to such circumstances in the future as he has done, or been forced to do, up to now. . . .We must remain continually alert and work indefatigably to make ourselves the strongest."[56] All well and good, but the opposition to reform had demonstrated its formidable strength.

Notes

1. Bapst, *Le Maréchal Canrobert* 4: 54–56.

2. The full Commission on the Reorganization of the Army included six members of the cabinet: Rouher, Marshal Vaillant, Marshal Randon, Fould, Chasseloup-Laubat, and Vuitry; plus Marshals Baraguay d'Hilliers, Canrobert, Regnaud de Saint-Jean d'Angely, MacMahon, Niel, and Forey; Generals de Palikao, Fleury, Lebrun, Allard, Bourbaki, Leboeuf, Frossard, and Trochu; and two intendants, Darricau and Pagès. Piétri to Stoffel, 21 November 1866, "Lettres au colonel Stoffel," 3: 721–22; *Le Moniteur*, 1 November 1866.

3. François-Charles Du Barail, *Mes souvenirs, 1820–1879* 3: 80–84; Bapst, *Le Maréchal Canrobert* 4: 56–62.

4. Piétri to Stoffel, 21 November 1866. Legge, The *Comedy and Tragedy of the Second Empire*, p. 326.

5. Ducrot to Trochu, ca. 7 December 1866. Auguste Poulet-Malassis, ed., *Papiers secrets et correspondance du Second Empire*, pp. 4–5 ; Lehautcourt, "La Réorganisation de l'armée avant 1870," pp. 536–37; Vincent Benedetti, *Ma Mission en Prusse*, pp. 202–04.

6. Piétri to Stoffel, 21 November 1866. Legge, *The Comedy and Tragedy of the Second Empire*, p. 327.

7. Etat des services. Dossiers Stoffel (lst dossier); Piétri to Stoffel, 3 January 1867. Piétri, "Letters au colonel Stoffel," 3: 724

8. Report of ? November 1866. Stoffel, *Rapports militaires*, *pp.* 48–62. The Prussian organization would be altered further by the Law of 9 November 1867.

9. Piétri to Stoffel, 20 December 1866. Piétri, "Lettres au colonel Stoffel," 3: 724.

10. Bapst, *Le Maréchal Canrobert* 4: 62–63.

11. Ibid. 4: 64.

12. Michael Howard, *The Franco-Prussian War*, pp. 29–31, 37. A brief but well-informed account of the reform movement.

13. *Oeuvres de Napoléon III* 5: 278, 282–84.
14. Piétri to Stoffel, 3 January 1867. Legge, *The Comedy and Tragedy of the Second Empire*, p. 329.
15. Adrien Dansette, *Du 2 décembre au 4 septembre: le Second Empire*, p. 287.
16. Raymond Cazelles, *Le Duc d'Aumale, prince aux dix visages*, pp. 350–52.
17. Duc d'Aumale to Cuvillier-Fleury, 2 April 1867, *Correspondance du duc d'Aumale et de Cuvillier-Fleury* 4: 161.
18. Du Barail, *Mes souvenirs, 1820–1879* 3: 232–33; Bapst, *Le Maréchal Canrobert* 4: 66–67.
19. Louis-Jules Trochu, *Oeuvres posthumes* 1: 62–65.
20. Ibid. 1: 65–75.
21. The conversation is said to have occurred on 11 April 1867. Bapst, *Le Maréchal Canrobert* 4: 64–67; Howard, *The Franco-Prussian War*, p. 37
22. Trochu, *L'Armée française en 1867*, pp . 3–7, 12.
23. Ibid., pp. 32–34.
24. Ibid., pp. 39–62.
25. Ibid., pp. 277–80.
26. Ibid., p. 68.
27. Ibid., pp. 68–70.
28. Ibid., pp. 70–81.
29. Ibid., pp. 120–28.
30. *Procès du Général Trochu contre MM. Vitu et de Villemessant du Figaro*, p. 60.
31. Trochu, *L'Armée française en 1867*, pp. 270–73.
32. Ibid., pp. 274–76.
33. Ibid., pp. 281–85.
34. For a balanced and succinct treatment of the Luxembourg crisis, see Otto Pflanze, *Bismarck and the Development of Germany* 1: 377–91.
35. Barthélemy-Louis-Joseph Lebrun, *Souvenirs militaires, 1866–1870*, pp. 24–27.
36. Ibid., p. 28.
37. Richard Holmes, *The Road to Sedan: The French Army 1866–1870*, pp. 15–17.
38. Ibid., pp. 129–51.
39. General Trochu to Marshal Leboeuf, 11 July 1870. Trochu, *Oeuvres posthumes* 1: 84–85.
40. Alfred, comte de La Chapelle, *Oeuvres posthumes et autographes inédits de Napoléon III en exil* 2: 23–58; Lebrun, *Souvenirs militaires*, pp. 45–49.
41. Report of 2 December 1867. Stoffel, *Rapports militaires*, pp. 64–77.
42. Piétri to Stoffel, 27 December 1867. Legge, *The Comedy and Tragedy of the Second Empire*, p. 330.
43. Piétri to Stoffel, 27 December 1867. Piétri, "Lettres au colonel Stoffel," 3: 727.
44. Piétri to Stoffel, 8 January 1868. Ibid. 3: 728–31.
45. Howard, *The Franco-Prussian War*, pp. 35–36.
46. Report of 20 February 1868. Stoffel, *Rapports militaires*, pp. 87–92.
47. Henri Haase to Napoleon III, 23 January 1868. Poulet-Malassis, ed., *Papiers secrets et correspondance du Second Empire*, p. 324.

48. Edmond Leboeuf to Napoleon III, 27 February 1868. Ibid., pp. 325–28.
49. Ibid., p. 328.
50. Report of 20 February 1868. Stoffel, *Rapports militaires*, pp. 93–94.
51. *Oeuvres de Napoléon III* 5: 298–99.
52. Ibid., p. 300.
53. Bernard Schnapper, *Le Remplacement militaire en France: quelques aspects politiques, économiques et sociaux du recrutement au XIXe siècle*, pp. 259–60; Adrien Dansette, *Du 2 décembre au 4 septembre: le Second Empire*, pp. 291–92; Chesney and Reeve, *The military Resources of Prussia and France*, p. 247, republished the Niel Law from the minutes of the Corps législatif; Richard D. Challener, *The French Theory of a Nation in Arms*, pp. 17–22.
54. Joseph-Edouard de La Motte-Rouge, *Souvenirs et campagnes* 3: 338–39.
55. Roger L. Williams, *The Mortal Napoleon III*, p. 126.
56. Piétri to Stoffel, 22 March 1868. Piétri, "Letters au colonel Stoffel," 3: 730.

Part III

The Gadfly:
Stoffel's Final Two Years in Berlin

During Baron Stoffel's years in Berlin, the French ambassador to Prussia was Vincent Benedetti, whose appointment dated from 5 October 1864. A Corsican by birth, comte Benedetti had enjoyed many years of successful foreign service. He became the first French envoy to the new Italian kingdom in 1861, after having completed negotiations for the Treaty of Turin by which Nice and Savoy were ceded to France in 1860. And he had long been an open sympathizer with Italian national aspirations. As such, he was associated with the Thouvenel faction in the French foreign office which worked to undermine the Vienna settlement of 1815. His appointment to Berlin in 1864 was seen correctly as a signal that Napoleon III sought rapprochement with Prussia: as indication that the emperor had not veered from his habitual antagonism to Austria.[1]

In those circumstances, Stoffel's association with Benedetti ought to have been cordial. Benedetti was sympathetic to Prussian goals, at least initially; and Stoffel, for all his apprehension about the failure of France to keep pace with Prussian military reform, was not anti-German. The circumstances had been altered, however, by Benedetti's failure to obtain Prussian compensation for France in 1866-67. He became the most immediate victim of Bismarck's refusal to permit French expansion into Luxembourg to compensate for Prussian expansion in North Germany. And he became the ultimate victim, too, by giving Bismarck, during the negotiations, a treaty draft in his own hand providing for French annexation of Belgium, no matter that the ideas therein had probably initially been Bismarck's. When that draft was exposed by

Bismarck in 1870, it would contribute to the isolation of France and to the destruction of Benedetti's reputation. Fearful that the balance of power was at stake, he had embarked upon a personal policy; for the annexation of Belgium was not a matter of official policy.[2]

Thereafter, Benedetti began to warn his foreign minister of the need for serious military preparations. The government, in other words, received consistent information from its chief diplomatic and military agents in Berlin. It appears, however, that in time, in 1868 and into 1869, Benedetti developed the suspicion that Stoffel was not reliable. The doubt was not transmitted officially, but evidently in verbal complaints which recommended Stoffel's replacement. The complaints added up to the charge that Stoffel was becoming more the agent of Prussia than the agent of France: that is to say, the dupe of Bismarck. One must read Stoffel's later reports (or the gist of them) with the knowledge that such charges were being made quietly, and that they would resurface in the years after the Franco-Prussian War.[3]

As there were no valid grounds for the charges, as anyone who has read Stoffel's reports could attest, what could have aroused Benedetti's antagonism? That Benedetti did not know German has always been known. As French was still the language of diplomacy, his lack of German was no obstacle to *official* communication. Stoffel's fluency in German, in contrast, gave him an obvious advantage in Berlin. He conversed freely with a variety of Prussian officers; he read technical publications on military affairs; and he read the local newspapers. The most pertinent advantage, which Benedetti sought to turn against him, was Stoffel's capacity to form friendships. He won acceptance with his bluff, engaging manner, and his professional competence. In moments of emotional intensity, he might revert to French; but he could make the Prussians comfortable through the mastery of their language. As he evidently assumed that these capabilities made his observations the more valuable, he made no effort to conceal his sociability. He was an occasional guest of Bismarck at Varzin,[4] which worried Benedetti considerably; and he became the friend of Kraft Karl, Prince zu Hohenlohe-Ingelfingen, one of Prussia's foremost artillerymen. Benedetti saw only danger in such familiarity.

Stoffel had to know, from the transparent attempt to remove him from Berlin late in 1867, that he had critics within the ministry of war. The appointment of Marshal Niel to head that ministry meant that Stoffel's critics were for the moment out of favor, and he knew that the emperor remained firmly behind him. But it is unclear whether Stoffel knew at the time, or even in later years, of Benedetti's displeasure.

Stoffel's second report in 1868, meanwhile, amounted to a long essay on the respective qualities of the Prussian and French armies. "What, in fact," he asked, "would be the situation if war were to break out tomorrow?" Some critical factors, such as who would be the French commander-in-chief, he could not know. Thus, he limited himself to the question: Which of the two armies is the finer? His appraisal was divided into two parts: *Moral factors*, by which he meant a nation's character (its traditions, history, temperament, and the level of general instruction). And *material factors*, meaning military organization, the material of war, and the level of military instruction given to *all* ranks.

The report deliberately focused primarily on Prussia on the stated assumption that the French already knew their own situation and on the evident assumption that he believed the Prussians to excel in most respects. He noted, however, that learned opinion in Prussia gave the individual French soldier high marks, holding him to be the world's best in individuality, lively intelligence, and élan. His jauntiness and high spirits were regarded to be precious qualities in war. He was thought to be more inventive than the Prussian soldier, and even a better marcher as many of the Prussians came from very flat country. The Prussians also recognized the superiority of his rifle. In Stoffel's opinion, that ended the list of French advantages.

Prussian moral superiority rested upon obligatory public instruction, in effect far more than thirty years. Except in the Polish provinces, the Prussians had extended public instruction to all classes, a success unequaled by any other European country. Stoffel believed that the cultivation of the mind in France was still, in 1868, mainly confined to the large cities; while, in North Germany, that cultivation was common in cities of third or fourth rank. How much the Prussians had achieved by 1866 became astonishingly clear during the interrogation of Austrian prisoners, many of whom were found to be so little schooled that they did not know the difference between the left and right hands.

Finally, as a moral factor, Stoffel cited the sense of duty that seemed to pervade the Prussian population including the bureaucracy. He claimed not to know the source of it (despite his discussion of obligatory service and obligatory instruction as civic duties), simply noting that the phenomenon was obvious. Everyone in government, right up to Bismarck he added, was quite aware of that quality.

As for the components of Prussian material superiority, Stoffel stressed, as in 1866, the advantages of establishing special services on a permanent basis: the companies of railroad crews, telegraphers, and stretcher-bearers. Despite the technical superiority of the *chassepot*, the Prussians believed that their infantry fire would be more disciplined and accurate than that of the French because of the great attention paid to instruction and target practice. He thought the superiority of Prussian artillery to be incontestable. The French had lighter gun-carriages, giving a greater mobility. But the Prussian guns had a faster rate of fire, longer ranges, and greater accuracy than the French; and Prussian gunners received more intensive instruction than the French.

Stoffel knew that the Austrian artillery had worked considerable damage on Prussian artillery during the campaign in Bohemia, a factor contributing to subsequent French complacence about Prussian gunnery. At the outbreak of the war in 1866, the Prussians had not completed their conversion to steel guns. About one-third of their guns were outmoded bronze smooth-bores, which fared poorly against the Austrian rifled-bores that had a longer range. Emerging on the offensive from mountain passes, the Prussians had difficulty finding suitable positions and were pounded by Austrian guns already in position and protected with breastworks. At the end of the battle, a portion of the Austrian gunners had showed a heroic firmness in covering the retreat, further contributing to the myth of Austrian superiority. In fact, Stoffel concluded, Prussian officers were better trained than their Austrian counterparts, and their equipment was now entirely superior.[5]

Stoffel had not wavered in his conviction that the greatest material advantage enjoyed by Prussia was the composition of her general staff. He had raised the matter in 1866; he returned to it here "to raise a cry of alarm and issue a warning. If the French do not do something to repair this particular inferiority, they may be in for a cruel repentance in the future."[6] The composition of the Prussian general staff had never been defined by a particular law or regulation. An assumption had been made that, of all the officers in the army, those on the general staff ought to be the most intelligent and the most learned; and that the general staff ought to function as the highest instructional unit in the army. Beyond the soundness of the institution itself was Moltke's personal merit. Given his almost absolute control of selection, promotion, and reassignment, he guaranteed the success of the system.

He redescribed its structure (see his report of 25 October 1866); but his ultimate point was that every lieutenant in the Prussian army, regardless of branch of service, was eligible to compete for the higher training in Berlin and for service on the general staff. The competition allowed Moltke to retain the very best at the top and to reassign the less able to suitable commands. "It is a merit system which teaches everyone that advancement depends upon intelligence and hard work. And no mediocrity can survive on the general staff, at least not so long as a Moltke is chief of the general staff!"[7]

What Stoffel had to say about the French general staff, in comparison, exposed his fear that the French would take no steps to remedy the insufficiency within the high command that had been obvious in 1859. At that time, the emperor, aware of his lack of field experience, appointed a major-general for guidance. His choice had been Marshal Vaillant, then age seventy, a choice that could hardly have been worse as Vaillant had been a soldier in name only. Vaillant had given up riding by then, so that an ancient horse, unable to move faster than a walk, was found for him on the campaign. When the emperor proceeded at a trot or at a gallop, the marshal could only follow on his distinctive beast, which strained to lengthen its stride. The poor man became the victim of persistent laughter within the headquarters staff. Moreover, as the minister of war immediately before the outbreak of war, Vaillant was held accountable for every deficiency in the preparations.[8]

Stoffel's determination to avoid a repeat performance aroused him to comments about the French general staff not likely to have been enjoyed by a majority of its members. The staff, he wrote, did include some officers as distinguished as the best of the Prussians (he mentioned no names). But he called many of them mediocrities: officers unable to read a map, with no knowledge of the various arms, who had never studied a campaign illustrating modern war. The War of 1859, he added, showed that some staff officers did not even know how to choose a suitable encampment for an infantry brigade or a regiment of cavalry, despite prior French experience in actual war. Such matters were taught in Prussia on field trips to officers in the Academy of War or on the general staff. A system must be devised, he concluded, which guaranteed the advancement of the army's best, and which precluded mediocrity from obtaining the best places for the duration of their careers. "Even to a point, indeed, where they are not physically able to ride a horse at a fast pace. Moltke would exclude from the general staff immediately any officer incapable of service on horseback."[9]

Stoffel, in sum, had become more worried by the comparative casualness with which the French general staff was composed than by any other French deficiency. No one seemed to be concerned whether a staff officer could go for several leagues at a full gallop; whether he could speak any foreign language (all Prussian staff officers were required to know French); or whether he had ever commanded a company, a battalion, or a regiment. For he had reached the conclusion that the Prussians had owed their victory over the Austrians primarily to their general staff officers, as well as to the excellence of their army corps staffs. "Let us beware of the Prussian general staff!"[10]

His other current worry was the influence of the growing peace movement in France. The Prussians had recently announced that about 12,000 men from the army would be sent home on furlough on 1 May 1868, a temporary measure for reasons of economy. Stoffel knew that the announcement had generated considerable discussion in the French press as to whether the measure implied hope for general disarmament, a discussion he thought to be notably devoid of common sense.

The peace movement was a small stream fed by diverse tributaries. It included intellectuals like Ernest Renan and Edgar Quinet who were sympathetic to Germany, impressed by the recent educational and intellectual ferment in the German world, which they hoped would strengthen the growth of liberal government and civilization in Western Europe. Prince Napoleon, the emperor's cousin and a friend of Renan, was counted within that group. His unofficial trip to Prussia in 1868 (he travelled incognito as the comte de Meudon) necessarily aroused speculation about a secret mission to reach a settlement with Prussia. But Napoleon III had long since learned not to entrust delicate enterprises to his unreliable relative. Piétri alerted Stoffel that the prince was on his own and without official mission. "Maybe the trip will open his eyes. He has been a bit too German."[11]

A similar group, hoping to bridge the chasm between France and the German world, was largely Alsatian in origin. The chief figures were Charles Dollfus, of the venerable industrial family, and the Protestant journalist Auguste Nefftzer. They had founded the *Revue germanique* in 1857, which Dollfus was still directing in 1868. Their editorial policy, meanwhile, had been carried into *Le Temps*, founded by Nefftzer in 1861 and regarded officially as an organ of Orleanist opinion.

The peace movement, in fact, was compromised by its frequent identification with enemies of the regime. The Ligue de la paix was founded at the time of the Luxembourg crisis in 1867 by Frédéric Passy, a political economist known to be a liberal Republican. One of his associates was Michel Chevalier, the prominent Saint-Simonian, whose loyalty to Napoleon III made him an exception to the rule in the peace movement. Similar peace groups were formed in Le Havre, Nantes, and Strasbourg, drawing their support mainly from Republican opponents of the regime. A leftwing journal, *Le Phare de la Loire*, campaigned for an international peace conference, the idea being to promote self-government and the creation of a European confederation, the United States of Europe. The movement exposed a common Republican assumption that the overthrow of monarchical governments was the necessary prelude to international peace: "peoples" would not fight each other![12]

Disarmament, whether partial or total, Stoffel commented, was conceivable or even possible in France, Austria, Italy, and Britain; but quite impossible in Prussia. The principle of obligatory military service was fundamental, not simply to Prussian military institutions, but to the social order of the nation. Even if the Prussians reduced the years of active service, and lengthened the number of years in the Landwehr to meet the constitutional requirement of twelve years of service, they would still have roughly 900,000 men available. They would not do so, he predicted, as it would mean a less efficient regular army and a greater dependence upon aging Landwehrians.[13]

Several weeks later he submitted another substantial report, which opened with a brief discussion of the military forces of the south German states. By treaties concluded in 1866, these states had put their forces at the disposition of Prussia in case of war (and depending upon the circumstances); so that Prussia had been pressing them to adopt Prussian organization, armament, and even the Prussian uniform. He provided reliable figures on south German military strength; and about which states had yielded (Baden and Hesse), and which were resisting (Bavaria and Württemberg).[14]

The bulk of the report was directed to the Artillery Committee, a response to questions about Prussian plans to perfect their rifle. Stoffel replied with his typical candor: He had accompanied the king during a military parade at Potsdam on 25 April 1868. After the review, the king asked him whether the French were no longer satisfied with their Model 1866 (as was being reported in the press) and were considering an order of 100,000 Remington rifles made in America. Stoffel replied that he had attended the exercises at the camp de Châlons the previous year, at which time the *chassepot*, despite imperfections, was said to be an excellent weapon. Many of the defects had since been remedied; but if others had recently surfaced, he did not yet know about them. The king had agreed that the rifle was an excellent arm, but added that the cartridge left much to be desired in his opinion. Stoffel promised to look into the matter.

Therefore, when the king asked Stoffel to sit next to him at lunch on 3 May, he returned to the question as frankly as possible. He had learned that certain people (unnamed) had taken it upon themselves to discredit the *chassepot* through negative articles in the press. In fact, he told the king, the rifle worked very well: very accurate with an effective range up to 1,000 meters. The cartridge did, indeed, require manufacturing improvement to obtain more exact dimensions. On occasion, the rubber ring, which sealed the breech, could be snagged by the firing pin. In cold weather the sealing of the breech was incomplete until two or three rounds had been fired, which permitted the rubber to warm and to seal completely. Such inconveniences were regarded as minor by the French, who were estimating they had an advantage over the Prussian rifle of about 10 to 7.

The French believed, Stoffel continued, that the Prussian rifle, because of the imperfect closure of the breech, could not be fired safely except at reduced loads. Any military rifle today, he told the king, must have sufficient muzzle velocity to give a flat trajectory and must be quick and easy to load to give the soldiers confidence in combat. Not only did the king agree, he added that the Prussian rifle was far from perfection by those measures. Improvements in muzzle velocity and rapidity of loading were being sought. But as the modification of a million rifles would be an expensive undertaking, nothing would be done until the benefits could be proven incontestably.[15]

This research alerted Stoffel to the persistent opposition to a breech-loading rifle in France despite the fact that he had undermined the opponents' arguments in his report of 8 September 1866. Consequently, he sought fresh information through an interview with General von Kessel, an infantry commander during the war of 1866. The principal objection to breech-loaders was that rapid fire would promote a waste of ammunition and quick deterioration of the arm. Kessel asserted that his troops had had recourse to rapid fire very rarely in Bohemia as proved by the small number of rounds expended on an average per man. Years of training had been given to convince the soldiers of the superiority of their rifles, and considerable practice on firing ranges had given the men confidence in their weapon. The advantage Prussian infantry had enjoyed in 1866 was not in actual rapid fire, but in their ability to reload easily and quickly. Austrian officers taken prisoner stated that their troops had been demoralized, not by the rapidity of Prussian infantry fire, but by the knowledge of their constant readiness to fire: their ability to reload while concealed, while the Austrians had had to expose themselves to reload. (A surprising percentage of the Austrian dead had been struck in the head.) Consequently, Austrian infantry believed themselves to be disarmed much of the time in the presence of an enemy always ready to fire. The key to success, Stoffel reasserted, with both rifle and artillery fire, is easy and quick reloading. And that meant breech-loaders.[16]

Stoffel had also been asked whether the Prussians meant to use explosive bullets (those which burst upon contact) against enemy personnel. Such bullets, he replied, were not issued to the troops. Each infantry officer carried five such bullets, but was trained to fire them only at enemy caissons to blow them up, the recommended range being 200 meters. As for so-called rifle-grenades recently mentioned in the press, they were not infantry arms, but rather what the Prussians called the Wallbüchse: a weapon to be used against ramparts in support of infantry, mounted on a light, maneuverable carriage and firing a ball which burst.[17]

The emperor continued to follow Stoffel's reports with the greatest attention and there could no longer be any question that the minister of war forwarded them immediately to the emperor after reading them himself. Marshal Niel expressed his appreciation of the reports, which contributed to the impression at the Tuileries that the emperor had found, in Niel, a minister capable of recognizing and eliminating deficiencies. Neither of them, moreover, had any second thoughts about Stoffel's reliability. "Your reports are valued in a manner very flattering to you," Piétri wrote; "and your personal letters are no less appreciated. Your association with the Bismarck family provides a magnificent position to observe and to make judgments, something unavailable to even the most crafty diplomatist."[18] We are left to wonder whether Piétri had received a hint of Benedetti's anxiety!

That very day, Stoffel was posting an additional report on the debate in Prussia about how much ammunition needed to be carried in the field. As the revolution in armament was bound to affect tactics, he advised that the French, too, ought to study the question about whether the revolution suggested that more, or less, ammunition ought to be carried with the armies. Stoffel had read a number of contradictory papers in German on the matter and talked to a number of intelligent officers. The argument for diminishing the supplies was based on the idea that the perfection of portable arms, along with the improvement in instruction at all levels, would result in a lower consumption of ammunition. Prussian figures for the Bohemian campaign, in fact, showed that the Prussian infantry on an average had consumed only seven cartridges per man. Was it not feasible to reduce the provisions to enhance mobility?

That average figure was troublesome as some of the infantry had never been in position to fire a shot. Moreover, as the new rifles and guns were rapid-fire pieces, prudence alone suggested increasing the amount of ammunition carried. The Prussians were also somewhat anxious about the fact that a French infantryman then carried more than the sixty cartridges commonly supplied to a Prussian infantryman in 1866. Each infantry battalion carried its reserve cartridges in a caisson that followed the battalion on the march and remained in its proximity during battle. The debate produced a compromise in 1868: A Prussian infantryman henceforth was to carry eighty cartridges, making possible a reduction in the reserves carried behind the lines; yet raising the total number of cartridges available per man from 163 to 168. Stoffel noted that a similar augmentation had been affected for artillery ammunition.[19]

During the summer of 1868, he composed several lengthy essays meant to undercut those in France who still did not take Prussia seriously. The first was a breakdown of the military forces then available to the North German Confederation (a total of 953,000 men), which demonstrated the enormous preponderance of Prussia within the confederation (amounting to 80% of the total population). None of the member states, and there were twenty-two of them, had a population sufficient to raise even one army corps except for Prussia and Saxony.[20]

In the second essay, Stoffel undertook to explain why the French, having fought two victorious wars in the previous fifteen years, had failed to recognize the advisability of reform; whereas the Prussians, victorious in 1866, recognized deficiencies to be corrected and had been making considerable progress in the two years since Sadowa. The critical difference, he argued, was the king's particular role in Prussia, a situation unique in Europe: His influence "goes beyond his technical capacity as chief of the army (der Kriegsherr as the Germans say); for the present king has a passion for the military métier, so much so that he is criticized for inattention to other matters. First as a prince, later as regent, and finally as king in 1861, he has been the man behind military reforms for fifteen years, notably the great reorganization of 1860. . . . He is the permanent inspector-general of the army, his eye on every unit, the inspections continual. . . . And he is a faithful attender of the Military Society in Berlin whose meetings occur every two weeks in the winter. . . . I often accompany the king on his inspections, for celebrations, not to speak of on military exercises."[21]

As a result, he concluded, the Prussians had become the most formidable of possible adversaries. Even Prince Napoleon, on his recent visit, had recognized that it no longer made sense "to make fun of Prussia." If war should break out, the Prussians would demonstrate an energy, a boldness, and a science of war that the French had not faced in Italy. "Would the Prussian troops preserve the precision of their movements in the face of our soldiers' élan? I do not know. In France, unfortunately, we have a school of officers who deny the advantage of precise movements; who go so far as to establish, as a principle, the impetuosity to be derived from disorder. Would to God that our generals would ponder what Napoleon I wrote about maneuvers and put their faith in what he said: he whose soldiers certainly had as much élan as our troops today. But it would be quite another thing against solid troops such as are the English or the Prussians. And it would then be too late for regrets!"[22]

It was possible to read the references to the king as a criticism of Napoleon III for his comparative inability to dominate the French military, or for his attention to internal affairs and constitutional reform, those "other matters" of little interest to the Prussian king. The emperor seems to have read the message otherwise, as a justification for his much criticized attempts to interfere; and he had Piétri send word of his great satisfaction to Stoffel. Piétri, who had no knowledge of military affairs, added his own opinion that Stoffel had been exaggerating the progress in Prussia deliberately to encourage greater French efforts. "These efforts have been made, and are being made every day. . . . We are ready for every event, big as it might be."[23] The tenacity of Piétri's optimism, expressed more than once in his letters to Stoffel, tells us much about the complacence at court despite the emperor's misgivings.

Accordingly, Stoffel regretted in late summer of 1868 that he must relay news that the partisans of steel artillery had lost ground to the partisans of bronze, and that a decision had just been made in Berlin to resume the manufacture of bronze guns. He knew the decision would weigh heavily on the similar debate in France and called it good news for the French *only* in that France did not yet have a foundry comparable to Herr Krupp's for the production of steel guns.[24]

He soon feared a new cause for French complacence. Among the papers found in the Tuileries and published in 1871 was a personal letter from Stoffel to Piétri, dated from Berlin, 20 November 1868. The letter had not been sent by the conventional route, but rather with a British courier; meaning that the letter had passed through Brussels and London before reaching Piétri through the ministry of foreign affairs. He had been approached by Gerson Bleichröder, Stoffel explained, the Berlin banker who managed Bismarck's personal finances. "He is the only Jew whom Bismarck receives personally, the only Jew at whose house he accepts invitations to dine."[25] Stoffel, who got on well with Bleichröder, knew that he provided Bismarck with confidential information and was used occasionally for confidential missions.

Bleichröder claimed to have been sent to Stoffel by Bismarck out of an urgent desire for peace. Did Stoffel think it would be a good idea to arrange a meeting between the king and the emperor as a means of putting out a peaceful signal that would set Europe at rest? In particular, Bleichröder added, Bismarck wanted it known that the North could not for the moment push for the annexation of the southern states; but he also believed that the unity of all Germany would someday come as a natural process. Bleichröder portrayed Bismarck as content to consolidate the gains of 1866 and to do nothing to accelerate what would inevitably come to pass in time. Bismarck's immediate associates were described as highly favorable to the proposed interview. They also believed that Napoleon III would not accept such a meeting unless Bismarck and the king gave serious guarantees, in writing, that it had nothing to do with an arrangement for the ultimate union with the South. Did Stoffel think, Bismarck wanted to know, that the emperor would agree to such an interview if such pledges were made?

Since the editor who later published this document did so to prove that Stoffel had been gulled by Bismarck's claim to want peace, Stoffel's evaluation of Bleichröder's mission requires notice. He thought it possible that Bleichröder had acted independently, taking an initiative quite on his own in order to play a larger personal role in the affairs of state. He thought it probable, however, that the initiative had been Bismarck's. For Bleichröder had said that he would be going to Paris toward the end of December and would seek an audience with the emperor if His Majesty had by then given a positive response. As Benedetti was at the moment absent from Berlin, it appeared to Stoffel that Bismarck had seized the opportunity to sound out the Tuileries unofficially. It belonged to the Tuileries, Stoffel added, to determine whether the trial balloon was proof of Bismarck's desire, sincere or not, to avoid all pretext for conflict. He had told Bleichröder, consequently, that such matters were not his province and evaded the question by claiming not to know what the emperor's inclinations would be.

The issue may not have been Stoffel's province, but his characteristic candor drove him to add personal observations which he had good reason to believe that Piétri would transmit to the emperor. Public opinion in Prussia was unchanged: suspicion and animosity when it came to France, the causes being very simple. "First incontestable fact: Prussia desires to unite all Germany, regardless in what form—a matter of indifference here. Second incontestable fact: What obstacle does Prussia see to the realization of this desire? France, and France alone. The logical conclusion: The entire Prussian nation is suspicious of us. Certain parties detest us; we are distrusted on all sides; and the least emotional at the very least see us as a barrier. In sum, animosity, mistrust, or irritation when it comes to France. Such is the fatal consequence of the events of 1866."[26]

The Bleichröder incident is curious in that it coincided with a French initiative to forge an alliance with Austria.[27] Piétri acknowledged receipt of Stoffel's letter, saying, "I have passed it on. We are all quite well-informed about the personage. He can present himself when he wants; we are forewarned, and we shall know how to cope."[28]

A recurrent theme in Stoffel's reports was the sense of continual preparation and of readiness that he met everywhere in Prussia. Everyone, from the king on down, seemed to be caught up in incessant labor. In his report of 12 December 1868, he cited the attention paid to railroads as another aspect of the mania for readiness. During 1868, a commission comprising general-staff officers had been reviewing all the railroads within the North German Confederation, preparing a recommendation on how they might best be used for military purposes. The federal chancery, Stoffel indicated, expected to have critical railway information brought up to date every two years, beginning with January 1870, enabling the government to propose improvements, extensions, the points possibly to be fortified, and so on.[29]

This attention to detail, Stoffel had learned, was fortified by the German passion for statistics. At some point during the summer of 1868, William I had talked to Stoffel of his pride in the character of his officer corps. Prussia had done as much as possible to recruit officers only from the ranks of the greater and lower nobility in the tradition of Frederick II, who believed that the nobility alone was moved by a sense of honor. William I was of similar mind, describing his officer corps as the elite of the nation in social position, instruction, and education, because of which "it is quite natural that it commands the other classes."[30] The ideal might have remained unchanged since the eighteenth century, but it was common knowledge that Prussia, having raised her forces to nearly one million men, had been suffering from a shortage of officers.

Consequently, Stoffel obtained a statistical report which revealed that the Prussians, in fact, had recognized that one could not expect to fill the voids from the nobility alone, especially in the event of a long and murderous war. Men of bourgeois origin had been invading the officer corps within the previous ten years in impressive numbers, a transformation substantially enhanced by the fusion of Prussia with the smaller states in the North German Confederation. By late 1868, only one-third of the officers in the federal army were of noble origin, two-thirds counted as bourgeois, out of a total of 13,000 officers.

Their distribution within the federal army attested to the survival of old social prejudices. Roughly 92% of the cavalry officers were noble; whereas middle-class officers had come to dominate the "special arms" three to one: artillery and engineering. The figures also showed that the nobility had not lost its preeminence in the upper ranks. The report gave a total of 1,382 general and field-grade officers in the federal army. Only 366 of them were of middle-class origin, 171 of them in the "special arms." And only seven middle-class officers had reached the rank of general! Stoffel, himself a baron and a field-grade officer, called this Frederician ideal a reasonable and just principle. He also recognized it to be inapplicable in a France that had undergone a social revolution: and the Prussian example showed him that the massive armies of the future would be fatal to the aristocratic monopoly.[31]

While Stoffel had survived transparent attempts by his critics in the past to remove him from Berlin, the backbiting went on, not the least of it within the imperial court. The emperor was well-known to have a high opinion of Stoffel's mind and abilities. Not only did he read Stoffel's reports from Berlin, he studied and annotated them. It was said at court that his preoccupation with them had become virtually a mania. Yet, high officers of the crown sought to undermine the authority of those reports. The duc de Gramont, French ambassador to Austria, complained about their pessimism and urged the appointment of a military attaché of a sunnier disposition. General Bourbaki, one of the emperor's aides-de-camp in 1869, insisted that Stoffel had a highly exaggerated view of the qualities of the Prussian general staff. During a visit to Paris that spring, the outspoken Stoffel did not hesitate to confront Bourbaki on the topic of the French general staff; and only the intervention of the Empress Eugénie prevented the incident from becoming a vociferous wrangle.[32] There is some evidence that the emperor sought to quiet the opposition to Stoffel by adding a second military attaché in Berlin; but, in the end, the appointment was not made. Stoffel's trip to Paris, otherwise unexplained, may have been for a consultation about the criticism.[33]

His knowledge of the criticism deflected him not a whit from his assigned task. The first report to follow his trip to Paris proclaimed that the Germans were very critical of French ignorance of geography and history. He had found that they applied themselves with greater intensity than the French, not merely to the study of those subjects, but to publication. Their books in general, he noted (not just history, geography, or military books), were not crawling with numerous mistakes about proper names, whether of people or localities. Even such a deluxe edition as the *Commentaire de Napoléon I*, published by the Imperial Printery, he had found to be full of mistakes with proper names. He had even found errors in the published lectures meant to be read and studied within the French army (*Conférence de l'organisation militaire de l'Allemagne*). The bridgehead for Mainz, as an example, had been named Cassel instead of Castel, a significant mistake as it suggested Cassel, the capital of Hesse-Cassel. Such errors dishonor a book, Stoffel remarked. They can also contribute to a loss of time when one attempts to read a map, not to speak of inhibiting instruction![34]

During the early months of 1869, Stoffel had been constructing a more major report, which he would submit in August; and, as a major portion of the report amounted to a sharp criticism of the legislature for having gutted the military law of 1868, one has to believe that the issue had been raised during the spring visit with the emperor. The report ostensibly reflected the Prussian appraisal of the Law of 1 February 1868, but Stoffel left no doubt that he concurred entirely in it. When the law had been promulgated, the Prussians expected it would augment substantially the military resources of France. The law was even seen as progressive to the extent that it introduced the principle of universal military obligation.

Closer study of the law had considerably modified the initial Prussian reaction. What the Prussians do not understand, Stoffel explained, is how a legislator, having adopted that principle, would then deny the means to apply it, as the law did not permit giving anything resembling adequate military instruction to the national mobile guards. Far from adding to French power, the law now seemed likely to weaken French resources. We are given an auxiliary army of 500,000 men on paper, but the article severely limiting their training had made the law deceptive. "One is stunned to think," he added, "that such a senseless measure could have been seriously proposed and discussed in the chambers of a great country, or that a government could have found such a law acceptable. Was there no one to say that the law is a trap, that you are deceiving yourselves, not to speak of the country!"[35]

What of the argument that the mobiles could be given training once war should be declared—and then used as reserves? What if the war should be of short duration? he answered. What if there should be an initial disaster leading to an invasion of France? How then would such young men be given the necessary instruction, discipline, and cohesion? "Those who have studied this law [in Berlin] regard it to be sterile. It is said that the French nation is revealing ignorance and a presumptuous vanity. One reads in serious books here a poorly disguised pleasure over the alleged decadence of the Latin races."[36] Stoffel found the cause, not in decadence, but in French self-satisfaction. Given the eminent qualities that distinguished the French nation, the public had become indifferent to what transpired beyond the frontiers. Perhaps the worst feature of the Law of 1868 was its fortification of public ignorance; for Stoffel knew of popular confidence that the law had given the country a formidable strength, equal to, or surpassing, that of Prussia.

During Stoffel's trip to Paris that spring, the emperor had asked for his opinion on the likelihood of war. The second part of this report, entitled "On the Chances for War," was an account of what he had said to the emperor on that occasion. His argument had been founded upon four main points: (1) *That war was inevitable.* He reiterated the ambition of Prussia to be the embryo of a united Germany. When one raised the question about why Prussia, after Sadowa, had not simply swept up all the German states; or why she had not since shown more resolve in uniting the states of the south with those of the north, one got only one answer in Germany: the fear of a war with France. Since 1866, France was held to be the only remaining barrier to Prussian designs; but behind the moment lay an immense residue of resentment and envy, a conviction that France had always meddled—and would continue to meddle—in German affairs.

While Stoffel respected Prussian achievements in mobilizing the national strength; and while he emphasized the urgency to recognize Prussia as energetic, tenacious, and ambitious, with a population full of valuable and solid qualities, the report made it clear that he had not consequently come to like the Prussian population, calling it unpolished, fairly arrogant, and quite without generosity.

Stoffel had come to know Bismarck, the architect of Prussian policy, very well. He saw in Bismarck a remarkable balance between intelligence and strong will. Totally committed, in other words, to the Prussification of Germany; yet, too intelligent to allow impatience to lead him into error, and anxious not to put at risk what he had already accomplished in 1866. Stoffel predicted, consequently, that Bismarck, who believed time to be on his side, would not advocate war with France, even over the issue of German unity. He had said as much to Stoffel in recent conversation, saying that the French would have to begin the firing for such a conflict to develop. What made war inevitable, Stoffel concluded, was the persistence of explosive attitudes on both sides of the Rhine: suspicions, jealousies, and overheated susceptibilities. Under such circumstances, a war could be at the mercy of an incident. In making the prediction, he was quite aware that the more sophisticated in France would scoff at the idea of such superficial causation, always seeking more complex or murkier motives.

(2) *That Prussia had no aggressive plans.* He also knew that his second premise was not shared in France, attributing the contrary view to people who knew nothing about Prussia from the inside, and who assigned their own sentiments to the Prussians. No doubt, he hastened to add, that Prussia was ambitious; arrogance was certainly not lacking; her military preparations were unquestionably formidable. But why conclude, without any proof, that the preparations have an aggressive character? People who had taken the trouble to study German history (which he thought did not include many in France) all understood that the military activity, which dominated life in Prussia, dated from far back: that it was only a continuation of what was inherent in the life of that nation. In fact, the French had paid little attention to the reforms of 1860. Only the events of 1866, he concluded, gave birth to the belief in France that something entirely new had been born in Prussia, and that it was directed against France.

(3) *That there is great insight in Prussia* as to the national mission (*clairvoyance*). Even if not nourishing any aggressive designs, the Prussians were described as preparing for an inevitable war in France. "As a man who loves his country, I can only be saddened by the clairvoyance of our future enemies."[37] In contrast, he offered additional comments (4) *On the lack of clairvoyance in France*, which, when they were first discovered by those who overthrew the Second Empire in 1870, would be temporarily suppressed as obnoxious to those who had taken power. The French legislature, he wrote, "professes to represent the country and is, indeed, the image of the country ... in its determination not to see in Germany the development of a threatening cloud: its majority made up almost entirely of mediocrities, of men without character, without nobility, and without any of the expertise that makes a legislator; the opposition led by ambitious and puffed-up attorneys, who make a patriotism out of malignant recriminations or contrived malice. Men who conceal both incapacity and impotence with florid language, who assert that they alone are solicitous for the interests of the country, and who dispute every last soldier and cent with the government in their efforts to gain an artificial popularity! Men who would be execrated if the truth of their crimi-

nal conduct were understood: for they seek to weaken France and are betraying her to the benefit of her most fearful enemy.

"In Prussia, the press stops at nothing in exciting the public against France, in presenting France as the irreconcilable enemy of Germany; and it supports the government in every possible measure to prepare for any eventuality. In France, the press is at the service of parties rather than the country, a disunifying agency even in the face of danger from abroad."

Notice the contrast in the moral climate: Discipline, patriotism, and energy in Prussia; whereas in France the respectable is no longer respected: virtue, honor, love of country, the family, and religion have become subjects of mirth. . . . All the fine French national qualities: generosity, fairness, the charm of wit, the élan of the heart; all are being gradually enfeebled or effaced, especially at the hands of our novelists, to a point where the noble French race will soon recognize only its defects."[38]

As for possible regenerative institutions, he believed that obligatory military service and obligatory public instruction were fundamental. Did the French still have the necessary character to adopt obligatory military service? He had his doubts. The willingness to sacrifice, the sense of duty, were too eroded. Even in the case of Prussia, it had taken a Jena before she turned around to temper herself with invigorating and male institutions. France had had, in the aftermath of the February Revolution, one occasion for the adoption of obligatory service, to apply the principles of equality so passionately proclaimed at that moment. He referred to the effort of General Lamoricière's commission to abolish "the dreadful evil of military replacement. . . . The project would have been adopted save for the intervention of M. Thiers. The road to universal military obligation was thus blocked by this man whose nature is devoid of any sense of true greatness, of any strong convictions, who is incapable of profound thought, and who has been more fatal to his country than twenty disasters."[39] Can Colonel Stoffel have forgotten these intemperate sentences when he authorized the publication of his reports in 1871?

Thereafter, he turned to more politic topics, perhaps a reaction to the unanticipated death of Marshal Niel on 13 August 1869. His replacement at the ministry of war was General Edmond Leboeuf, an energetic officer who had given the emperor some assistance in 1865 in getting the *chassepot* tested. Stoffel, in fact, limited his next report in September to information on minor improvements in the Prussian rifle supplied to five battalions for tests on firing and service. The Prussians were described as concerned by the inferiority of their rifle to that of the French.[40]

When in Paris, Stoffel had talked to the emperor, the minister of war, and others about the increasing sophistication of the Prussian telegraph service.

He decided to make a formal report on the subject in the autumn of 1869, in part because the reorganized Prussian system had worked satisfactorily during the fall maneuvers of the II Corps in Pomerania, in part because he thought the French were not giving the topic sufficient study. The Prussians had had a military telegraph service in 1866, but its effectiveness left something to be desired. Its organization had proved to be faulty; and Stoffel had learned during his mission to Bohemia in 1866 that Prussian troops had not hesitated to cut telegraph poles for firewood or to use the lines to tie horses.

The reorganized system divided military telegraph service into two parts: one service was attached to the army and used exclusively for military operations. A second service, located in staging areas behind the lines, assured communication between the army and the state telegraphic network. As a detailed account of its operation had just been published, Stoffel included a copy with his report with a recommendation that it be translated for instructional use in France. He also called attention to the special telegraphic instruction by then provided in all military schools and in the large garrisons. And he noted that the engineering personnel, which operated the telegraph service, was drawn from the Landwehr (as in the case of other exceptional services such as medical teams and railway companies), so that the regular effectives of the standing army were not reduced.

The report concluded with a description of internal security in Berlin itself. Direct telegraphic communication had been established between every caserne in the city and the king's personal office and the ministry of war. Telegraph wires were understood to be vulnerable in an emergency, but they could be easily put underground for greater security. The prefecture of police in Berlin had also been connected by wire to all its police and fire stations. The Prussians remained astonished that Paris had nothing comparable.[41]

At that moment Paris was endeavoring to cope with internal security through constitutional reform, which would lead to the Liberal Empire on 2 January 1870. Piétri urged Stoffel to be patient, describing it as a moment of great uneasiness, of domestic crisis, as the regime was undergoing fundamental transition. Stoffel had been negotiating with Heinrich Kiepert, the eminent German geographer, for a position at the Ecole pratique des hautes études. The minister of public instruction was willing to provide a salary of 7,500 francs, plus an allocation for books and equipment. And Stoffel was told that, if Kiepert hesitated over the terms, the emperor would provide funds to raise the salary to 12,000 francs a year; for Kiepert was very much wanted.[42]

As the use, or misuse, of cavalry by both sides in the Franco-Prussian War would doom traditional cavaliers, Stoffel's assessment of their future at the beginning of 1870 bears note. It was most likely provoked by an imperial order of 27 December 1869 making free and obligatory instruction in swordsmanship available in the French army to increase the skill of French cavalrymen. Most of the cavalry engagements in 1866 had turned into a free-for-all once the opposing forces had collided. Prussian regimental commanders had concluded that their horsemen needed to develop greater skill and agility and were now paying more attention to swordsmanship and gymnastics. Stoffel believed that the Prussian conscript generally became a better horseman than the French conscript; but that the French cavalryman, on balance, was superior to his Prussian counterpart because of far superior swordsmanship. Prussian officers complained in particular about their inability to get their men to use the point of the sabre. They were said to have an irremediable determination to strike great blows, thus leaving themselves open to thrusts. The recent French order, Stoffel concluded, would only increase the French advantage.

On the other hand, the Prussians generally believed that the role of the horse in warfare was decreasing, not only because of improved infantry and artillery weapons, but because the immense improvement in communications (rail and wire) implied less dependence upon cavalry as the eyes and ears of the army. The Prussian decision after 1866 to augment the proportion of its effectives assigned to cavalry did not seem to square with the general assumption about the future of the horse; and Stoffel could only surmise that the vaster scale of modern warfare implied a much greater need for intelligence and information. Henceforth, the traditional formation of large masses of cavalry would be abandoned in favor of supporting each infantry division with a brigade of two or three cavalry regiments.[43]

The last word Stoffel would have to say about the future of artillery indicated that the proponents of steel were sensing victory by early 1870. The Prussians had paid close attention to recent Austrian tests on large-calibre guns for naval ships. It appeared that the Austrians would abandon bronze for guns of steel manufactured by Krupp, a result seen as a new victory for Prussian intelligence and industry in Berlin. It would mean the adoption of Krupp guns by four countries: Germany, Russia, Belgium, and Austria. Another series of experiments, carried out on iron guns at Finspang in Sweden, had also gone well. Consequently, they had been adopted not only for Sweden-Norway, but by the Dutch and the Danes. As the iron guns were less expensive to produce than those of steel, the Prussians worried they might yet deal Krupp a mortal blow.[44]

The advent of the Liberal Empire on 2 January 1870 brought Emile Ollivier into power, a man long identified with those liberals who had advocated friendship with Germany, not to speak of disarmament. He saw no danger to France in a unified Germany and, as a member of the Republican opposition in 1867, had opposed the emperor's effort to enhance French security through the annexation of Luxembourg. He embodied, in short, that wing of the peace movement which sought the abolition of war through the promotion of liberty and democracy. During Ollivier's first weeks in office, the ministry moved to open talks for international disarmament; and, despite the emperor's objections, announced a reduction of 10,000 men in the contingent to be drafted in 1870 as a measure of good faith. The new tone in Paris encouraged even Bismarck to believe—in February of 1870—that he might bring off the unification of Germany without the risk of war.[45]

But what would be the reaction in Germany to the disarmament initiative? the emperor wanted to know. And would it have any influence upon Bismarck?[46] Stoffel's answers occupied two new reports. The south German state of Baden had just reduced its period of active military service from three to two years, and it was speculated that Bavaria and Württemberg would follow suit. Those in Prussia, Stoffel explained, who anticipated the annexation of the south German states to the North German Confederation, admitted that it would be necessary to bring those states in with their own military laws. And annexation under those circumstances might give impetus to those Prussian liberals who had been advocating a similar reduction in Prussia. The Prussian government was determined not to bend on the issue, regarding the three-year term as essential. Stoffel believed that the matter would become an explosive issue in 1871 when the Reichstag would be legally required to fix again the size of the standing army and what each member state must contribute.[47] Stoffel cautioned against underestimating the significance of Baden's action, and his report surely forecast greater obstacles to the unification of Germany than Bismarck's recent optimism warranted.

As for the matter of European disarmament, Stoffel had not changed his views about what Prussia's response would be since he first reported on the matter on 23 April 1868. "It makes no sense to believe," he reiterated, "that the country would willingly abandon a principle that underlies her other fundamental institutions, such as universal suffrage and obligatory instruction; and which has contributed so obviously to the development of national strength and greatness, and, thus, to the intellectual and moral development which makes Prussia the most enlightened and disciplined people in Europe."[48] The army was not simply a military institution, but a social institution: the fruit of royal paternalism. Not only was disarmament then an impossibility for Prussia; but "it means that, sooner or later, no matter the cost, all great powers will be driven to adopt the principles of Prussian military organization."[49]

In the spring of 1870, not long after submitting his report on disarmament, Stoffel went to Paris for consultations. "The emperor wants to see you tomorrow morning at ten," Piétri wrote. "Be on time and stay to lunch with us."[50] Although he returned to Berlin to complete several more technical reports in June and July, they came too late to have aroused any interest. The emperor had him promoted to the rank of colonel on 24 June 1870, a moment when neither man suspected the imminence of war. Stoffel's report of 1 July 1870, in fact, provided his government with the dates and locations planned for the maneuvers of various German units for the autumn of 1870.

Notes

1. Willard A. Fletcher, *The Mission of Vincent Benedetti to Berlin 1864–1870*, pp. 1–6.

2. Ibid., p. 276 ; Théodore Juste, *Napoléon III et la Belgique, le traité secret*, pp. 56–57; Hubert-Joseph-Walther Frère-Orban, *Le Temps*, 18 April 1892.

3. Emile Ollivier, *L'Empire libéral* 12: 326–28; Henri Welschinger, *La Guerre de 1870, causes et responsabilités* 1: 260.

4. Stoffel, *Rapports militaires*, p. xix.

5. Report of 23 April 1868. Ibid., pp. 97–110.

6. Ibid., p. 112.

7. Ibid., pp. 113–24.

8. Bapst, *Le Maréchal Canrobert* 3: 196–97.

9. Report of 23 April 1868. Stoffel, *Rapports militaires*, pp. 125–27

10. Ibid., pp. 128–31.

11. Piétri to Stoffel, 22 March 1868. Piétri, "Lettres au colonel Stoffel," 3: 730. See Ernest d'Hauterive, ed., *Napoléon III et le Prince Napoléon*, p. 294.

12. Taxile Delord, *Histoire du Second Empire* 5: 178–79; Fernand L'Huillier and Pierre Benaerts, *Nationalité et nationalisme*, pp. 181–82.

13. Report of 23 April 1868. Stoffel, *Rapports militaires*, pp. 31–34.

14. Report of 8 May 1868. Ibid., pp. 137–39.

15. Ibid., pp. 141–44.

16. Ibid., pp. 145–47.

17. Ibid., pp. 148–49.

18. Piétri to Stoffel, 28 May 1868. Piétri, "Lettres au colonel Stoffel," 3: 732–33.

19. Report of 28 May 1868. Stoffel, *Rapports militaires*, pp. 151–58.

20. Report of 24 June 1868. Ibid., pp. 163–84.

21. Report of 22 July 1868. Ibid., pp. 190–200.

22. Ibid., pp. 201–05.

23. Piétri to Stoffel, 17 August 1868. Legge, *The Comedy* and *Tragedy of the Second Empire*, pp. 334–35.

24. Reports of 29 July and 31 August 1868. Stoffel, *Rapports militaires*, pp. 210–11, 215.

25. Stoffel to Pietri, 20 November 1868. Poulet-Malassis, ed., *Papiers secrets et correspondance du Second Empire*, p. 132.

26. Ibid., p. 134.

27. Pflanze, *Bismarck and the Development of Germany* 1: 428–29.

28. Piétri to Stoffel, 6 December 1868. Piétri, "Lettres au colonel Stoffel," 4: 121.

29. Report of 12 December 1868. Stoffel, *Rapports militaires*, pp. 263–65.

30. Ibid., pp. 266–67.

31. Report of 19 December 1868. Ibid., pp. 277–81.

32. Mme A. Carette, *Souvenirs intimes de la cour des Tuileries* 2: 27–28; Cécile Aubry-Vitet, *Souvenirs de Froehner*, pp. 21–24; Legge, The *Comedy and Tragedy of the Second Empire*, p. 323.

33. Piétri to Stoffel, 27 May 1869. Piétri, "Lettres au colonel Stoffel," 4: 123.

34. Report of 14 June 1869. Stoffel, *Rapports militaires*, pp. 286 88.

35. Report of 12 August 1869. Ibid., pp. 289–91.

36. Ibid., pp. 292–96.

37. Ibid., p. 314.

38. Ibid., pp. 301–21.

39. Ibid., pp. 325–27.

40. Report of 20 September 1869. Ibid., p. 336.

41. Report of 17 November 1869. Ibid., pp. 346–54.

42. Piétri to Stoffel, 10 December 1869. Piétri, "Lettres au colonel Stoffel," 4: 124–25.

43. Report of 9 January 1870. Stoffel, *Rapports militaires*, pp. 362–68.

44. Report of 22 January 1870. Ibid., pp. 378–81.

45. Theodore Zeldin, *Emile Ollivier and the Liberal Empire of Napoleon* III, pp. 168–75; Pierre de la Gorce, *Histoire du Second Empire* 6: 175–81.

46. Piétri to Stoffel, 4 February 1870. Piétri, "Lettres au colonel Stoffel," 4: 125.

47. Report of 14 February 1870. Stoffel, *Rapports militaires*, pp. 382–84.

48. Report of 23 February 1870. Ibid., p. 392.

49. Ibid., p. 403.

50. Piétri to Stoffel, 9 April 1870. Piétri, "Lettres au colonel Stoffel," 4: 126.

51. Etat des services. Dossiers Stoffel (lst dossier).

52. Report of 1 July 1870. Stoffel, *Rapports militaires*, pp. 432–38.

Part IV

The Outbreak of War

The story of the Hohenzollern candidacy for the Spanish throne, and how it was manipulated to produce war between France and Prussia on 15 July 1870, is too well-known to require repetition here. We may even say with some assurance that the personal responsibilities for the conflict have been definitively established by distinguished recent publications.[1] The threatening language used by the French foreign minister on 6 July, to signal the intention of the new liberal regime to stand firm, inflamed war sentiment in France and rendered rational negotiation with Prussia unlikely.

On 12 July 1870, when a war seemed to be imminent, General Prince zu Hohenlohe, who commanded the Guard Corps artillery brigade, had what he called an unforgettable conversation with Colonel Stoffel. He asked Hohenlohe for an invitation to the next artillery firing practice, which Hohenlohe found surprising given the circumstances. Yet, the two were friends, and Hohenlohe granted the request for a firing practice two weeks hence. "Well," Stoffel replied, lapsing into French, "I shall be there in two weeks. I have to see how you are going to kill us." Hohenlohe said he had no intention of talking about that sad possibility, but added that Stoffel would have to admit that the coming war would be unnecessary.

At that, Stoffel cried out, again in French: "It's the greatest stupidity imaginable! Do you understand that this is something I cannot conceive of! Our emperor is a calm and reasonable man; and Ollivier is both calm and reasonable and a bit timorous. Yet, those two are making blunders which are going to plunge us, heads-up or heads-down, into a vast pit."[2] Stoffel's anxiety mounted daily until, by 15 July, he was nearly beside himself in Hohenlohe's opinion.

Not so distraught, however, as to neglect his duty: for on 16 July he reminded the ministry of war, by telegraph, of his earlier report on the timetable of Prussian mobilization. "One should expect," he repeated, "that it will take eight or nine days for the several army corps, mobilized in the various provinces, to be transported by rail to the designated point of concentration. Counting, therefore, from 15 July, Prussia will have several armies of 100,000 to 120,000 men each after twenty days on different points of our frontiers."[3] His calculations were precise, as the battles of Wissembourg, Froeschwiller, and Forbach would be fought between 4 and 6 August.[4]

In planning the disposition of Prussian forces, the Prussians had been troubled by the possible use of the French fleet to land Franco-Danish troops in Hanover in expectation of Hanoverian sympathy. It was known that the parties concerned had undertaken negotiations, and Prussia was aware that many Hanoverians would welcome the opportunity to recover their independence from Prussia. But no firm plans were in place at the outbreak of war.[5] The rough treatment Colonel Stoffel experienced in Berlin after the outbreak was linked in an odd way to the Hanoverian question; that is, the persistence of a separatist movement in Hanover that had opposed annexation by Prussia in 1866.

Prince Napoleon became the principal advocate of what he called a Baltic diversion once war became a certainty. During the previous weeks, he had been enjoying a trip in Scandinavia en route to the Arctic with Ernest Renan. They had had word of the Spanish crisis, but hoped, in Renan's words, that nothing would interfere with the steady progress of all peoples toward civilization and liberty.[6] A telegram announcing the likelihood of war reached them at Tromsö in Norway, a profound shock to a man like Renan who believed that the threat of war had been removed indefinitely, perhaps forever.[7] The prince was instructed to return to Paris at once.

Upon his return, the prince was joined by General Trochu to advocate the Baltic diversion. Trochu estimated that is would require 30,000 French infantry, a division of cavalry, and supporting artillery. The Danes would be asked to furnish the rest: about 40,000 men plus materiel. They anticipated, of course, the cooperation of Hanover. General Trochu was to be placed in command of the ground forces, while Prince Napoleon suggested himself as commander of the fleet, an idea the minister of the marine, Admiral Rigault de Genouilly, called preposterous. Marshal Leboeuf, knowing he would be outnumbered on the Rhine, claimed he could not spare the forces requested, especially in view of the fact that the operation had not been adequately planned and would have to be improvised. The idea of such a strike probably had merit; its effectiveness depended upon the immediate implementation that only careful prewar planning could have provided. In his later years,

General Trochu became increasingly convinced that the expedition would have altered the outcome of the war and attributed the rejection of the plan, not to its infeasibility, but to its advocacy by outsiders.[8]

At the moment of the declaration of war, Bismarck inspired articles in the press meant to arouse German patriotic anger against known Hanoverian separatists. But Hanoverians loyal to the North German Confederation, anxious to put themselves in a good light, gave Bismarck misinformation to the effect that the Stoffel reports had been among the decisive factors leading to the French declaration of war. The reports were said to have been deliberately inaccurate to encourage the French to believe that the lack of Prussian preparations made it opportune to attack. Only many months later, when those reports had been published, would Bismarck learn that they had been sound and Stoffel to be a man of "respectable character."[9]

For the moment, the Hanoverian charges convinced Bismarck that Stoffel had betrayed their friendship. On 18 July, when Georges Le Sourd, the French chargé d'affaires, delivered the declaration of war to Bismarck (Benedetti being at Ems), he also told Bismarck that the embassy staff would leave Berlin the following evening, and that Stoffel would accompany the staff. Bismarck did not find that arrangement satisfactory, saying that if Stoffel were still in Berlin on the 19th, he would be considered a prisoner of war. Le Sourd, having no inkling of Bismarck's motive, presumed that Moltke had demanded Stoffel's immediate ouster.[10]

Stoffel supposed that the unusual treatment indicated the Prussian government had long since penetrated the supposedly secret dispatches he had been sending from the French embassy to the ministry of war in Paris and knew, therefore, of the *accuracy* of his reports on Prussian preparations. It does not appear that he ever understood the real reason for his treatment, which was so different from the friendly terms expressed by William I on taking leave of Benedetti at Ems.[11] As instructed, he left his house on the evening of the 18th for the railway station, escorted and protected by police to avoid being stoned by the ruffians who had been threatening him since the outbreak of hostilities.[12] On the following day, Bismarck gave notice in the press that no further incidents would be tolerated, that such excesses were highly reprehensible, and that Stoffel's departure from the country was not to be hampered. "The former representatives of France are under the protection of international law and of the honor of Germany until they have crossed the frontier."[13]

Stoffel reached Paris about five o'clock on the morning of the 19th and went directly to St.-Cloud to report to the emperor. Stopping for a bit of breakfast in the kitchen before going in to see the emperor, he was questioned by General Bourbaki, the aide-de-camp on duty that morning. "Well Stoffel, tell us squarely, just between us, who is going to get the thrashing?" Stoffel:

"General, I have no hesitancy in answering your question. I do believe that France will finish on top, but don't think that it is going to be easy! Prussia is remarkably well prepared. The fight is going to be long and murderous."[14] His optimism, albeit qualified, was the spontaneous optimism of responsible leadership. In a crisis, no matter the odds, the trumpet must not give an uncertain sound. We can only surmise that he repeated his prediction to Napoleon III that morning, noting that it reappeared in the emperor's order of the day issued at Metz on 28 July: "You are about to contend with one of the best armies in Europe, but others equally brave have not been able to resist your courage. . . . The war about to commence will be a long and a severe one."[15]

Stoffel had been on detached service from the 15th Regiment of Artillery since the spring of 1862, serving the emperor personally in several capacities. In effect, his military career had been subtly politicized. Because he had worked conscientiously on those tasks assigned him, all of them duties unsolicited, he does not seem to have suspected the possibility of adverse consequences. His recent promotion to the rank of colonel (24 June 1870) had been accompanied by reassignment to the 8th Regiment of Artillery, although still on detached service as he was in Berlin. He would have had reason to suppose, when his mission was terminated by the outbreak of war, that he would be ordered to take command of his regiment. Instead, after his interview with the emperor on 19 July, his detached service was extended by assignment to general headquarters of the Army of the Rhine but without a specific task.[16]

The ambiguity of his new situation may have escaped him, but probably not its irony; for he had been thrust into the very heart of the institution he believed to be the critical weakness of the French army. The motive for his assignment (which can only be reasonably deduced from explanations given for a subsequent assignment) was his intimate knowledge of the enemy forces, a useful supplement to the French intelligence service. Given Stoffel's insight, it is a pity that no record of his activity, not to speak of his judgments, remains for those early calamitous weeks of the war. The emperor, having been rebuffed in his earlier proposals to reform the general staff and to provide a permanent major-general or chief-of-staff, had appointed Marshal Leboeuf, his minister of war, to that post at the outset of the war, but without eliminating his ministerial duties. Leboeuf, an abler man than his postwar critics knew, was crippled by the burden.

The emperor's decision to be the commander-in-chief, with the major-general as his adviser, has been rightly condemned by those who recognized his lack of field experience, and by those who came to know that his particular malady made service on horseback nearly unendurable. It is said that he took command, because he shared the empress' view that a Napoleon had to be at the head of his armies. That argument would seem to be undercut by the fact that he had not taken command in the Crimea. If he ultimately came to a point of contemplating going to the Crimea, his reason was to impose unity upon bickering generals. The appointment of General Jacques Pélissier, who tolerated no dissent, got the campaign off dead center; and his ultimate victory at Sevastopol won him the marshalate. All the same, his transparent indifference to instructions from Paris had raised unforgettable doubts about his reliability.[17] In the War of 1859, he was given command of the army of observation on the Rhine, while the emperor assumed supreme command in Italy. Was it not indication that he had failed to find a senior officer in whom he had complete trust!

In the years since 1852, most of the ranking generals had opposed systematically his projected military reforms, giving him good reason to doubt their capacity for modern war. Among the few who had backed the desired reforms, Marshal Canrobert, having long since recognized that he was unfit in temperament for supreme command, would not accept appointment. Death had taken Marshal Niel. The trusted Fleury had been sent to Russia as ambassador in 1867 and had been an immense personal success.[18] Trochu, after his indiscretions of 1867, would not have been acceptable to the army. That left Leboeuf and Lebrun, and Leboeuf had seniority. Given the options, the appointment of Leboeuf was logical; but he ought to have been freed at once from his ministerial responsibilities. That he was not given supreme command outright was a measure of the emperor's apprehension. He had not wanted the war, and he had put more stock in Stoffel's warnings than in Leboeuf's assurances of absolute readiness.

Napoleon III's lack of field experience has often obscured the fact that he possessed considerable military knowledge. In 1830, at the age of twenty-two, he became a captain of artillery in the Swiss militia. In 1833, he produced a manual entitled *Considérations politiques et militaires sur la Suisse*,[19] which won praise in its day. As a prisoner at Ham, he undertook his *Etudes sur le passé et l'avenir de l'artillerie*,[20] which ended at 1638 when he turned his attention to more immediate political matters in 1845. We have already noted those articles in *Le Progrès du Pas-de-Calais* (1843) which reveal how early he recognized the importance of numbers in future warfare; and noted those occasions when he overrode the intransigence of committees to force the adoption of rifled artillery and the *chassepot*. His taste for technical innovation and his political skills could have made him a first-rate military administrator. His penchant for reflection, his unwillingness to reach decisions hastily, meant that he could not be a good general on the battlefield.[21]

General Faverot de Kerbrech, a captain in 1870 and in the emperor's personal service on campaign as an equerry, had been dismayed by the number of generals in the emperor's immediate circle who nearly lost their heads on 6 August 1870 in the face of the initial military reverses, showing none of the firmness or calm that the situation required. The most extreme of them had been General Lebrun, reviling the beaten generals as ignorant and incompetent in the presence of the emperor. The coolest and sanest heads in the crisis belonged to General Eugène Pajol and the emperor himself. Faverot believed, as did Marshal Canrobert, that the man the emperor most needed at that moment was General Fleury, who was in St. Petersburg.[22]

Napoleon's decision to relinquish personal command of his armies, and accomplished on 12 August, was an intelligent, if belated, response to military reality. The decision was also influenced by his knowledge of intense political agitation in Paris. He knew the situation must be retrieved or his regime might be lost. The Ollivier cabinet had already been turned out (9 August) by a coalition of authoritarian Bonapartists and liberal Republicans, and the demands that Marshal Leboeuf resign as major-general had become irresistible. Consequently, the emperor shifted the supreme command in the field to Marshal Achille Bazaine, a choice popular in Paris; for Bazaine enjoyed a reputation for great physical courage, and the Left in particular championed him as a commoner who had risen to the highest rank.[23]

The Army of the Rhine, originally comprising seven army corps and the Imperial Guard, had become divided into two parts as a result of the battle of Wörth. One part, later known as the Army of Metz, remained under Bazaine's personal command. The other part, later known as the Army of Châlons, was entrusted to Marshal Maurice de MacMahon, until then the commander of the 1st Corps.[24] MacMahon was retiring upon the Camp de Châlons in order to regroup his beaten troops and to receive reinforcement. As Napoleon believed that he, himself, could not return to Paris under the cloud of failure, he chose to meet MacMahon at Châlons—but not to resume command. Bazaine remained the supreme commander in the field. Yet, before leaving for Châlons, the emperor also ordered Bazaine (whose forces were retreating toward Metz) to rejoin MacMahon at Châlons. The ambiguity of the emperor's situation was obvious to everyone: under the constitution he was commander-in-chief. He had now delegated that responsibility to Bazaine, yet remained present within the army.[25]

The headquarters personnel, originally assembled at Metz for the emperor and Marshal Leboeuf, no longer had any function once the transfer in command had been completed. Colonel Stoffel was among those staff officers who were directed to Châlons in search of a new assignment. The continuing irregularity of his service only compounded the ambiguity of his military career. When MacMahon reached Châlons on the night of 16-17 August, his personal headquarter's staff had already been constituted. Wanting to utilize Stoffel's knowledge of the German armies, MacMahon simply instructed Stoffel orally to provide him information on the composition and the movements of the enemy forces, but evidently saw no reason to assign him a particular position within the chain of command.[26] He became merely a consultant: an outsider on the inside. From the start, therefore, he had to rely upon the telegraph to obtain information from those departmental authorities whose areas were about to be invaded by the Prussian Second Army commanded by Prince Frederick Charles.

On 17 August, the emperor called a meeting at Châlons to devise new plans. Quite by chance the participants, including the emperor himself, all had been more or less openly opposed to the war; whereas those who then comprised the government in Paris had generally favored its declaration. While it was not the moment for mutual recrimination, the dichotomy was a silent barrier to candid collaboration. The emperor's meeting was attended by Marshal de MacMahon, by Prince Napoleon (who had just arrived from Paris), by General Berthaut (commander of the inadequately-trained Garde Mobile), by General Trochu (commander of the newly-formed 12th Corps) and his chief-of-staff, General Schmitz; and by General de Courson from the emperor's personal staff.

The resolutions taken at the conference—made under the impression that Bazaine's forces at Vionville had been successful the preceding day—were both wise and bold. Trochu gave up his command and accepted appointment as Governor of Paris, departing immediately to direct preparations for the defense of the city, taking with him the unreliable troops of the Garde Mobile. MacMahon's army was then to retire upon Paris to provide substantial strength for the capital's defense. The discussion had been led and dominated by Prince Napoleon, as the emperor appeared to be passive and preoccupied.[27]

Within a few hours of these decisions, word came that Bazaine, despite his apparent success, was retiring upon Metz to revictual, an ominous hint that perhaps the truth of his situation was being withheld. The uncertainty was compounded later that night by a telegram from Palikao, the new minister of war, protesting the decision to retire upon Paris and urging an offensive in support of the retreating Army of Metz. On the following day, 18 August, Bazaine's aide-de-camp reached Châlons to confirm that the marshal, after two days of reorganization, would resume his retirement in the direction of Châlons. MacMahon's dilemma was agonizing: to retire upon Paris under such circumstances would be to abandon Bazaine; and, as the Crown Prince's army was only a few marches from the camp de Châlons, MacMahon believed that his battered troops faced disaster if he sought to rejoin Bazaine. In either case, MacMahon had determined that his army could not move before 21 August. During the interim, the enemy cut the telegraph between Metz and Châlons. Thereafter the two commanders had to rely upon messengers adept at slipping through enemy lines.

On 21 August, still without reliable information from Bazaine and with enemy cavalry said to be within twenty-five miles of Châlons, MacMahon moved his army toward Reims. The move bought time, for from that base he could either advance toward Bazaine or retire upon Paris. Eugéne Rouher arrived from Paris that day representing the views of Palikao and the empress to the effect that Bazaine must be rescued. He departed convinced by MacMahon that Bazaine would have to capitulate before any substantial aid could reach him, reconciled to the view that a retirement upon Paris was the wisest course.[28]

Meanwhile, a variety of emissaries had been employed to obtain direct news from Metz, customs agents and forest guardians among others, beginning on 18 August before the evacuation of Châlons. Colonel Stoffel had the idea of hiring bold and intelligent police agents, such as one saw in Paris, who might have better success in reaching Metz. MacMahon approved the idea at once. Stoffel then telegraphed the prefect of police in Paris, specifically asking for two agents with a familiarity with the German language. The two, Miès and Rabasse, from the Sûreté générale, reached him on 19 August at Châlons. They were briefed on the situation by Stoffel, warned that they would be risking their lives, and promised a large compensation should they succeed in sending back, or bringing back, definite news from Bazaine to MacMahon. They started northward that very day by rail.

Stoffel then warned Marshal de MacMahon that the Prussian cavalry, reported to be approaching Châlons, was more than capable of sweeping across the camp (which was located on a flat, open plain) to cause a panic. The heights between Reims and Epernay provided more defensible terrain, a more suitable place to wait for news of Bazaine. The move was made on the 21st, as we know, general headquarters becoming established in the château de Courcelles, a suburb of Reims. Several of the officers on the marshal's personal staff, along with Stoffel, had to be billeted in a house owned by M. Cliquot, five or six hundred steps from the château.[29]

On 22 August, toward ten o'clock in the morning, the emperor received a dispatch from Bazaine, dated 19 August, which had been forwarded from Paris. The message was immediately given to MacMahon. The language was seemingly clear and the tone unambiguous. Bazaine meant to retreat from Metz to Châlons, either going via Montmédy and then south to Sainte-

Menehould and Châlons; or, if that route should be too strongly occupied by the enemy, to go beyond Montmédy to Sedan or even Mézières in order to reach Châlons. MacMahon, deducing from this news that Bazaine did not mean to remain entrenched in Metz, immediately concluded that he must now make an effort to join Bazaine. He cancelled the plan to retire upon Paris and notified both Bazaine and the minister of war that he would move his army in the direction of Montmédy.[30]

Later that evening, still 22 August, an additional message from Bazaine, sent on 20 August, reached MacMahon's headquarters. It repeated what had been promised in the message of 19 August (thereby revealing that Bazaine had not yet begun his retreat), but added the following stipulation: "The enemy is steadily increasing around us; and to join you, I shall very probably follow the line of the fortified towns on the Nord [Railroad], if, that is, I can undertake [the movement] without compromising the army."[31]

Stoffel's agents, Miès and Rabasse, at that point in Longwy, had played a part in the transmission of this second dispatch to MacMahon's headquarters. They had learned by chance that an emissary from Metz had reached Longwy bearing three dispatches from Marshal Bazaine. Managing to induce the local commandant to entrust them with the dispatches, they proceeded to the local telegraph office. Conforming to the instruction that Colonel Stoffel had given them, namely, to send him personally any news from Bazaine they were able to obtain, they addressed to Stoffel, at Reims, the dispatch meant for Marshal MacMahon. Thus was the stage set for what would become the Stoffel affair in 1873.

The message, in code, was dated from Longwy, 22 August 1870, at 4:50 p.m. It reached its destination directly at 6:50 p.m., not having passed through Paris. When it was brought to the château de Courcelles, which housed both general headquarters and the marshal's personal staff, Colonel Stoffel, according to his own testimony, was not present, but had gone to his quarters nearby: "At the dinner hour, I returned to the marshal's quarters where the officers of his personal staff took their meals in common. Upon entering, I was immediately told of the arrival of a dispatch from the police agents addressed to me containing a message from Bazaine to MacMahon. I cannot remember which officer or officers I talked to, but I asked at once if the dispatch had been deciphered and given to the marshal. The response was affirmative; and, in fact, I then found a complete translation of the dispatch on my work table."[32]

In a deposition given later in 1873, Marshal MacMahon would claim not to have seen this critical dispatch; but that, had he seen it, he would probably have proceeded at least to the Meuse to see what could be done at that point.[33] In any case, MacMahon set the Army of Châlons on its fateful march on 23 August, the very day that the Prussian investment of Metz was completed. As for Bazaine, he did not promptly learn that MacMahon was underway, not receiving MacMahon's dispatch for a week. His consequent inaction would leave him open to the charge that he had led everyone to believe that he meant to break out of Metz, when, privately, he had resolved not to do so.[34]

Given the disaster in the making, the uncertainties and vacillations of those August days were certain to attract the attention of later apologists and historians. Had Marshal de MacMahon not seen the dispatch of 20 August? or had he failed to appreciate Bazaine's apparent equivocation in the message? Had the officers on his staff misperceived the possible significance of Bazaine's *if*? or were they justifiably confident he would send word instantly of any change in his plans? For that matter, had any of them actually seen the dispatch of 20 August as Colonel Stoffel would assert?

As for Bazaine, who had already withdrawn his forces from the field of an apparent success, and who seemed to be obsessed by the need to rest his troops, had he ever seriously expected to risk a retreat upon Châlons? Or had he simply begun to waiver after the composition of the dispatch of 19 August, ultimately to opt for the relative shelter of Metz? Had he, finally, deliberately lied to MacMahon and the emperor about his plans? or had the awesome demands of his command so far outreached his capacity that his decisions were no longer a matter of rational calculation?

The eastward movement of the Army of Châlons was pathetically slow, but one should not have hoped for more with demoralized troops and inadequate preparation. By the evening of 27 August, when MacMahon was at le Chêne-Populeux, he knew that he was approaching overwhelming enemy forces in the Ardennes and that Châlons and Reims to his rear had been occupied by Germans. He concluded that he must fall back in a northwestward movement toward Mézières, especially as he had no news from Bazaine since the dispatch of 19 August. He telegraphed his decision that night to the minister of war. The reply from Palikao reached le Chêne about 1 o'clock in the morning: "If you abandon Bazaine, Paris will be in revolt and you yourself will be attacked by all the forces of the enemy. Paris will protect itself from the outside. The fortifications are completed. . . . [Our information] indicates that the Crown Prince, sensing the danger to which your flanking movement exposes his army and the army blockading Metz, should change direction and march toward the north. You have at least 35 hours advance on him, perhaps 48. You have before you only a portion of the forces blockading Metz. . . . Everyone here feels the necessity of relieving Bazaine, and we follow your course with extreme anxiety."[35]

Despite the language in that dispatch, Palikao would always deny that the government had feared a revolution in Paris and that the march upon Metz had been advised for dynastic reasons. When he wrote his apologia in 1871, Palikao knew that those charges had been made in an anonymous brochure by an officer who was severely critical of the decision to attempt the juncture with Bazaine.[36] Palikao argued to the contrary that the dispatch had been written with the knowledge, as of 22 August, that Bazaine would move northward from Metz and out of conviction that a successful juncture of the armies was possible.[37] His critics conceded that a well-planned swift march might have had some chance, but knew—as did MacMahon—that the Army of Châlons was no longer an instrument capable of such a stroke. We know today, furthermore, that Palikao issued his recommendations based upon defective information about the enemy strength. He supposed that MacMahon had merely to evade the Third Army commanded by the Crown Prince of Prussia. He did not know that seven army corps had been detached from the First and Second Armies besieging Metz to form a new army called the Army of the Meuse, commanded by the Crown Prince of Saxony.[38]

Despite his misgivings, MacMahon obeyed Palikao's instructions. The retreat towards Mézières was countermanded with orders to resume the march toward Montmédy. The emperor sent his aide-de-camp to tell MacMahon that he regarded that movement to be extremely dangerous. But MacMahon replied that he had weighed all the alternatives and was going to persist in his resolution to push forward.[39] Had he been named commander-in-chief on 21 August as Napoleon III had recommended, perhaps MacMahon's conduct would have been different. As it was, he was subject to Bazaine, to the minister of war, to the cabinet, and to the empress's privy council; and he felt obliged to obey. He would later complain to family and friends that he had been handicapped by orders, counter-orders, opinions, and summations coming from a variety of authorities, but not by the presence of Napoleon: "The emperor never openly opposed the movements I ordered. At Reims, at le Chêne-Populeux, the emperor believed that the army should fall back upon Paris. But I alone prescribed the movement in the direction of Metz."[40]

We shall never know whether MacMahon, had he been commander-in-chief, would have assumed greater responsibility for the integrity of his army. His harshest critics would claim that he had already shown himself to be too irresolute to be an effective commander-in-chief. Others, more sympathetic to his dilemma, would argue that military chiefs had always been held responsible for executing the orders of their government. Such opinions, moreover, would always be influenced by an author's particular view of Bazaine's conduct. Was his inertia the ultimate factor that enabled Moltke to pin down the Army of Châlons in Sedan?[41]

Once Moltke understood that MacMahon was not retreating northwestward as anticipated, he grasped the opportunity to trap MacMahon between the Third Army and the Army of the Meuse: the former, having passed south of MacMahon, was by then pivoting around to be on his west; the latter was blocking the French advance from the east. That advance was checked at Beaumont on 30 August, where the French sustained serious losses. MacMahon at once issued orders for his army to retreat northward to the fortress of Sedan.[42]

By then the minister of war had taken another step that would remain forever controversial. He had recalled General Emmanuel-Félix de Wimpffen from Algeria, who reached Paris on 28 August. Palikao had long known Wimpffen and believed him to be an energetic, aggressive general. Neither man's account of what had transpired between the two in Paris inspires much confidence, not simply because of evident contradictions, but because their motives were deliberately concealed. One can only deduce from their postwar accounts that Palikao and the empress-regent had been anxious to get their own general into position to take command in case anything happened to MacMahon, and not to allow either MacMahon or the emperor to appoint the replacement. The need to replace General Pierre-Louis-Charles de Failly as commander of the 5th Corps[43] offered Palikao a welcome pretext to send Wimpffen into MacMahon's army as the corps commander. When leaving Paris for the front, Wimpffen also carried secret orders, signed by Palikao, giving him command of the Army of Châlons in the event MacMahon should become incapacitated. Wimpffen had obviously been informed of governmental dissatisfaction with MacMahon's operations and believed that the emperor's interference had been the cause of MacMahon's vacillation.[44]

The particular choice of Wimpffen for the assignment was further evidence of Palikao's lack of faith in MacMahon's judgment. For it had been general knowledge in the service that there was bad blood between MacMahon and Wimpffen. As a brigadier, Wimpffen had served with distinction under MacMahon in the Crimea. When MacMahon had become governor-general of Algeria in 1864, he revamped the administration; and, out of sentiment, he gave Wimpffen command of the Alger Division. Wimpffen was a general officer of some professional merit, but his character did not measure up to his intelligence. He lacked, what is more, certain social proprieties indispensable to someone of his new position. In time, MacMahon was driven to remove Wimpffen from the scene, and he was sent out to be commander of the province of Oran. In 1870, MacMahon left him in Algeria, meaning to deny him a responsible part in the campaign. Consequently, MacMahon was irritated at Palikao's interference when Wimpffen put in his appearance at Sedan on 31 August, doubly so as it was hardly the moment to change a corps commander, whatever may have been Failly's inadequacy. It tells us much about Wimpffen's character that he did not tell MacMahon at once about the secret order he carried.[45]

The battle for Sedan opened early on the morning of 1 September, a day that Marshal de MacMahon had hoped could be a day of rest for his battered forces. General Henri Castelnau, accompanying the emperor that morning as an aide-de-camp, noted in his journal that, as they rode out to the front, they met the wounded Marshal de MacMahon being brought into the city on a van. He had transferred command of the army to General Auguste-Alexandre Ducrot, the corps commander in whom he had the greatest confidence. Ducrot, knowing that the Army of Châlons would be enveloped if it remained around Sedan, favored an immediate withdrawal toward Mézières where a new army corps had been assembled to provide reinforcement. He faced resistance from some of his generals whose troops were holding firm, which delayed the proposed withdrawal; but at 8 o'clock he gave the order for the retreat to the northwest. Somewhat later in the morning, Castelnau and the emperor returned to the city to see MacMahon. At his headquarters they met Colonel Stoffel and learned that the wound was not serious, but incapacitating.[46]

Meanwhile, news of the impending retreat led General Wimpffen to throw off the wraps. After announcing that he was assuming command of the army on the grounds of his appointment by the minister of war, he then issued orders canceling the retreat. Ducrot, although he had to submit to the orders of the minister of war, argued furiously with Wimpffen against the countermand, but to no avail. Wimpffen had his mind set on a breakthrough to the east, namely, an offensive aimed at a juncture with Bazaine. As the countermand caught troops already on the move, the ensuing confusion was dreadful; and the attempt to breakout toward the east was soon overwhelmed. Wimpffen had asked the emperor to put himself at the head of the troops for the attack, but the emperor had refused, knowing the futility of the assault and already determined to put an end to the bloodshed. Wimpffen would later cite that refusal as the ultimate cause of the French disaster. While no one today would attribute the loss of the battle of Sedan to Wimpffen alone, he had revealed his fabled irresponsibility in asserting his right to command when nothing had prepared him to take it on, having arrived on the scene only the day before. And, in suspending the retreat ordered by Ducrot, Wimpffen surely contributed to the disaster. For the retreat had been the only possible way to save the remnants of the army.[47]

At the moment when Napoleon III gave the order to hoist a white flag in

Sedan, the Prussians had no idea that the emperor was still within the Army of Châlons. During the cease-fire, General Philip Sheridan, who had chosen to follow the war from the German side, remarked to Bismarck that Napoleon III would likely be one of the prizes. Bismarck thought not: "The old fox is too cunning to be caught in such a trap; he has doubtless slipped off to Paris."[48] The reception of Napoleon's letter to William I, offering his sword in defeat, proved Sheridan to be right. Once it could be ascertained that the emperor's offer of surrender encompassed only the Army of Châlons and himself, and not the rest of France, the Prussians imposed an unconditional surrender. On the following day, 2 September 1870, Wimpffen had no choice but to accept the terms by which the remnants of the Army of Châlons passed into captivity.[49]

While the army surrendered as prisoners-of-war, along with all arms and materiel, one concession was granted which later contributed to considerable hard feeling. French officers who gave their parole "not to take up arms against Germany nor to act in any way prejudicial to her interests until the close of the present war" were permitted to go free.[50] Colonel Stoffel was *not* among the 550 officers who took advantage of the concession. Most of those who did not either preferred to share the fate of their men or refused the commitment not to take up arms again. In time, a few of them managed to escape to rejoin the fight, only to find themselves censured in Germany for having violated their parole. The two officers most frequently cited as guilty of dishonorable conduct were General Ducrot and Colonel Stoffel, both of whom had escaped, but under different circumstances. As the provisional government in Paris restored such escapees to active service, a common assumption in Germany was that the French condoned breaches of parole.[51]

Aside from the fact that the terms of surrender offered the ultimate possibility for confusion over which officers had, and which had not, given their parole, a subsequent circumstance also promoted ambiguity. Sedan, being close to the Belgian frontier, was not a convenient location from which to transfer more than 100,000 prisoners for internment in Germany. Most of them had to be taken first to a staging area established at Pont-à-Mousson just south of Metz. To facilitate the movement, some French generals were free on parole to pass through Belgium to a specified German city as the place of captivity, the route Napoleon III followed. General Ducrot, however, was within one of the groups of officers who were given safe-conduct passes to get themselves from Sedan to Pont-à-Mousson for embarkation to Germany. They gave their word not to escape; and they all went as promised to the railway station in Pont-à-Mousson where they turned in the passes to the

German military and once again became *guarded prisoners*, as they had been in the holding-camp in Sedan before setting out. During their progress from Sedan to Pont-à-Mousson, the officers had taken pains to avoid contact with the regular troops, some of whom were bitterly resentful and dangerously undisciplined.

Once they reached the railway station, Ducrot asked to board the car meant for him and his staff as quickly as possible to avoid unnecessary unpleasantness. The German general in charge ignored the request and, when pressed on the matter, shouted that he did not know any French generals, and that they would board when their turn came. Ducrot paced back and forth in increasing irritation, finally gathering a group of his officers around him to tell them to do whatever they could to escape and to head for Epinal. A few of them managed to escape and later published the details of their flight.[52] Others, like Colonel Pierre-Joseph Robert, who found no opportunity to slip away, would sign a letter of protest on 14 October 1870, when interned at Stettin, after reading statements critical of General Ducrot in the international press. These French versions of the escape denied there had been any violation of parole; whereas in Germany any escape, no matter the circumstance, was held to be a dishonorable violation.[53]

Colonel Stoffel's escape was of a different order. He remained forever discreet about the details, saying only that he had escaped from Sedan and had gone to Paris hoping to be useful again in the defense of the country.[54] The story was only revealed after the turn of the century in General Hohenlohe-Ingelfingen's *Aus meinem Leben*. He had heard it at some point from General von Hindersin, whose task it had been to organize the holding-camp for French prisoners at Sedan. Hindersin had been Inspector-General of Artillery and an early advocate of steel guns. Stoffel knew him well from his days in Berlin. Hindersin, on horseback, met Stoffel in the camp, recognized him and greeted him. Stoffel, also on horseback, but unarmed, rode along with Hindersin until they reached the guards on the exterior of the camp. In fact, they rode beyond the limits of the camp, which Hindersin did not seem to notice, and the guards dared not to raise any objection as the French officer was accompanied by their commanding general. Soon after, they separated, and Stoffel simply disappeared.[55] If he remained silent thereafter as to whether his escape had been inadvertent or assisted, he did tell Franceschini Piétri, who was interned with Napoleon in Germany and had heard that Stoffel had violated his parole, that he had not violated any pledge—nor taken one—and that his situation had been unique. Replied Piétri: "In *our* country, there can only be approval for your having gone back to Paris to take part in the fight."[56]

Notes

1. See in particular Georges Bonnin, ed., *Bismarck and the Hohenzollern Candidature for the Spanish Throne. The Documents in the German Diplomatic Archives*; Theodore Zeldin, *Emile Ollivier and the Liberal Empire of Napoleon III*, pp. 168–84.
2. Kraft Karl, Prince zu Hohenlohe-Ingelfingen, *Aus meinem Leben: Aufzeichnungen aus den Jahren 1848–1871* 3: 402–03.
3. Telegram of 16 July 1870. Stoffel, *Rapports militaires*, p. 464.
4. Henri Welschinger, *La Guerre de 1870, causes et responsabilités* 1: 11.
5. Michael Howard, *The Franco-Prussian War*, pp. 59–60, 74–75.
6. Ernest Renan to Princesse Julie, la marquise Roccogiovine, 11 July 1870. Renan, *Correspondance* 1: 324.
7. Renan to Sir Mountstuart Grant Duff, 19 August 1870. Ibid. 1: 326–27.
8. Louis-Jules Trochu, *Oeuvres posthumes* 1: 89–94.
9. Moritz Busch, *Bismarck: Some Secret Pages of his History* 1: 37 39
10. Emile Ollivier, *L'Empire libéral* 14: 509–11; Mme A. Carette, *Souvenirs intimes de la cour des Tuileries* 2: 92–93.
11. Willard A. Fletcher, *The Mission of Vincent Benedetti to Berlin 1864–1870*, p. 259.
12. Stoffel, *Rapports militaires*, pp. v–vi.
13. Busch, *Bismarck: Some Secret Pages of his History* 1: 39–40.
14. François-Nicolas-Guy-Napoléon Faverot de Kerbrech, *Mes souvenirs, la guerre contre l'Allemagne*, pp. 15–16.
15. Blanchard Jerrold, *The Life of Napoleon III* 4: 489–90.
16. Etat des services, 21 July 1870. Dossiers Stoffel (lst dossier).
17. F. A. Simpson, *Louis-Napoleon and the Recovery of France*, pp. 311–14.
18. François Charles-Roux, *Alexandre II, Gortchakoff et Napoléon III*, pp. 465–67.
19. Napoléon III, *Oeuvres* 2: 325–412.
20. Ibid. 4: 1–420.
21. Henri Bonnal, *Le Haut commandement français au début de chacune des guerres de 1859 et 1870*, pp . 15–47, 57; Emile-Félix Fleury, *Souvenirs* 2: 13, 42–76, 107–113; Adrien Dansette, *Du 2 décembre au 4 septembre: le Second Empire*, p. 284.
22. Faverot de Kerbrech, *Mes souvenirs*, pp. 30–31.
23. Howard, *The Franco-Prussian War*, pp. 133–35.
24. Helmuth von Moltke, *The Franco-German War of 1870–71*, pp. 419–32.
25. Emile-Auguste Zurlinden, *La Guerre de 1870–1871. Réflexions et souvenirs*, p. 307.
26. Stoffel, *La Dépêche du 20 août, 1870, du maréchal Bazaine au maréchal de MacMahon*, p. 7; Welschinger, *La Guerre de 1870* 1: 275.
27. Trochu, *Oeuvres posthumes* 1: 114, 118, 127, 132.
28. Déposition de M. Rouher. *Enquête parlementaire sur les actes du Gouvernement de la Défense Nationale*. D. T. 1: 238–39; Welschinger, *La Guerre* de 1870 1: 275–76.
29. Stoffel, *La Dépêche du 20 août*, pp. 17–21.

30. Déposition de M. le Maréchal de MacMahon. *Enquête parlementaire sur les actes du Gouvernement de la Défense Nationale.* D. T. 1: 31; Serré de Rivières, *Rapport complet, Procès du Maréchal Bazaine,* p. 103.

31. Howard, *The Franco-Prussian War,* pp. 189–90.

32. Stoffel, *La Dépêche du 20 août,* PP. 29–32.

33. Amedée Le Faure, *Procès du Maréchal Bazaine,* p. 31.

34. Bonnal, *Le Haut commandement français,* pp. 158–60.

35. Déposition de M. le Maréchal de MacMahon, D. T. 1: 32–33.

36. [Colonel Pierre-Joseph Robert], *La Campagne de 1870 jusqu' au ler septembre, par un officier de l'armée du Rhin,* p. 82.

37. Palikao, Charles Cousin de Montauban, comte de, *Un Ministère de la guerre de vingt-quatre jours, du 10 aout au 4 septembre 1870,* pp. 110–12, 117.

38. Moltke, *The Franco-German War of 1870–71,* pp. 64–65.

39. Déposition de M. le Maréchal de MacMahon, D. T. 1: 33.

40. Léon Laforge, *Histoire complète de MacMahon* 1: 248–50.

41. For opposing views on these questions see Maurice d'Irisson d'Hérisson, *La Légende de Metz,* pp. 151–58, which is anti-MacMahon; and Emile-Auguste Zurlinden, *La Guerre de 1870–71,* pp. 217, 307, which condemns Bazaine's conduct.

42. Howard, *The Franco-Prussian War,* pp. 197–203.

43. Failly's failure to support MacMahon earlier at Froeschwiller had been widely criticized as the source of MacMahon's defeat and subsequent retreat. Failly's removal, consequently, had become a political necessity.

44. Palikao, *Un Ministère de la guerre de vingt-quatre jours,* pp. 120–22; Emmanuel-Félix de Wimpffen, *Sedan,* pp. 50, 106.

45. François-Charles Du Barail, *Mes Souvenirs, 1820–1879* 3: 36; Wimpffen, *Sedan,* pp. 143–150; Pierre de La Gorce, *Histoire du Second Empire* 7: 302, 336.

46. Georges-A.-M. Girard, *La Vie et les souvenirs du général de Castelnau, 1814–1890,* p. 201.

47. Du Barail, *Mes Souvenirs* 3: 36; Howard, *The Franco-Prussian War,* pp. 203–14.

48. Philip Henry Sheridan, *Personal Memoirs of Philip Henry Sheridan* 2: 402–403.

49. C.-P.-Victor, comte Pajol, *Lettre de M. le général [Eugène] Pajol sur la capitulation de Sedan,* pp. 4–6; B.-L.-Joseph Lebrun, *Bazeilles-Sedan,* p. 130.

50. Howard, *The Franco-Prussian War,* p. 222.

51. Grégoire-Gaspard-Félix Coffinières de Nordeck, *Capitulation de Metz,* p. 22; Moritz Busch, *Bismarck in the Franco-German War* 2: 127–28.

52. Auguste-Alexandre Ducrot, *La Journée de Sedan,* pp. 147–54; Faverot de Kerbrech, *Mes souvenirs,* pp. 100–101.

53. Colonel Robert had been an aide-de-camp to General Ducrot and would publish, anonymously, *La Campagne de 1870 jusqu'au ler septembre, par un officier de l'armée du Rhin,* severely critical of Marshal de MacMahon. The book had to remain unacknowledged as Robert later, by then a general, served as a political partisan of President MacMahon. See Adolphe Robert et al., *Dictionnaire des parlementaires français* 5: 159–60.

54. Stoffel, *Rapports militaires*, p. vii.
55. Willy Schädler, *Les Barons Stoffel* 2: 136–37.
56. Piétri to Stoffel, 5 March 1871. Piétri, "Lettres au colonel Stoffel," 2: 127.

Part V

The Defense of Paris

Two days after the capitulation at Sedan, the imperial regime was overthrown in Paris by the Parisian deputies of the Republican opposition. They called themselves the Government of National Defense (4 September 1870) and asked General Trochu to assume the presidency of their council. Despite his prior employment by the imperial regime, Trochu had become well-known as a critic of the military establishment, from which it was thought to follow that he must be sympathetic to a Republic. That assumption was made not only by the Republicans newly in power, but by the politicians who had supported the fallen regime. One ought to be struck by the tendency to ascribe political motives to those who were not politicians. Officers like Trochu, Ducrot, and Stoffel, who had survived the debacle to fight again in the defense of Paris, were profoundly professional. They served the national, rather than party, interests primarily and could be driven to exasperation when military decisions had to serve political policies. No one among them had been closer to the fallen emperor than Colonel Stoffel. Yet, he returned from Sedan to Paris expecting immediate employment and evidently without a thought that his past service could have made him unreliable as a soldier.

Wilhelm Froehner was the first of Napoleon's former research assistants to pay the penalty for that association, vulnerable in particular under the circumstances because of his German birth, although he had been naturalized in 1866. On 5 September 1870, he was arrested as a probable German spy and held in the Conciergerie for three days. As he was allowed to send out letters, he immediately wrote of his plight to Stoffel and several former officers of the Maison de l'Empereur. On the second day of his incarceration two policemen took him to see Jules Simon, the new minister of public instruction, whose province included cults and fine arts. Simon rambled on at length about the seriousness of the charge that had been made against Froehner, but neglected to be specific. He did grant Froehner's request to check on whether he had received answers to his letters on the way back to his cell.

Accompanied by his guards, Froehner went directly to the Taverne Anglaise in the rue Boissy-d'Anglas where several of his friends habitually lunched. He found Stoffel and Oppermann at table. After a short discussion, they agreed that the best course was to approach Léon Gambetta, the new minister of the interior. Stoffel undertook the mission and obtained immediate results. The charge against Froehner was that he had been designated by the Germans to pick out the most valuable treasures in the Louvre for transfer to Berlin. As Gambetta put the matter in a letter to Jules Simon, *if* the Venus de Milo should be stolen by the Prussians, and *if* you have evidence at that time that M. Froehner is their accomplice, *then* you should have him arrested. A copy of the letter was read to Froehner on the afternoon of his third day in jail by Emile de Kératry, the prefect of police, who signed his release. Even so, Froehner was replaced at the Louvre that month without explanation and never recovered his position. Long after the event, he learned (from Saint-René Taillandier, the literary scholar) that the denunciation had come from Frédéric Villot, a malicious colleague.[1]

The ministry of war, meanwhile, moved quickly to recognize Stoffel's presence in Paris.[2] Although still officially listed as attached to the 8th Regiment of Artillery, Stoffel was put at the disposal of General Adolphe-Simon Guiod, the commander-in-chief of artillery for the Army of Paris.[2] At that moment, the defense of Paris seemed to be feasible despite the loss of the Army of Châlons. The city had been powerfully fortified and vast numbers of men brought into the city, most of them, to be sure, untrained. But the fortified perimeter of the city was thirty-eight miles, which would require an enormous enemy force to sustain a successful investment.[3] With Marshal Bazaine in Metz with five army corps, over 150,000 well-armed men supported by cavalry and artillery, Moltke could not devote his entire strength to the siege of Paris. The government, moreover, began assembling an army for the relief of Paris in the valley of the Loire, providing a further diversion of enemy strength. Yet, Bazaine proved to be unequal to a sortie from Metz, and his ultimate capitulation on 29 October 1870, without having made a determined effort to escape from the city, was a rude shock to the capital. While we attribute Bazaine's conduct today to incompetence and the collapse of his morale, the immediate explanation was that he had betrayed the revolutionary government in Paris.

Despite Colonel Stoffel's immediate request for service under the new regime and his acceptance without reservation, he soon found that public opinion in a besieged city can be anything but rational. He was also denounced in the more radical newspapers as one of the principal authors of the defeat on the grounds that he had furnished the imperial government with false reports about the preparations of the Prussian army, which fed the popular assumption that he had been one of many traitors. Even after his appointment to be chief-of-staff for artillery under General Guiod, 11 November 1870, thus a major figure in the defense of Paris,[4] rumors were published to the effect that he continued to be in secret communication with the enemy.

While the charges did not deflect him from what he believed to be his duty, he was seared by the experience. The new regime was seemingly powerless to prevent such outrages by maintaining public order. Stoffel would emerge from the siege of Paris politicized for the first time. Having always been an outspoken man with a keen sense of honor, he would publish in 1871 an extreme statement that was offensive to all French republicans. Namely, that in the course of the siege of Paris, he had developed a violent dislike for the Government of National Defense, calling its members a collection of chattering attorneys who had reached power by an act of criminal usurpation, leaving France without a real government in the most critical moment of her history.[5] The indictment seemed to exempt General Trochu. Yet, he had proved to be more verbal and more eloquent than any of the lawyers in his cabinet. What is more, as General Du Barail would later say, Trochu was too good a soldier to have had any substantial faith in the enterprise he headed and in the value of the means at his disposal. But in the face of so many illusioned Parisians, he could not bring himself to say with firmness: you are wrong; you dream of an impossible resistance; make peace![6]

Meanwhile, Stoffel's appointment to be chief-of-staff of artillery in the Army of Paris was merely one piece in Trochu's plan to break out of Paris to link up with the French forces on the Loire. The original idea had been to break out westward down the valley of the Seine; but General Ducrot, who was to be given command of the operation, believed that the only possible chance of success lay on the eastern side of Paris, in the loop of the Marne between Champigny and Bry. Both flanks of his army could then be covered by the river: the St. Maur peninsula on one side and the Avron plateau on the other. The location would also offer the advancing infantry artillery cover from the eastern forts of the Paris perimeter. The initial objective was the plateau of Villiers and Coeuilly from which the force would pivot to the right and drive southward to join the Army of the Loire that was expected to reach the Forest of Fontainebleau. The attack was scheduled for 29 November.

The Avron plateau was at that moment not occupied by either the French or the Germans, which meant that the entire operation, difficult enough in itself, could not begin until the French established artillery positions on the plateau. This was to be accomplished via the Fort de Rosny, the nearest fortification; and Trochu, on 27 November, ordered Colonel Stoffel to assume personal command of the guns in the Fort de Rosny, surely a mark of confidence.[7] The same day, he received detailed instructions for the operation on the Avron plateau from General Pierre Schmitz, Trochu's chief-of-staff. They indicated that Trochu would come to the Fort de Rosny during the night of the 28th when engineering operations were to begin. Positions were to be prepared on the plateau for both heavy naval siege guns (which had been brought into Paris before the enemy investment) and field artillery. While Stoffel was to command the artillery, he was ordered to work closely with Admiral Théodore Saisset to be sure that the siege guns were in place by daybreak on 29 November to support troop movements.[8]

As for the actual employment of the guns, Stoffel's instructions were written by Trochu: "As soon as it is sufficiently light to see objectives on 29 November, you will commence a very slow fire, but sustained and carefully aimed, at the first enemy positions, namely: on the Maison Blanche and the Villa Evrard [both mental asylums], on Neuilly-sur-Marne, Bry-sur-Marne, the Le Plant woods, the L'Huillier woods, and the village of Champigny, a point north of the Chennevières plateau, west and below Coeuilly. During this time, various columns will be advancing, concealed as much as possible and in a manner not to interfere with the artillery action. Their riflemen will be deployed, but will remain prone or well concealed.

"After a cannonade of about an hour and a half, General Ducrot will give the order to have five colored rockets fired from Fort de Nogent. In the meantime, during this cannonade from both the forts and the established batteries, positions prepared on the right bank of the Marne and in the loop [of the river] will be found and occupied to join in the firing. But, upon the signal of those five rockets, all artillery fire directed at [those initial targets] will cease immediately. The columns, preceded by their skirmishers, will assault their first objectives. After a cessation of ten minutes, our artillery will resume its fire with great rapidity upon the next objectives, namely: on Noisy-le-Grand, Villiers, Coeuilly, and Chennevières. The firing will last exactly one hour, timed by your watch. Then it will cease, and the columns will assault the second objectives.

"From that moment on, our batteries will have to seek and follow the movement of troops, watching them at quite a distance. You will be limited to supporting them on their flanks and by searching the terrain ahead of them, but at a distance sufficient so as not to make them anxious. It is quite understood that, if the enemy batteries, whether from fixed positions or employed as field guns, open fire, all of our artillery should concentrate its fire upon the enemy guns. And our columns should advance only when the enemy fire shall have been nearly halted. Then, our own artillery may again begin to batter the designated targets."[9]

Trochu's schedule was interrupted at the outset by a sudden rise in the level of the Marne on the night of 28 November, making the pontoons placed for the crossing of infantry unusable. The attack had to be postponed until the morning of the 30th and cost the French all possibility of surprise. Given that circumstance, the initial thrust went surprisingly well with the attacking forces occupying both Bry and Champigny, their first objectives. The advance had been effectively supported by fire from the fortresses and the Avron plateau; but, thereafter, the Germans were able to mount a devastating counterbattery fire. General Hohenlohe, who commanded the Prussian artillery, discovered only later that "his old friend" Stoffel had commanded the French guns which took a fearful pounding.[10]

General Ducrot, who had had some previous experience with the superior range of Prussian artillery at Sedan, had anticipated that his troops might be pinned down; in which case General Exéa was expected to cross the river with the 3rd Corps on the extreme left at Neuilly-sur-Marne and to attack Villiers from the north. But Exéa vacillated, fearful to commit additional troops to what appeared to be a lost cause, and failed to provide adequate support in time. General Ducrot, meanwhile, meaning to encourage his troops, emerged from a building at one point holding his sword high, followed by all his staff officers and his escort. He provided the unexpected sight of a commanding general in combat with a Saxon footsoldier, whom he killed.[11] In this action on 2 December near Villiers, the oldest of the French generals, baron Renault, and a number of senior officers were killed. The fighting was fierce, the casualties heavy; and Ducrot knew by 4 December that his troops, who were not carrying the usual baggage, could no longer survive the bitter cold and the want of food. He gave the order to retreat into Paris.[12] On the following day, 5 December, Moltke informed Trochu that the Army of the Loire had already been defeated and turned back. The Battle of the Marne had been in vain.

Trochu lost no time in seeking the names of those whose valorous conduct merited recognition. Aware that naval personnel had also participated, he asked Admiral Saisset to propose sailors, who had manned the naval guns either in the eastern forts or on the Avron plateau, for decoration. Inasmuch as Colonel Stoffel had commanded the naval guns as well as those of the army, Saisset went beyond the confines of Trochu's request by recommending Stoffel's promotion to the rank of brigadier-general; and without waiting to see what Trochu's reaction would be, Saisset notified Stoffel of the proposal.[13] Trochu, who had had decorations rather than promotions in mind, named Stoffel to be commandeur de la Légion d'Honneur.[14] Despite this distinction, Stoffel must have felt slighted; but there is no reason to believe that the matter was personal. Promotion at the upper ranks had become something of a moral dilemma for Trochu during the siege. His own chief-of-staff, Schmitz, had refused both a decoration and a promotion to the rank of division-general, explaining that he was personally devoted to the emperor and wanted his military efforts in the defense of Paris to be nothing but a demonstration of that attachment. "No personal rewards!"[15] Had Stoffel known of Schmitz's attitude, he might well have adopted it.

What evidence remains indicates that Trochu had both respect and regard for Stoffel, at least in 1870. How else to explain his appointment to command the guns on the Avron plateau? Trochu's good will was further evident in a letter later that month which gave Stoffel information about the projected offensive against Le Bourget on 21 December. Stoffel's role was to be chiefly diversionary: to make visible preparations on the night of the 20th so as to mislead the enemy about the point of attack, but to be ready to provide artillery support to the main thrust if called upon. What is striking about the incident (beyond the dismal fact that the offensive proved to be another costly failure) is Trochu's choice of words in his instructions. They were addressed to "Mon cher Colonel." And the closing read, "Je vous renouvelle, mon cher Colonel, l'assurance de mes sentiments affectueux."[16] As the two men had never before been closely associated in the military service, those words seem to indicate that Trochu had lately become informed about the character of Stoffel's reports from Berlin. Although as yet unpublished, those reports had been found by officials of the revolutionary government after 4 September 1870. The reports revealed that Trochu and Stoffel, whatever their differences in the particular, had been akin in their criticism of the prewar imperial army.

After Ducrot's withdrawal into Paris on 4 December, Stoffel's gun positions on the Avron plateau were extremely vulnerable: poorly sheltered and exposed to German fire from three sides. Yet, he held on, attentive to frequent reports on casualties, the consumption of munitions, and the destruction of guns from his subordinate officers.[17] On 27 December, enemy artillery fire sharply increased, directed initially upon the Avron plateau and the eastern forts at Rosny, Noisy, and Nogent, an aggressiveness that reflected the Prussian desire to force a conclusion of the siege. Parisians who followed the news of military activity were by then aware that Colonel Stoffel was in charge on the Avron plateau.[18] His guns replied as best they could, but the enemy pieces were superior in number and calibre. The temperatures were Siberian at the time, making it virtually impossible to repair at night the damage done to gun emplacements during the day. Trochu ordered the plateau abandoned on the night of 28 December after the loss of more than 100 men. The quick success encouraged the Germans to believe that a bombardment of the city itself might be equally effective, and it began on January with Hohenlohe-Ingelfingen in command of the guns.[19]

Far from crushing civilian morale, the bombardment produced popular demands for more sorties just when Trochu had concluded that his remaining forces must be guarded. He was overruled by his civilian colleagues in the cabinet, and a new assault was prepared for 19 January by generals junior to Trochu, this one aimed at German headquarters in Versailles. The ensuing fiasco may have proved Trochu to be right, but the majority in the cabinet removed him from further military command. That majority, on the other hand, had finally recognized that it must accept armistice terms, perhaps not principally for military reasons, but because the regime was threatened by insurrection led by radicals demanding extreme military efforts. That could have led to both a total collapse of public order and to the ultimate necessity to accept an unconditional surrender. Negotiations for an armistice opened at Versailles on 23 January and concluded on the 28th.[20]

Among the terms of the armistice was a provision to disarm all but 12,000 men of the Paris garrison, who were to be taken to Germany as prisoners-of-war only if peace had not been concluded by the end of the armistice period. Small arms were to be stacked. All siege guns had to be dismantled from the city walls and—along with field artillery—laid at the foot of the ramparts for delivery to the Germans.[21] It fell to Colonel Stoffel to prepare the lists of equipment to be surrendered from the city, lists he turned over to "his old friend" General Hohenlohe.[22]

None of the Prussians declined to meet with Stoffel on the grounds he had violated his parole, from which we may deduce that the legitimacy of his escape had come to be understood, at least at the highest ranks. But Ducrot's escape was still held to have been dishonorable, and the French had been unable to employ him as a military expert during the negotiations for the armistice. During later discussions, in fact, Bismarck noticed that Ducrot's name had not been included on a list of high-ranking French officers to become German prisoners. Jules Favre, the French foreign minister, had explained that, as Ducrot had given up his command before the armistice had been signed, he had not been on active duty. Bismarck accepted the explanation saying it would simplify matters, as otherwise the Prussians would have a sensitive matter to settle with Ducrot about his escape.

When Ducrot learned of the remark from Favre, he wrote to Moltke to say that he would not hide behind the technicality and asked to be included on the list of prisoners. And, as prior explanations seemed not to have changed the minds of German officers on the issue, he asked that a court-martial be constituted as a *tribunal d'honneur* to pass on the charges made against him and the four fellow officers who had escaped under the same circumstances. Moltke at once agreed to the requests, adding that the court-martial would be constituted as soon as practicable.

As Ducrot had been elected to a seat in the National Assembly, he felt obliged to notify Moltke that he would go to Bordeaux to take his seat, but that he would still make himself available when a court-martial should be convened. Bismarck replied, extending Ducrot permission, as a German prisoner-of-war, to go to Bordeaux. In time it became clear that the Germans had quietly dropped the matter. Determined to clear the honor of his name, he later appealed to the Commission on Capitulations, established by the law of 8 August 1871, to review the case. The commission, chaired by General Changarnier, found that Ducrot had escaped as a "guarded prisoner," and that his behavior had been quite correct.[23] Exonerated, and despite his known antipathy to the Republicans who had taken power on 4 September 1870, he continued his military service without harassment, at least for a number of years.

But Trochu's and Stoffel's military careers were among those which did not survive the disaster of 1870-1871. Trochu, the mulish Breton of profound religious conviction, won a seat in the National Assembly from his native Morbihan and meant to serve only until reformist military legislation could be enacted. Once that had been accomplished in 1872, he made good on the decision he had reached on 4 September 1870: that if he survived the governorship of Paris, he would retire permanently from the army, from public affairs, and from society. He told Adolphe Thiers, who endeavored to dissuade him, that he must go as a beaten man, defeated in defending a cause he knew in advance was so likely to fail that he had accepted the obligation to disappear upon the completion of the task. An even larger matter loomed in his mind: "After forty years in public life, amidst many revolutions and wars whose causes and consequences I have endeavored to judge, I have acquired the firm conviction that the country, made such as it now is, no longer wants servants made such as I am."[24] In truth, his popularity *had* vanished and, with it, his public authority; but he won respect for his dignified and austere retirement. The premature loss of Trochu's moral and intellectual strength, as General Du Barail would put it, was one of the painful prices of the defeat of 1870, and not the least painful of the prices![25]

Colonel Stoffel was a man of different style and temper; and, having never enjoyed public popularity or authority, he was unmoved by the consequences of their loss. Trochu, in a sense, had always been an outsider, which he had recognized in his comment to Thiers. Stoffel, if an outsider within the army, had served the emperor faithfully since 1861 and had known that his services had been esteemed. He had known, more than Trochu could have known, that the emperor had always been in their camp as a military reformer. After 4 September 1870, as a consequence, he grew increasingly partisan in mind as he experienced attempts, not merely to discredit his reports, but to pin the blame for the defeat upon the fallen emperor. It is apparent that he did not mean to fade away in response to the criticism, but to fight back. It is less clear whether he had already decided to seek an early retirement when undertaking his polemic (as has been surmised),[26] or whether early retirement became the necessary consequence of the polemic. In any case, we are at the genesis of the Stoffel affair.

Immediately after the Revolution of 4 September, the Government of National Defense had appointed a commission to collect, sort, and publish papers seized in the Tuileries. As the idea was to discredit the fallen regime, the commission hastened to get material into print, publishing the initial installment on 24 September. Others followed in rapid succession; and, before the end of 1870, bound volumes of the incriminating papers had been put on sale.[27] There can be no doubt that Stoffel's military reports from Berlin were found in the emperor's office. Alexandre Estancelin, a legislator, was present at the time of their discovery;[28] but the commission withheld the material from publication, either recognizing that it reflected poorly upon those who had just taken power, or that it might be used in the emperor's favor.

On the other hand, even a hasty appraisal of the reports would have revealed Stoffel's thorough knowledge of the Prussian army and his warnings about the probability of war. Within a few weeks, as we already know, he was given a critical command in Paris, which overlooked not only his recent attachment to Napoleon III but his total want of command experience. His performance on the Avron plateau certainly confirmed Trochu's confidence in him. Yet, the failure to publish even the truth about the reports, if not the reports themselves, left the door open for the false rumors and the malicious attacks that so stung Stoffel during those weeks of his active service. Even the Germans, though well aware that Stoffel had not been one of their agents, had begun to speculate about the nature, or the fate, of his reports. From their point of view, the initial French operations in August of 1870 reflected a serious lack of information about the true state of Prussian preparations and the probable speed of Prussian mobilization. How could this ignorance be explained, the Germans wondered, when Colonel Stoffel had been assisted by his complete mastery of the German language, his amiable and friendly demeanor, a clever intellect, and untiring energy? He had known the Prussian army more thoroughly perhaps than any other foreign officer ever had. Hohenlohe's eventual explanation revealed one of the postwar rumors in Paris: "This enigma was not solved until after the war," he wrote, "when his most important, accurate, and detailed reports, every line of which cautioned his countrymen against war, *were found unopened*. They had not been read!"[29]

The failure to reveal the truth about the Stoffel reports, if seemingly a practical decision by the commission under the circumstances, in fact also expressed a desire to destroy his reputation. For the commission did publish his personal letter to the emperor's private secretary, Franceschini Piétri, dated 20 November 1868 from Berlin, referring to the proposed visit of Bismarck's banker, Gerson Bleichröder, to Paris. The editorial preface to the letter claimed the letter proved that Stoffel had been as blind as Benedetti to Bismarck's intentions. While a close reading of it showed just the opposite, a hasty reading by the average reader could well have verified the editor's claim. The document provided ammunition for those who sniped at Stoffel during the siege. One can understand his growing impatience with the tactics of the regime he was risking his life to serve.[30]

The National Assembly at Bordeaux swallowed the anguishing peace terms on 1 March 1871, which meant no further fighting, at least between Germans and French. After mid-April, Stoffel was notified that a decision had just been made to put him on limited service (which meant on half-pay) as of 15 March 1871, the date that Thiers and his ministers had resumed residence in Paris.[31] One cannot tell from the notification whether Stoffel had requested the change, but that would not appear to be the case as he was shortly thereafter assigned to command the 14th Regiment of Artillery, to be stationed at Toulouse, thus to active service.[32] In the interim, he had evidently decided that the status of limited service was either desirable or advantageous, so he declined the appointment and was again put on limited service as of 24 May 1871.[33]

What had happened to alter his outlook? Several unauthorized brochures had recently appeared reproducing bits and pieces of Stoffel's reports. Recognizing the inadequacy of publication by snippet, the publishing firm of Garnier Frères decided to approach Stoffel, who by then was residing in Versailles with his widowed mother, for permission to publish the reports in their entirety and with his assistance. He gave permission immediately on the grounds that the reports were public property. By then, he had also received a remarkable letter from Franceschini Piétri, still a captive in Germany, but anticipating imminent release from exile with the imperial couple in England:

"I have always done you justice. Today more than ever I recognize that you were right. If you had been listened to, we should not be where we are. But everyone was blind: ministers, statesmen, the deputies in the Majority, and those who formed the Opposition. Each one saw no farther than his own personal interest, either to protect a personal position, or to remain on good terms with his constituents, or to checkmate the government on the road to overturning it. Thus, everyone worked against the country. Perhaps only the emperor saw correctly; yet, blocked every moment by the remarks of some and by the ill-will of others, he was unable to carry out many of the plans he had formed. I quite understand that he must bear the responsibility, for in this world there must always be a scapegoat. In time, public opinion will calm down and, by degrees, will appreciate more fairly everyone's responsibility. The emperor's responsibility will then be lessened."[34]

Colonel Stoffel, in order to set the record straight, lent Garnier Frères his own drafts of his reports from Berlin, forty-five of them, but noted that some of them contained technical material not likely to interest the public. He gave the publisher the discretion to omit any reports thought to lack interest. All he required was that the documents to be published, including those previously published without his consent, which had been altered or edited to suit the needs of the newspapers which had published them, be printed exactly as he had written them.

The editors had hoped Stoffel would write a short history of Prussian military institutions and organizations as an introduction to the volume. He declined, citing a profound disinclination to revisit the bitterest years of his life after what had happened to France. He had lived among the Prussians when writing his reports and had recognized "their crushing superiority" long before the outbreak of war. "I foresaw an imminent struggle between a vigorous, educated, disciplined people, imbued with patriotism and faith, governed by strong and time-honored institutions respected by everyone; and our unfortunate nation, ignorant, skeptical, egotistical and vain, respecting nothing, and having made a game of overturning all institutions which had governed them for the previous eighty years!"[35]

In this vein, he proceeded to write a lengthy letter to the editors, which he meant them to use as the introduction to the reports. The raw candor, which had characterized his reports, was more extreme than anything the reports had contained. We are bound to wonder whether he believed that remaining on limited service would protect him from reprisal, or whether the anger in his soul had simply blotted out all consciousness of the risks he ran. His critique began, as was conventional in that era, with a judgment of the French Revolution. He thought that the French had been dwelling upon the glories of the Revolution and the imperial years—resting on their laurels—for nearly eighty years, indifferent to the fact that, thanks to the Revolution, France had been denied a sound religious education.

In its place, the deplorable system of public instruction, which had continually mouthed formulas about everything French being the best. We have lived in ignorance of what goes on elsewhere and have even failed to study foreign languages. We are, as a result, and despite our intelligence and wit, the most foolishly vain, the most idle, and the most inane of the peoples of Europe. It is the fault of an educational system that teaches us to admire ourselves and prevents us from looking abroad.

The respect paid to school teachers in England, Germany, and Switzerland, he added, helped to guarantee both a desirable morality and a respectable level of instruction in those countries. There had been at least some truth, therefore, in the axiom that the Prussian schoolmaster had won the battle of Sadowa. In France, he continued, those in charge of moralizing and teaching the young had been themselves the product of an education without sufficient morality and of an instruction too limited and misguided. A vicious circle!

The want of discipline within the army had been attributed to insufficient severity on the part of officers. Stoffel asserted that the foundation of discipline comes out of the family and from within society. He traced the origin of indiscipline and instability within nineteenth-century France to that article in the Civil Code which constrained the right of the head of the family to dispose of his fortune arbitrarily. The upshot, he argued, had been new grounds for conflict within families and a reduction in the respect for parents by children. Outside the family, meanwhile, whether in public or private schools, little or nothing was any longer done to encourage a respect for parents, or a belief in God, or a sense of duty, or an obedience to authority or the law. The problem had first come into focus for him when he began his studies of the Prussian army in 1866. He noticed that punishment was infinitely less frequent in the Prussian army than in the French army, for the reason that the discipline imposed in the French army was artificial and sufficed only so long as the discipliners were in control. The salvation of the French, he concluded, required a return to religion.[36]

In sum, he addressed issues that had divided France ever since 1789, and he was bound to get disagreement from those who cherished liberty and equality more than authority, or who reckoned the right to religious indifference as a critical liberty. Only when he turned his attention to the conduct of the late war did he go beyond the limits of conventional dispute and into the realm of defamation. "We have been nourished on lies, not only for a long time, but more recently. Ollivier and Gramont provoked this cursed war by claiming that the French ambassador had been insulted by the king of Prussia.

A lie! Benedetti was never insulted by William. From the opening of the war into the first days of September, the government [in Paris] never frankly admitted [the extent of] our disasters. Lies! On 4 September, the deputies of Paris usurped power and gave themselves the name of Government of National Defense. A lie! Men without a mandate do not constitute a government; and in what way could incompetent lawyers, vulgar souls, deprived of patriotism, contribute to defending the country? One of those attorneys [Jules Favre] declared boastfully that he would cede neither an inch of territory nor a stone from our fortresses. Lie! Five months later, he put his signature to a treaty which ceded Alsace, Lorraine, and Metz! The governor of Paris will not capitulate, Trochu proclaimed proudly. Lie! For no one doubts that he would have capitulated had he not so adroitly resigned his functions in good time.

"He had earlier protested his devotion to the empress-regent, saying he would defend the dynasty if it required being killed on the steps of the Tuileries. On 4 September he betrayed that oath to his sovereign. Why should anyone have believed his later pledge?[37] During the siege, Jules Favre told us we were winning the respect of the entire world. A lie! We might have gained that respect had we had at our head men of intelligence, heart, and energy, instead of students of rhetoric. On 19 February, Trochu explained to the Parisians that, under the agreement, the enemy had no right to enter Paris as they had not broken through the walls. Words at the very least maladroit! Monsieur Thiers spoke before the Assembly at Bordeaux of the concessions he had obtained from Bismarck. Lie! Monsieur Thiers obtained nothing worthy of that name." There was more, but that is enough to establish the tone and to suggest the likelihood of retaliation.[38]

The book, with its letter-preface, appeared in June of 1871. It marked his public emergence as a political Bonapartist. Some of that persuasion, such as the emperor's former *chef de cabinet*, Charles-Etienne Conti, found Stoffel's criticism sharp, very severe, but also very justified.[39] Saint-Marc Girardin, the Rightist who was presiding over the parliament commission of inquiry on the day in July the commission took testimony from Benedetti, remarked that the Stoffel reports had just been published in "an interesting volume." The publication of the book, in fact, provided Benedetti evidence to back up his claim that the government had been completely informed about the true strength of Prussia.[40] The two historians, who would publish the most extensive, multi-volume works on the Franco-Prussia War in the period before 1914, were impressed by the high quality of the information Stoffel had provided. He had foreseen the war with Prussia and had recognized the superiority of the enemy in both preparation and discipline. Even so, they were conscious of widespread belief that he had provided false information and had fulfilled his mission poorly.[41] It would be extreme to claim that his letter-preface was responsible for the later hostility to him. His proximity to Napoleon III in the climate of postwar France would have been sufficient to breed suspicion. And there remained the not inconsiderable fact that he had been right and the army chiefs, for the most part, wrong. The intemperate letter-preface merely provided the first opportunity to strike back.

In the aftermath of the suppression of the Commune, Thiers had shuffled his cabinet. He had given the ministry of war to a personal friend, General Ernest-Louis-Octave Courtot de Cissey, a moderate conservative. Cissey, who had commanded the 2nd Army Corps of the Army of Versailles in the suppression of the Commune, was probably well-qualified to undertake the rehabilitation of the army; but he had also gained a reputation for being ruthless in his vigor.[42] It is obvious that Thiers discussed the slander in the letter-preface with Cissey, and they decided to respond to the charges by forcing Stoffel to quit the army; certainly the gossip in military circles attributed the initiative to Thiers.[43] At some point in July, Cissey invited Stoffel to request retirement, citing unauthorized publication as grounds. Cissey then wrote a personal letter to the head of the ministry's personnel division to have Stoffel's service record *examined* and to make a proposal about Stoffel's retirement from the service. The letter-preface, he explained, had been having a very annoying effect.[44]

General Renson, head of the personnel division, seems to have understood the word *examine* to mean *tinker with* or *alter*. The report he submitted to General de Cissey was completely at odds with Stoffel's actual service record and patently contrived to damn him. As Stoffel's annual service evaluations before 1860 are missing from the files—and those after 1860 are highly laudatory—one must suspect that the earlier evaluations were deliberately destroyed for the purposes of Renson's report, which was to make a case for Stoffel having always been a scoundrel until he was rescued by the emperor. But Renson also cautioned Cissey against putting Stoffel into retirement, claiming it would have the opposite effect from what Cissey meant to attain. He would be portrayed as a victim, and certain people and newspapers would treat him as a politician, evidently his aim. No doubt, the blunt criticism had produced a sensation, and it was a serious matter coming from an army officer. But Renson claimed that the very violence of the letter-preface was self-condemning, and that a majority of readers had disapproved it. Better, therefore, not to do anything that would inflame the issue further.[45]

As for the personnel report Renson submitted to Cissey, it summarized Stoffel's military service up to 1859 as bad: he had not been decorated before that year;[46] he had been rated as lacking in zeal, as ignorant of the details of his profession; his conduct had been criticized as irregular, and he had been infamous for bad debts. Had he remained within his regiment, in all probability he would not have been promoted beyond the rank of major. Only the benevolence of the emperor had saved Stoffel from his difficulties!

Renson called Stoffel a gifted and intelligent man, very clever, and a writer of distinction. He had made himself prominent during the siege of Paris by having bits of his reports from Berlin published in newspapers. The tactic made him known and produced considerable reaction in France and abroad. He had recently enhanced that notoriety in a more extreme fashion through a letter introducing the principal reports from Berlin. The letter, if containing the truth about certain parties, was quite unacceptably violent. On 30 July 1871, the *Journal de Paris* expressed the view that Stoffel, while he had not done a good thing, had at least had an excuse: the refusal of General Trochu to promote him to be brigadier-general. And that was the crux of the matter. Stoffel had realized that his military advancement was over by the end of the siege of Paris, or at least very compromised. So he burned his bridges! Since then, he had refused to take command of the 14th Artillery, preferring to wait until he had completed two years in grade to retire, 24 June 1872.

Yet, having made the charge that Stoffel had been dishonest, incapable, and in violation of army regulations, qualities that would have prevented his promotion beyond the rank of major, Renson reiterated his recommendation against giving the case further publicity by retiring Stoffel at once. Wait another year until Stoffel had reached the moment when he could be retired with a colonel's pension, as he had requested. By then, the fact that he had attacked General Trochu, Jules Favre, and the Chief of the Executive Power (Thiers) would be somewhat forgotten, the issue passé, and the affair could be put to bed quietly.[47]

General de Cissey accepted the recommendation of the personnel division, and the retirement procedure was postponed for a year. The correspondence within the ministry of war confirms that General de Cissey took the initiative when that moment came, and the motive was in his hand: "I have told this superior officer that I would put him on retirement for his unauthorized publications."[48] The service record shows that Stoffel applied for retirement about ten days later on grounds of longevity of service.[49] Analyses of comment that appeared subsequently in the British press betray a legitimate concern that French official versions of the retirement might not be universally accepted. In the main, it *was* inferred that Cissey had warned Stoffel that, if he should publish certain criticisms concerning the late war, he would not be able to return to the army. A more troubling reaction was that the only man in France who had foreseen the truth about the French military system would inevitably win no friends in the French military and would find himself in disgrace: a monstrous business! Nor did the real instigator of the retirement escape detection: "Thiers has given evidence of his penchant for arbitrary and despotic government."[50]

There remains a document evaluating Stoffel's service record and eligibility for retirement. His total length of service had been 31 years, 16 days, plus 4 years of preliminary schooling, at the moment of his formal retirement, 16 October 1872. At 51 years of age, the army had been his life. He had been in grade 2 years, 3 months, and 25 days, therefore had the right to a pension in grade. The pension was conceded on 28 December 1872: a grant of 3,413 francs a year.[51]

A few days thereafter, 9 January 1873, Napoleon III died in the course of a series of operations to remove a bladder stone. Colonel Stoffel signed the official register at the funeral, but not everyone present (roughly 3,000) had that opportunity. One expects to find many notables on such an occasion, but the list included many commoners who necessarily identified themselves with the name of their trade or craft. The absence of notables was also noted and, in several cases, much resented, Marshal de MacMahon in particular. Generals Ducrot, Trochu, and Wimppfen were not present; but Generals Castelnau, Lebrun, and Marshal Leboeuf paid their respects.[52]

Prince Napoleon went to England for the funeral, but was on his customary bad behavior. Having hankered for the throne himself, he had been irritated by the birth of the prince imperial in 1856 and made no effort to conceal his dislike of the empress thereafter. After arriving for the funeral, he had demanded to see the will of Napoleon III and became enraged to find no mention of himself in it. After the funeral, the empress expressed her desire for a reconciliation, and Colonel Stoffel accompanied Prince Napoleon to Camden Place in the hope of forging some Bonapartist unity. The demands he made upon the empress as the price of his friendship (that he be recognized as the head of the Bonapartist party, and that the prince imperial be given over to his care) were indignantly refused; so the feud continued.[53] Stoffel remained near Camden Place for some days after the incident, and the empress had him invited to lunch to talk to the prince imperial.[54]

In the spring of 1873, the chances of founding a permanent republic seemed promising. The monarchical factions had been unable to reach a compromise, Gambetta had been conducting an effective campaign for dissolution of the National Assembly and for new elections, and Thiers had recently made public his preference for the republic as the form of government that divided the French the least. Consequently, the monarchists were eager to bring him down before their own cause was lost. Most of the conservative Bonapartists, including Colonel Stoffel, were ready to cooperate with the

Right. A by-election in Paris, scheduled for 27 April 1873, had aroused considerable interest in that it pitted Charles de Rémusat, Thiers' foreign minister, against Désiré Barodet, a Gambettist republican. Only toward the end of the campaign, on 22 April to be precise, did a conservative alliance select Stoffel as its candidate. As Paris had long been profoundly republican, the Right cannot have had any expectation of victory. But Stoffel was believed to enjoy some good will in Paris because of his insight into Prussian preparations before the war, and his recent removal from the service had made him appear a victim of the Thiers regime. His electoral committee, which was chaired by Charles, duc de La Rochefoucauld-Bisaccia, a Legitimist, hoped that Stoffel's candidacy would serve to draw conservative support away from Thiers.

As the candidate of a coalition, Stoffel refrained from calling himself a Bonapartist. The announcement of his candidacy referred to him as independent and conservative: "I am charging my thirty-five years of loyal military service to speak to the voters for me. I hope they will vouch for the sense of discipline and duty I shall bring in exercising the mandate of a deputy. Born in Paris, I shall be proud to represent the decent and hardworking part of this great city, which will only recover its prosperity through the complete reestablishment of moral and material security. I shall devote all my efforts, as a deputy from Paris, and all my intelligence to maintaining order in the streets and to restoring a calmer state of mind. I am a soldier, I speak as a soldier, and I shall behave as a soldier."[55]

Napoleon III, before his death, had recommended against such an affiliation with the Right, and a leftwing faction of Bonapartists refused to join the coalition. Representing a kind of Caesarian socialism, this faction was led by Jules Amigues, a former republican. He made no pretense of running for the Parisian seat in 1873, so that his electoral committee, made up largely of artisans, put out a statement in support of his view that none of the candidates represented the views of the People and advised abstention. His campaign posters advertised him as the rare candidate who did not want to be elected. Opinion was divided as to whether he was a potential menace or a harmless eccentric.

Neither Amigues nor Stoffel affected the outcome of the by-election. Of the 342,656 votes cast, Stoffel received only 26,644. Most of the votes were divided by Barodet and Rémusat, with Barodet winning by about 54,000 votes. Although the vote was more likely a demand for dissolution of the Assembly and new elections than an expression of hostility to Thiers, the defeat of Rémusat led directly to the overthrow of Thiers by the Right in late May and his replacement by Marshal de MacMahon.[56]

Colonel Stoffel's problems with the ministry of war did not end with the concession of his pension on 28 December 1872. He was pursued thereafter for recovery of money the intendancy (quartermaster-general) claimed he owed the state. It may be that Stoffel brought the situation upon himself by requesting indemnification for earlier financial losses. Such indemnities did figure in the final settlement of the claims. But Stoffel's political activity in the recent Paris election may have reinforced the government's desire to punish him. Among the surviving documents about the controversy, the initial letter certainly suggests a fixation on Stoffel's association with the recently deceased emperor whose funeral Stoffel had attended. Reference was made to advances Stoffel had presumably received at Sedan, whether from the liquidation of the imperial civil list, or from deposits made in his name with the deposit and consignment office. How much of that money remained on deposit? He was also asked for detailed evidence concerning indemnities paid to him during his mission to Berlin and for travel expenses for his return from Berlin to Paris in July of 1870.[57]

Ten days later the intendancy made an additional claim for 588 francs, the amount Stoffel was said to have overdrawn in forage rations from 1871 into 1873. He refused to pay the claim, preferring to have it deducted from his pension; and the controller was authorized to make such a deduction.[58] A few weeks later, the intendancy fell upon an additional 109 francs Stoffel presumably owed for the same reason and evidently handled the debt in the same manner.[59] No letters of explanation or protest from Stoffel were preserved in this particular file despite evidence that Stoffel had responded to the claims.

But the adjustment of the major claim for reimbursement dating from 1870 was not prepared for another year; and, meanwhile, Stoffel had become a figure in the court-martial of Marshal Bazaine late in 1873 and again subject to censure. One cannot be certain, therefore, whether the long delay in enforcing the claim was nothing more than bureaucratic inefficiency, or whether it reflected a revival of military vengeance against Stoffel. He was alleged to have received 27,300 francs at Sedan. Subtracting from that figure the pay he had been entitled to, plus indemnification for the loss of his personal effects and for two of his horses killed during battle, in addition to unpaid expenses in Berlin between 1 and 19 July 1870, the intendancy calculated that Stoffel owed the State 21,799 francs.[60] Adding to that the reimbursement for forage, the figure came roughly to 22,500 francs to be recovered from an annual pension of 3,413 francs.

The initial official assumption was that the debt would have to be repaid in installments deducted annually from the pension, 682 francs annually, reducing his income by 20%. Given the circumstances of his age, the bureaucrats in the office of control and accountability recognized that it would be difficult, probably impossible, ever to recover the debt entirely. A check of personnel records was therefore authorized to determine whether Stoffel had ever revealed information about personal or real properties that might be seized.[61] Such a check was feasible in that the forms used by the inspector-general's teams in their annual service evaluations provided a space for a statement about private fortune. The archivist found that Stoffel usually had made no declaration of his private means. In 1844, when he had been assigned to his first regiment, he had noted his dependence upon a family which was "not very rich." Ten years later, at the time he had inherited the barony, he had admitted to some private means, a statement he had reiterated in 1865.[62] As Stoffel's widowed mother still lived in Versailles, the authorities must have concluded that she still controlled whatever inherited wealth the family might have. In the end, they settled for the annual 20% reduction of his pension.

That is the way matters stood for the next fourteen years, and we only know Colonel Stoffel's version of the matter from a statement he would make in 1888. At the outbreak of the war in 1870, he had been functioning as military attaché in Berlin in his capacity as ordnance officer to the emperor. After his expulsion from Germany, he had been granted a long audience by the emperor on 20 July and was made to understand that the emperor was giving all his ordnance officers a campaign allowance of 15,000 francs. Stoffel was instructed to draw his money from the treasurer of the civil list. As he had no urgent need for the allowance, he put off drawing it. The emperor had enjoined him to make his preparations for departure quickly so that he could rejoin the emperor's Maison militaire at Metz without delay.

"At the end of a week, I left for Metz. Marshal Leboeuf, major-general of the army, there informed me that he had just obtained the emperor's authorization to attach me to his personal staff because of my knowledge of the German army. When Marshal Leboeuf gave up his functions as major-general, I found myself without employment. The emperor ordered me to rejoin the officers of his Maison militaire and to return with him from Metz to the Camp de Châlons. There, Marshal de MacMahon assigned me to his personal headquarters staff. I remained in that capacity until the battle of Sedan.

"On that day, 1 September, there remained four million francs in the coffer of the Army of Châlons. To avoid the necessity of turning the money over to the enemy, an order was given during the morning of 2 September to the paymaster to pay the troops any back pay due them, to pay indemnities for losses of any sort, and even to give officers advances, reducing as much as possible the sum in the army's treasury." (We know from General Ducrot that army paymasters were on the scene, as Stoffel claimed, and that they had been directed to retire into Sedan on the night of 30-31 August.[63]) "As the time was short, being the moment when the capitulation was about to be signed, the officers of every rank were alerted to have themselves paid for the month of August as well as in advance for the month of September, and to claim indemnification for losses of personal effects, horses, and so on.

"In these exceptional circumstances, I had no qualms about taking—in addition to my pay and various indemnities—the 15,000 francs the emperor had awarded me as a campaign allowance at the outset of the war. Nor did I foresee, despite the fact that I regarded the end of the imperial regime as very near on 2 September, that the State would later demand restitution of a sum I was not entitled to, as I regarded myself as still entitled to that money from the emperor's civil list. After the war, the Commission on the Liquidation of Army Expenses recognized me, with reason, as a debtor to the State; and the Minister . . . required repayment of 21,779 francs, to be deducted from my pension, reducing each payment by one-fifth."[64]

That final sentence intimates that Colonel Stoffel, far from seeing the financial settlement as further retribution by the State, had recognized it as just and proper. The circumstances under which he wrote his explanation, and to which we shall later return, could suggest otherwise; and that in his later years he had learned to be more circumspect in dealing with the army.

Notes

1. Cécile Aubry-Vitet, *Souvenirs de Froehner*, pp. 34–37.
2. Ministry of War to General Guiod, 12 September 1870; Ministry of War to Colonel Stoffel, 15 September 1870. Dossiers Stoffel, Cote 76381/2 (lst dossier).
3. See Michael Howard, *The Franco-Prussian War*, pp. 317–23, for an excellent summary of defensive preparations.
4. Ministry of War to Colonel Stoffel, 11 November 1870. Dossiers Stoffel (lst dossier).
5. Stoffel, *Rapports militaires*, pp. vii–ix.
6. François-Charles Du Barail, *Mes Souvenirs*, 1820–1879 3: 233.
7. General Guiod to Colonel Stoffel, 27 November 1870. Dossiers Stoffel (lst dossier).
8. General Schmitz to Colonel Stoffel, 27 November 1870. Ibid. (3rd dossier).
9. General Trochu to Colonel Stoffel, 28 November 1870. Ibid. (10th dossier).
10. Kraft Karl, Prince zu Hohenlohe-Ingelfingen, *Aus meinem Leben*: *Aufzeichnumgen aus den Jahren 1848–1871* 4: 327.
11. Louis-Jules Trochu, *Oeuvres posthumes* 1: 439–40.
12 Léonce Rousset, La *Seconde campagne* de *France. Histoire générale de la guerre Franco-Allemande, 1870-71* 3: 243; Howard, The *Franco-Prussian War*, pp. 342–46.
13. Admiral Saisset to Colonel Stoffel, 8 December 1870. Dossiers Stoffel (5th dossier).

14. Commandeur de la Légion d'Honneur, 8 December 1870. Ibid. (lst dossier).

15. *Procès du Général Trochu contre* MM. *Vitu* et de *Villemessant du Figaro*, p. 58.

16. General Trochu to Colonel Stoffel, 20 December 1870. Dossiers Stoffel (10th dossier).

17. Ibid. (2nd and 9th dossiers).

18. Edmond and Jules de Goncourt, *Journal, mémoires de la vie littéraire*, 27 December 1870, 9: 142.

19. François-Nicolas-Guy-Napoléon Faverot de Kerbrech, *Mes souvenirs, la guerre contre l'Allemagne*, pp. 224–25; Howard, *The Franco-Prussian War*, pp. 356–57.

20. Roger L. Williams, *The French Revolution of 1870–1871*, pp. 106–110.

21. Rousset, *La Seconde campagne de France* 3: 407.

22. Hohenlohe-Ingelfingen, *Aus meinem Leben* 4: 459.

23. Faverot de Kerbrech, *Mes souvenirs*, pp. 273, 279–81; Auguste Alexandre Ducrot, *La Journée de Sedan*, pp. 155–59.

24. Trochu, *Oeuvres posthumes* 1: 621–22.

25. Du Barail, *Mes Souvenirs, 1820–1879* 3: 233, 241.

26. Willy Schadler, *Les Barons Stoffel* 2: 152.

27. For a list of the various collections, see R. L. Williams, *The Mortal Napoleon III*, pp. 197–98.

28. Du Barail, *Mes Souvenirs, 1820–1879* 3: 142–43.

29. Hohenlohe-Ingelfingen, *Letters on Strategy* 1: 308; Emile Ollivier, *L'Empire libéral* 12: 326–27.

30. Poulet-Malassis, ed., *Papiers secrets et correspondance du Second Empire*, pp. 131–34. See the fuller treatment of this letter in Part 3.

31. Ministry of War to Colonel Stoffel, 19 April 1871. Dossiers Stoffel (lst dossier).

32. Ministry of War to Colonel Stoffel, 12 May 1871. Ibid.

33. Etat des services, 6 August 1872. Ibid. (3rd dossier).

34. Piétri to Stoffel, 14 March 1871. Piétri, "Lettres au colonel Stoffel," 4: 129.

35. Stoffel, *Rapports militaires*, pp. i–iv.

36. Ibid., pp. x–xi, xviii–xxiii.

37. Trochu would defend himself successfully against the latter charge. See R. L. Williams, "General Trochu v. 'Le Figaro'," *Manners and Murders in* the *World of Louis-Napoleon*, pp. 151–91.

38. Stoffel, *Rapports militaires*, pp. xii–xiv.

39. Piétri to Stoffel, 14 July 1871. Piétri, "Lettres au colonel Stoffel," 4: 135.

40. Déposition de Vincent Benedetti, 22 July 1871. *Enquête parlementaire sur les actes du Gouvernement de la Défense Nationale*; D. T. 1: 88–89.

41. Rousset, *La Second campagne de France* 1: 127–29; Henri Welschinger, *La Guerre de 1870* 1: 10–11.

42. Robert Tombs, *The War Against Paris 1871*, p. 186; Du Barail, *Mes Souvenirs* 3: 291; Jacques Chastenet, *l'Enfance de la troisième 1870–1879*, p. 111.

43. Faverot de Kerbrech, *Mes souvenirs*, p. 16.

44. General Courtot de Cissey to General Renson, 30 July 1871. Dossiers Stoffel (1st dossier).

45. General Renson to General Courtot de Cissey, 3 August 1871. Ibid.

46. Chevalier de la Légion d'Honneur, 21 June 1859; Médaille de la Valeur militaire de Sardaigne, 23 March 1860; Officier de la Légion d'Honneur, 12 August 1866; Commandeur de la Légion d'Honneur, 8 December 1870. None of these decorations were noted in the report. Dossiers Stoffel (3rd dossier).

47. Personnel Report on Colonel Stoffel, 3 August 1871 (General Renson to General de Cissey.) Ibid.

48. Report to the Ministry of War from the Personnel Division (signed by General Renson), 2 August 1872. Ibid.

49. Etat des services, 13 August 1872. Ibid. (1st and 3rd dossiers).

50. Dossiers Stoffel (1st dossier).

51. Ibid.

52. Marie-Jean-Pierre, duc de Cambacérès, *Funérailles de Napoléon III*, pp. 42, 58, 60, 72.

53. Edgar Holt, *Plon-Plon*: The Life of Prince Napoleon, pp. 250–51.

54. Piétri to Stoffel, 25 January 1873. Piétri, "Lettres au colonel Stoffel," 4: 136.

55. Jules Claretie, *Histoire de la Révolution de 1870–1871* 2: 614–15.

56. Ibid. 2: 615–21; John Rothney, *Bonapartism After Sedan*, pp. 92–97, 114.

57. Assistant Intendant to Colonel Stoffel, 13 June 1873. Dossiers Stoffel (1st dossier).

58. The Intendancy of the Ministry of War, 23 June 1873. Ibid.

59. The Intendancy of the Ministry of War, 15 July 1873. Ibid.

60. Office of the Controller, Ministry of War, 9 April 1874. Ibid.

61. Office of Control and Accountability to the Ministerial Archives, 26 May 1874. Ibid. (3rd dossier).

62. Ministerial Archives to the Office of Control and Accountability, 30 May 1874. Ibid. (1st dossier).

63. Ducrot, *La Journée de Sedan*, p. 120.

64. Colonel Stoffel to the Minister of War [Charles de Saulces de Freycinet], 2 November 1888. Dossiers Stoffel (3rd dossier).

Part VI

The Bazaine Trial

The chances are that Colonel Stoffel would have lived out his years in obscure retirement after 1873, as in the case of General Trochu, had it not been for the decision to bring Marshal Bazaine to trial for treason. Inasmuch as contemporary scholarship has absolved Bazaine from the charge of treachery, if not from the charge of incompetence,[1] how may we account for the widespread assumption of his treachery after his surrender of Metz at the end of October in 1870? The loss of the best army the French had, barely eight weeks after the capitulation at Sedan, was undeniably a crushing blow and inexplicable for the vast majority who had so recently taken French superiority and invincibility for granted. How else to explain such a reversal, as the truth of the matter was inadmissible, except to assume a betrayal!

Members of the Government of National Defense, who had hoped to secure quick and easy peace terms by portraying the war as having been the sole responsibility of Napoleon III, had meanwhile been dismayed to find the severity of German intentions. In consequence, negotiations had deadlocked as the French groped for modifications that would not compromise the revolutionary regime. Bismarck countered in October with threats to negotiate with the exiled empress to force acceptance of his terms; and, from the viewpoint of Gambetta in Tours, Bazaine's capitulation was easily interpreted as a political act to undermine the new Republic and to support negotiations with the fallen regime. Gambetta, struggling both to organize the national defense and to secure the foundations of the Republic, struck back by making the charge of treason official and by accusing the old army of having merely been an instrument of governmental tyranny under the Second Empire:

"A general upon whom France was counting, even after Mexico, has just deprived the imperiled fatherland of more than 100,000 defenders. Marshal Bazaine has committed treason. He has made himself the agent of the man of Sedan and the invaders' accomplice, indifferent to the honor of the army entrusted to him. . . . For twenty years, France has been subject to a corrupting power which dried up all the sources of greatness and life. The French army, deprived of its national character, unwittingly became an instrument of that reign and of servitude. Now, despite the heroism of the soldiers, that army has been engulfed through the treason of its leaders, the fatal epilogue of the military coup de main of December [2, 1851]."[2]

Both Bismarck and Thiers had been angered by Gambetta's proclamation, presuming it had been contrived to make an armistice impossible. While Gambetta would claim that the proclamation had been meant to arouse public anger and to prevent any general collapse into despair, the fact was that Bazaine's treachery had not been proved. Gambetta had simply seen an irresistible opportunity to link the vanquished at Sedan with the vanquished at Metz to compound the ruin of the Bonapartist party. As many Bonapartist senior officers like Stoffel still served in the armed forces, they resented the implications of the blanket indictment. Admiral Martin Fourichon, a member of the governmental delegation in Tours, had refused to countersign the proclamation. Subsequent telegrams from departmental prefects showed that the proclamation had excited some patriotism, but had also excited some of the public against army officers in general, hardly contributing to morale.[3]

We are, in fact, so accustomed to sympathize with Republican hostility to Bazaine after 1870, on the grounds that his surrender had been meant to wound the budding Republic, that Bonapartist hostility to him, which was just as real, can easily be overlooked. Bazaine had his apologists within the party, to be sure. But many senior army officers had disapproved of Bazaine's management of his command; and some of them, aware that Bazaine had nursed a grievance against MacMahon dating from much earlier days in African service when Bazaine had been MacMahon's subordinate, could not rid themselves of the suspicion that Bazaine's inaction at Metz had been meant to settle a personal score. Such criticism of Bazaine by the military, however, had not encompassed the charge of treason, made by politicians for political advantage. The French ultimately became so accustomed to sympathize with Republican attacks upon the Bonapartists as losers of the war that Bonapartist hostility to the Republicans as people who had exploited the war and the defeat to gain office was largely ignored. As a consequence, the issue of Bazaine's guilt or innocence, by the time of the court-martial, was considerably more convoluted than is generally remembered.[4]

The idea of a marshal of France put on public trial for possible condemnation and degradation was repugnant to Thiers personally and likely to be demoralizing to the army and the country at the very moment when he sought to generate national revival. But Bazaine, badly advised and revealing once again a certain insensitivity or lack of insight that had been remarked earlier in his career, asked that he be tried for the sake of his honor and to clear his name of the criticism first published by Gambetta. Bazaine expected to be exonerated, regarding himself simply as a victim of the passions raised against the fallen Empire, not as a general who had failed in his duties. It may be that Thiers, who believed the same thing, inadvertently contributed to Bazaine's illusion.[5] On 29 May 1871, Thiers brought the public clamor to try Bazaine to a head by declaring before the Assembly that Bazaine himself had requested a trial on the events leading to the capitulation of Metz, adding that he believed this request for justice should not be denied him. "I transmit his request to you; I leave to the Assembly the responsibility for responding to it."[6]

Military regulations, in fact, required an official investigation of every capitulation after a war, just as every naval captain who has lost a ship must pass before a board of inquiry. Such investigations merely established the circumstances of a capitulation, after which the investigators rendered an opinion about the circumstances. Such an inquiry was *not* a court-martial, and no sentence could be passed. Accordingly, a commission on capitulations was established by the Assembly on 30 September 1871 and put under the presidency of the aged Marshal comte Baraguay d'Hilliers, a man known to have had no prior hostility to Bazaine. In Italy, Bazaine had commanded a division within Baraguay d'Hilliers' corps and had won praise for his courage.

The commission report ultimately expressed the opinion that not only had Marshal Bazaine's conduct caused the loss of Metz with its army of 150,000 men; but that, his dispatches of 19 and 20 August 1870 had been the critical factor in determining Marshal de MacMahon's march from Reims to the Meuse, and that MacMahon's march had not been adequately supported thereafter by *serious* attempts to break out of Metz. Thus, the report also held Bazaine in great part responsible for the loss of the Army of Châlons. We should note that the commission evidently believed that both of Bazaine's dispatches had led to MacMahon's decision. Yet, in the same month that the commission had been appointed, Marshal de MacMahon, when testifying before the parliamentary commission investigating the actions of the Government of National Defense, mentioned only the dispatch of 19 August 1870. The commission on capitulations obviously knew that the second dispatch had at least reached MacMahon's headquarters, and that its contents had been known. If the opinion of the commission was severe in its report on

Bazaine's conduct, at least the report did not reflect some ancient animosity. What is more, as Baraguay d'Hilliers was held to be Bonapartist, the negative report could not be attributed either to Republican or to Monarchical machinations.

And there the matter ought to have been closed as Thiers hoped it would be. But Bazaine, still hoping for eventual exoneration, did not withdraw his request for a court-martial; and Thiers had no choice but to honor Bazaine's request. Formal charges were brought against Bazaine on 7 May 1872 by the minister of war, General de Cissey. The *instruction* (legal inquiry) was entrusted to General Séré de Rivières, whose name, as commanding the engineers, had recently been linked to the final disaster of the Army of the East in January of 1871. Bazaine was placed under house arrest in Versailles for the many months that Rivières required to prepare the indictment, while the ministry of war pondered the delicate matter of membership on the court-martial. The Thiers regime fell in the spring of 1873 before all arrangements had been completed, and it is said that Bazaine's hopes for a favorable outcome were strengthened by the elevation of a fellow marshal, MacMahon, to the presidency of the Republic. Whatever may have been the bad blood between them, MacMahon would not likely look kindly upon the degradation of a French marshal. Cissey, as a personal friend of Thiers, was no longer wanted by the new regime, and he was replaced at the ministry of war by General François-Charles Du Barail.[7]

The choice of Du Barail remains curious, and so it seemed to him at the time. While he had had a distaste for Thiers, regarding him to be a self-seeking schemer, that would not seem to have been sufficient to outweigh the facts that he had been sympathetic to Napoleon III and was only a brigadier-general. The new regime was not only monarchist, but more specifically Orleanist; and it is true that Du Barail had served under the duc d'Aumale in Africa twenty-five years earlier and had anticipated an Orleanist restoration in 1871 when two princes of that house took seats in the National Assembly.[8] If he suspected that the Orleanists sought an under-ranked, compliant minister of war with the Bazaine affair still to be settled, he did not say so. Having been given the command of the 3rd Corps (Cavalry) during the suppression of the Commune, he had reason to believe that he enjoyed MacMahon's confidence; and he may have found it both understandable and proper that MacMahon might expect to exert exceptional authority in the direction of military affairs.

As for the composition of the military tribunal, the military code then in effect did provide for the court-martial of senior generals and marshals (the Military Law of 1857); but the code was unequal to the actual situation, which was unprecedented. The pertinent clauses included Article 11: to judge a division general or a marshal of France, the marshals of France were to be called to sit on a court-martial in order of seniority. Article 12 permitted the substitution of full admirals for marshals. Article 24 eliminated from the court any general who had participated in any prior inquiry into the case. And Article 36 was particularly troublesome in stating that when a division general or a marshal of France was to be brought before a court-martial, after having commanded an army or an army corps, "none of the generals having been under his orders in the army or army corps may sit on that court."

In May of 1872, when charges were brought against Bazaine and the *instruction* opened, France had only four marshals besides Bazaine himself. Baraguay-d'Hilliers had chaired the commission on capitulations which had been investigating the capitulations of fortified posts, including that of Metz. Leboeuf and Canrobert had served at Metz under Bazaine's command. MacMahon had become subordinate to Bazaine once Napoleon III had given up supreme command (and could not have been called in any event after he assumed the presidency of the Republic in 1873). The country had only one full admiral, François-Thomas Tréhouart, who was aged and infirm, indeed, near death. Accordingly, General de Cissey had understood at once the need to modify the military code, in particular Articles 11 and 12, to make a trial possible, and he proposed the alterations that became the Law of 16 May 1872.

This authorized the seating of general officers who had served as commanders-in-chief in the face of the enemy. The new criterion, in other words, required having had experience in making command decisions when under fire. But it meant that a marshal of France could now be judged by men who were not his peers. A second reform, voted on 2 August 1873 after Du Barail had become minister of war, authorized the minister to appoint supplementary or substitute judges who could be ready to sit in case of the indisposition of the regular judges, passed obviously in anticipation of a lengthy court-martial. The task of selecting a court was further complicated by the fact that a number of generals had been elected to seats in the National Assembly and were using that situation as a claim for exemption, though it was not, in truth, disqualifying.[9]

Both Cissey and Thiers had to know, in modifying the military code, that it would have the dramatic effect of catapulting the duc d'Aumale to center stage because of his seniority as a division general. While Thiers preferred the Orleans family to any other dynasty, he no longer believed that monarchy was possible and had discouraged the aspirations of the prince de Joinville and the duc d'Aumale who had taken seats in the Assembly in June of 1871.[10] (The actual Orleanist heir was their nephew, Philippe, comte de Paris.) As Thiers' own aspirations had become linked to the preservation of the Republic, to put the matter more precisely, he had been denying the duc d'Aumale a military command commensurate to his rank. The denial was political, no matter that Aumale's actual military experience hardly qualified him for the senior appointment he sought.

He had entered the army in 1838 as a 2nd Lieutenant for service in Algeria at the age of seventeen. He demonstrated great personal bravery, but surely the brilliance of his rapid promotion owed something to his membership in the royal family: captain in 1839, battalion commander in 1840, maréchal de camp in 1842, and lieutenant-general in 1843! From 1847 until the fall of the regime in 1848, he was governor-general of Algeria. After the February Revolution, he resigned his function and moved to England where he occupied himself with historical studies, in particular with a multi-volume history of the princes of Condé. During the Second Empire he was denied the right to publish in France until after the press reforms in 1868, and the reader may recall that he had rather deftly entered the dispute on the correct location of Alesia in 1858, taking Stoffel's side in the debate, but had had to do so anonymously.

After the initial French military reverses in 1870, he requested military employment but was denied for political reasons by the imperial regime. He was among the many who, even after Sedan, believed that Bazaine would retrieve the situation. "I know him," Aumale wrote. "He is the first soldier of France, our supreme hope, the only man who can still save us."[11] Elected to a seat in the National Assembly on 8 February 1871, he could not take the seat until the abrogation of the laws on exile on 8 June. The 23-year exile meant he had not taken part in the Crimean War, in the Italian campaign, or in the Franco-Prussian War. Yet, he had resumed military service in March of 1872 as a division general a few weeks before Cissey's modification of the military code.[12]

Inasmuch as Thiers knew full well by then that Aumale was part of the parliamentary faction that sought his ouster, why did he countenance an alteration in the law that could lead to immense publicity for Aumale? Thiers presumed that if Aumale should refuse the presidency of the court, it could be said that he had declined to do his duty, and one could then continue to deny him the position of command commensurate to his rank he had been seeking. If he should accept the appointment, then he would bear the opprobrium within the army of having judged an unfortunate colleague; and it would also appear to be an act of Orleanist revenge against the fallen regime. Aumale was aware of the trap and told both Thiers and Cissey that, as a member of the Assembly, he did not belong on a military court. But the reform measure they put through in May of 1872 made such deputies specifically eligible for service on military courts.[13]

Even though the makeup of the court was not announced until August of 1873, namely, after the completion of the *instruction*, it was generally assumed that the duc d'Aumale would preside at the court-martial. In fact, there remained two sticky factors which had to be overcome. Aumale's seniority in rank rested upon what some thought was a deliberate misreading of the Law of 19 May 1834, which had stated that time spent on inactive status could only count in figuring an officer's retirement pension. The ministry of war had counted inactive service in calculating longevity, and contrary interpretations of the law did not appear in print until much too late to question Aumale's claim. Even General Du Barail, in whose term of office the court was actually appointed, seems to have accepted the legitimacy of Aumale's seniority; but Du Barail had also hoped that the *instruction* would terminate with a judgment of nonsuit so as to avoid the court-martial of Bazaine.

The second possible inconvenience was the legal dean of the division generals, Jean-Paul-Adam Schramm, a retired relic of the First Empire, who, at 84, proved to be jealous of his seniority despite his retirement. He was the only division general senior to Aumale. He protested the choice of Aumale and was told by Du Barail that his advanced age had recommended against giving him the presidency of the court—but that he would be seated as a member. Beyond which, Du Barail had added, the matter was out of his hands: the council of ministers had already selected Aumale. Schramm replied that, if he was too infirm to preside, he was also too infirm to sit merely as a judge.[14]

In sum, the appointment of the duc d'Aumale, whatever might be the fairness of his conduct during the trial, could not escape the suspicion that the prosecution of Marshal Bazaine was meant to serve Orleanism by associating Bazaine's alleged treason with Bonapartism. The focus upon Bazaine's shortcomings, moreover, also served to attenuate MacMahon's responsibility for the defeat; and we must assume that the Orleanist cabinet was solicitous to embellish the new president's reputation. The eventual insertion of Colonel Stoffel into the affair, through a tortured interpretation of the evidence during the *instruction*, was designed to excuse MacMahon. But this attack upon Bonapartism, by vilifying both Bazaine and Stoffel, if meant to serve Orleanism, could benefit Republicanism just as well. Gambetta had made the initial charge of treason, and the Gambettists remained active in promoting Bazaine's prosecution. Whatever party hoped to benefit from it, the fact is that Bazaine would not have been tried had he not demanded the court-martial. The old notion that Bazaine became the victim of a royalist plot is considerably off the mark.

The military court appointed by General Du Barail in August of 1873 comprised the duc d'Aumale, as president, and six division generals as judges. The six were divided into two fractions: the first fraction included three generals who had acted as commanders-in-chief in combat; the second fraction included three generals who had commanded a division, but who were at that moment assigned to the First Military Division, the region in which the court-martial was to be held. An additional three division generals were made available to the court as substitute judges. Given the limitations imposed by the military code, Du Barail found it impossible to appoint men who had what he called the *moral* authority to judge a marshal of France, except for the duc d'Aumale whose authority he called *personal*.[15] Most of the judges were elderly, called out of retirement in 1870 either for the defense of Paris or for commands in the Army of the Loire.[16]

It is sometimes said, perhaps because of the presidency of the duc d'Aumale, that Bazaine, a commoner, was confronted by a jury of aristocrats, who sought to bring him down for having dared to aspire to supreme command. Of the ten generals chosen by Du Barail, only half bore noble titles. Without any question, Aumale sought to avoid the appointment. Marshal Baraguay d'Hilliers, having recently done his unpleasant duty by investigating the capitulation of Metz, told Aumale that he must now do *his* duty, however onerous.[17] General de La Motte-Rouge's reaction to his appointment to the court was anything but bloodthirsty. "I cannot escape this difficult mission by reason of my seniority," he wrote to his former aide-de-camp. "Thus, I must prepare myself to fulfill this duty with the calm, impartiality, and the spirit of justice that must be, and which should be, the basis of my conduct in this enormous trial, which it would perhaps have been useful to avoid."[18]

The prosecutor chosen for the trial (known as the commissaire du gouvernement) was General Joseph-Auguste-Jean-Marie Pourcet, who had achieved the rank of division general in 1869. He had been posted in Algeria in 1870 and had not been recalled until October of that year for service as a corps commander on the Loire. Brigadier-General Raymond-Adolphe de Séré de Rivières, in charge of the *instruction* and formally called the reporter, was the descendant of a family ennobled in the 18th century and a military engineer. Bazaine chose the well-known Bonapartist defense attorney, Charles-Alexandre Lachaud, to represent him.

Aside from General Du Barail, who had retained a fond memory of his youthful service under Aumale's command in Africa, and who had had great difficulty in finding qualified judges for the court, the Bonapartists in Paris watched the gradual assembly of the judicial mechanism with a mixture of anxiety and contempt, no matter their individual views of Bazaine's conduct. The general public, by and large, eager to see Bazaine convicted, remained indifferent to the manner in which that end was to be accomplished. It may be, moreover, that a long history of celebrated trials, in which guilt or innocence had been overlooked in a contest for political advantage, had long since accustomed the public to expect the courtroom to be a political theater. Bazaine's choice of Lachaud as his attorney was clear indication that both sides in the case had perceived the likelihood of, or the opportunity for, a political trial.

The duc d'Aumale may have borne a great name (Henri-Eugène-Philippe-Louis d'Orléans), and the name may have lent luster to the trial in the eyes of the public; but all too many army officers, who had taken an active part in the war, risking their lives, only to find themselves linked with treason by Gambetta, were contemptuous of a general who owed his rank to paternal favor, granted at the age of twenty contrary to all rules and regulations. The trial, as one Bonapartist later put it, provided the spectacle of a general, whose closest sight of fire had been his cigarette and fireplace, presiding over a court made up of old soldiers who had won their stars in the midst of shot and shell, and passing judgment on a marshal of France.

Perhaps more serious for the integrity of the proceedings were the legal qualifications of Generals Séré de Rivières and Pourcet, who were responsible to prepare and prosecute the case against Bazaine. Senior officers were expected to be familiar with the military code, to be sure; but neither man was an attorney nor at home in legal proceedings. Pourcet, who had accepted a command from Gambetta in the latter days of the war, was thought to be susceptible to Gambetta's influence. Séré de Rivières, an engineering officer, was rumored in military circles to have found the literary composition of his report beyond his powers and to have turned to Challemel-Lacour for help. The rumor implied that the report, if signed by Séré de Rivières, had been skillfully molded into a Republican indictment of Bazaine; and it accounts for an angry and impolitic outburst Colonel Stoffel would make during the Bazaine trial.[19]

For Paul-Armand Challemel-Lacour, a philosopher and old-line Republican, had accepted appointment to the prefecture in Lyon under the Government of National Defense. His conduct under the most threatening circumstances won him Gambetta's deep respect. Toward the end of 1871, when Gambetta founded his paper, *La République Française*, in his campaign to convert the nominal republic into an actual republic, Challemel-Lacour had become one of Gambetta's numerous collaborators. Gambetta had imposed a rule of anonymity upon his collaborators to provide party discipline and to avoid individual self-promotion. He, himself, wrote very little for the paper, but he met with his collaborators every evening to direct and influence the tone and content of the principal articles, which were unsigned.[20] Bonapartist officers, aware of Challemel-Lacour's seniority at *La République Français* and convinced (probably correctly) of his anonymous collaboration with General Séré de Rivières, had no doubt that the general had allowed himself to be used by the Gambettists for political purposes.

Well over two years elapsed between Marshal Bazaine's request for a trial in 1871 and the opening of the court-martial in 1873. To account for the delay, recall that the commission on capitulations had been required to make its report on Metz, after which the *instruction* had been opened. Several hundred witnesses were interrogated, and all statements were required to be verified through the confrontation of the accusers with the accused. All relevant documents also had to be examined before the report could be put in writing. Rivières signed it, with his recommendation to prosecute, on 6 March 1873. The minister of war tarried until 24 July to authorize seating the court, but the government, for reasons of dignity and propriety, meant to postpone the actual proceedings until all German troops had been withdrawn from the country. Some members of the government, including General Du Barail, even hoped that Bazaine, meanwhile, would manage to escape house arrest in Versailles and flee the country, making it possible to sentence him *in absentia* and to avoid the spectacle of a marshal on trial. But Bazaine remained confident of his eventual vindication and awaited his day in court. The last Prussian crossed the frontier on 16 September, enabling the authorities to announce that the trial would commence on 6 October at the Trianon.[21]

The reading of Rivières report, the Acte d'Accusation, occupied the first six sessions of the court and was not completed until 11 October. We shall only be concerned here with that portion of it that involved Colonel Stoffel, namely, with the fate of the dispatches sent from Metz by Marshal Bazaine on 20 August 1870. The reader may recall that the emperor had received a dispatch from Bazaine on 22 August, dated 19 August, which had been at once given to Marshal de MacMahon. Bazaine had indicated his clear intention to retreat from Metz to Châlons by one of several possible routes. MacMahon, judging from the news that Bazaine did not mean to remain entrenched in Metz, concluded that he must make an effort to join Bazaine and cancelled his plan to retire upon Paris. He notified both Bazaine and the minister of war that he would move his army in the direction of Montmédy.

In the meantime, Bazaine had sent out three more dispatches in cipher on 20 August as follows:

> To the emperor: My troops still occupy the same positions. The enemy appears to be preparing batteries for the likely support of his investment [of Metz]. General Marguenat has been killed on the 16th, and we have here more than 16,000 wounded.

To the minister of war: We are under the fort of Metz, resupplying in rations and munitions. The enemy is continually increasing and appears ready to begin an investment. I am writing to the emperor, who will communicate my letter to you. I have received a dispatch from MacMahon to whom I have responded about what I expect to be able to do in a few days.

To Marshal de MacMahon: I have had to take a position *near Metz* in order to rest the soldiers and to resupply them with rations and munitions. The enemy continually increases around me; and, in order to join you, I shall probably follow the line of the places on the Nord, and shall inform you of my march, if, that is, I can undertake it without comprising the army.[22]

General de Rivières: While all three messages were informational and distinct, only the dispatch to MacMahon contained the reservation, "if I can undertake it without compromising the army", which hinted that the march toward MacMahon might not be possible. During the interrogations, Marshal Bazaine explained that the first two dispatches were simply informative, whereas the one to MacMahon was a directive given by a commander to his subordinate. Unfortunately, MacMahon did not receive it, as it was intercepted. The *instruction* established that all three dispatches had been carried from Metz to Thionville by a woman, Louise Imbert, and that duplicates had been carried by a police agent named Flahaut. The latter also carried a letter from General Coffinières de Nordeck [commander of the post of Metz] to Colonel Turnier, commander of the post at Thionville. All of the dispatches reached Turnier.

As the telegraph line had recently been cut, Colonel Turnier had them taken to Longwy for transmission by a commissaire de police named Guyard, but only after having had copies made of them. Turnier entrusted the copies to a student of the Ecole polytechnique named Bazelaire, who was leaving for Paris. (Bazelaire transmitted them the following day, 22 August, from the telegraph office in Givet.) Meanwhile, the originals reached Colonel Massaroli, commander of the post at Longwy. It happened that two police inspectors, named Rabasse and Miès, on a mission from army headquarters, were also in Longwy. Colonel Massaroli had them transmit the messages to the three destinations. These agents, however, telegraphed what they called a true copy to Colonel Stoffel as the chief of intelligence on MacMahon's staff rather than to MacMahon himself, indicating that they were retaining the original dispatch. Both the emperor and the minister of war received their dispatches; but MacMahon, during interrogation, said that he had not received his, and that he would not have forgotten a dispatch of such importance. Two of his staff officers, Colonels d'Abzac and de Broyé, also testified that they had had no knowledge of the critical dispatch.

Rivières continuing: The two police inspectors were agents of the sûreté in Paris whom Colonel Stoffel had requested on 18 August from [Joachim] Piétri, the prefect of police. Stoffel instructed them on the 20th to seek a route to Marshal Bazaine in order to obtain dispatches from him. They were to address all information they gathered to Stoffel personally. Thereafter, they set off for Longwy where they happened to arrive about the same time as Guyard, the commissaire de police, coming from Thionville with four messages dated 20 August. After taking possession of them, the two agents sent copies of the documents to Colonel Stoffel and then waited for further instructions from him. In due course, Stoffel sent acknowledgment of their receipt along with an order to rejoin the army. They regained the army on 26 August at Rethel, turning over the originals of the dispatches to Stoffel. Thus, this critical dispatch to MacMahon had been intercepted at least twice: on the 22nd when it had been received by telegraph, and on the 26th when the agents placed the original in Stoffel's hands. "At least twice," Rivières emphasized, because the message transmitted by young Bazelaire also had not reached MacMahon "and must have been intercepted as well by Colonel Stoffel."[23]

When General Rivières asked Colonel Stoffel about the incident during the *instruction*, Stoffel was taken by surprise. According to Rivières, Stoffel did not immediately recall the matter and disputed the possibility that he could have intercepted the dispatch. When increasingly pressed on the issue, Stoffel persisted in his denials "but in a very embarrassed manner." There could be no doubt about it, Rivières concluded: Colonel Stoffel had intercepted a dispatch addressed to Marshal de MacMahon, and evidently he had received instructions to do what he did! But from whom? Whoever it may have been, Stoffel had associated himself with a maneuver meant to mislead his own chief to whom he owed, more than to anyone else, the truth. Having been ordered to gather intelligence by MacMahon, Colonel Stoffel had committed an outrageous act.

Rivières quite realized (or those who had assisted him did) that the charge brought against Stoffel could have the undesirable effect of mitigating Bazaine's primary responsibility for the catastrophe at Sedan; and it was Bazaine, after all, who was on trial, not Stoffel. Why, the reporter thus asked, had Bazaine not adequately expressed his reservation about being able to retreat in his other two dispatches of 20 August? Had he not owed the truth of his situation equally to the sovereign and to the minister of war? But, as for mitigating circumstances, the reporter had to add in all fairness that MacMahon, when asked what he would have done had he received the critical dispatch, that is, would he have believed it necessary to wait for additional information from Bazaine? responded that in all probability he would have continued his march toward the Meuse, deciding only there what could be done. The response may well have been ingenuous; but Rivières, not believing it, called it a generous declaration, but not really absolving Bazaine from the primary responsibility for the debacle at Sedan. "For he had learned on 23 August that the Army of Châlons was already marching toward the Meuse."[24] [The latter statement was erroneous, based upon the testimony of Bazaine's most bitter critics. The trial would prove that the actual date was 30 August.]

The charge made by General de Rivières against Stoffel was read in court during the session of 7 October, the second day of the trial. A torrential rain had kept the curious at home, and the gallery was virtually empty.[25] The press, however, took immediate note of the charge, and Stoffel felt obliged to respond. Despite the thrust of Rivières' questions during the *instruction*, Stoffel had not anticipated that a serious charge against him would be made in the report. To respond, he wrote a letter to the director of *Le Bien Public*, one of the papers which had taken the charge at face value, and one of the papers that had supported Charles de Rémusat in the recent by-election in Paris. No one, he argued, had the right to judge him before he had the opportunity to give his own testimony, adding that his loyalty and his *parole de soldat* were beyond question. He found it difficult to understand, moreover, why he should be attacked *for political reasons*. "Like you, I am the outspoken enemy of all anarchy. I served my country for 35 years under the flag of Marengo and Friedland. And, at the time of the elections last May, I put my name at the service of the cause of order." At a moment when a faction within the Assembly was "intriguing" to impose a restoration of monarchy, he thought that the peril mandated the cooperation of all patriots to defend the national sovereignty.[26] His argument was flimsy in that he had been the candidate of the Monarchical-Bonapartist coalition in that election. What he meant now to illustrate was that he was a conservative, a Bonapartist no doubt, but that he preferred a republic to a monarchy: the flag of Marengo, not the fleur-de-lis.

The Acte d'Accusation read in the courtroom and reported by the press amounted to a summary of the evidence General de Rivières had collected and written into his report. More than half of the material in the report, a mixture of documents, statistics, testimonials, and narrative, was probably unknown to Colonel Stoffel when he wrote his letter of protest. While this additional material was presented to support the various charges made in the Acte d'Accusation, a review of that portion of the material which concerned Stoffel provides the first of three checks on the validity of the charge made against him. (The second will be the testimony given by witnesses in the court-martial itself; the third, a pamphlet published after the trial by Stoffel.)

At the outset of the campaign in 1870, the narrative began, Colonel Stoffel was an aide-de-camp to the commander-in-chief, Napoleon III. [An error: he had been assigned to the staff of the major-general, Marshal Leboeuf.] Thus, he was without real employment once Marshal Bazaine took over that function. At Châlons on 17 August, he was attached to Marshal MacMahon's headquarters as chief of intelligence service thanks to Prince Napoleon's initiative. [An error: he was assigned to MacMahon's headquarters because of his knowledge of the enemy forces, but he was not chief of the intelligence service, nor did he even occupy a line position within headquarters.[27] While it is true that Prince Napoleon had been briefly at Châlons, reaching the camp shortly before Napoleon III arrived on 16 August, and attending a meeting called by the emperor on the 17th with MacMahon, Trochu, and Berthaut,[28] there remains no evidence that Prince Napoleon influenced the appointment.]

On 18 August, Monsieur Claude, chief of the sûreté générale at the prefecture of police, assigned two of his inspectors, Rabasse and Miès, to Colonel Stoffel. They reached the camp de Châlons on 19 August. Stoffel sent them out on the following day with instructions to use every possible means to obtain information about Marshal Bazaine's situation and intentions. In particular, they were ordered to send Stoffel, personally, any information, correspondence, or dispatches they were able to procure, whether received directly from the marshal or through intermediaries.

Depositions were obtained from Miès and Rabasse during the *instruction* to ascertain how they obtained Bazaine's dispatches of 20 August from Colonel Massaroli at Longwy. As for the dispatch intended for the ministry of war, they telegraphed it to the ministry; the one written to MacMahon they telegraphed to Stoffel, both on 22 August. The dispatch meant for the emperor was telegraphed by Colonel Massaroli. The original dispatches were retained by the two agents who asked whether they should return to headquarters. An answer came from Marshal de MacMahon, then at Reims, to Colonel Massaroli by wire: "Please tell the two telegraphic inspectors from the staff to rejoin headquarters which tomorrow will be in Bétheniville-sur-la Suippe."

Massaroli replied by telegraph that the two agents, in compliance, had departed carrying the originals of the messages. Then, he had to send a second message to indicate that the two agents were making a long detour given the importance of the dispatches, via Arlon, Namur, and Givet, to avoid capture by the Prussians. As a result, they did not reach headquarters until the night of 25 August—at Rethel. About 8:30 the following morning, the narrative continued, Colonel Stoffel learned of their presence and called them to headquarters. He was breakfasting alone on the ground floor of the house the marshal occupied. The original documents were given to him. After looking at them he said, "There is nothing new here. These are the dispatches that you sent to me by telegraph."

Marshal de MacMahon had not seen the dispatch addressed to him. Questioned about the matter during his second deposition, the marshal said, "This dispatch is so important that it would have struck me, and I do not recall it at all." Pressed, later on, about the same subject, MacMahon said, "The dispatch sent to Colonel Stoffel was serious enough that it would have captured my attention if it had been submitted to me." Two of MacMahon's aides, Colonels d'Abzac and de Broye, also were asked during the *instruction* whether they had seen the dispatch of 20 August from Bazaine to MacMahon, and both said *no*. Abzac in particular had remembered the police agents, recalling he had heard Stoffel complain that they had not brought him any information.[29]

General de Rivières also interrogated Stoffel during the *instruction*, initially recalling the reception of the dispatch of 19 August 1870 [on the morning of 22 August] from Bazaine to the emperor at the camp de Châlons, and recording the following exchange:

Rivières: Did any other communication from Marshal Bazaine arrive that day or on succeeding days? In other words, was the dispatch of the 19th the last that Marshal de MacMahon received from Marshal Bazaine?

Stoffel: I had no knowledge of other dispatches arriving subsequently.

Rivières: Is this memory precise in your mind?

Stoffel: Very precise.

Rivières: I find evidence in this dossier that two police agents from la sûreté had been put at your disposition. Are you able to give me some details on the mission you assigned to them, and on the result of that mission?

Stoffel: In fact, I sent two agents provided me by M. Piétri to get news about Marshal Bazaine. I promised them a significant sum if they should be able to reach Metz, but they were unable to succeed.

Rivières: I find the following dispatch in the dossier. (He then read the telegram sent to Colonel Stoffel by the two police agents from Longwy on 22 August, with its indication that they retained the original dispatch, plus the question whether they should return to headquarters. He also read to Stoffel Marshal de MacMahon's order to Colonel Massaroli to have the agents return.) What do you know about those dispatches?

Stoffel: I declare most formally not to have received that first dispatch [by telegraph]. As for [MacMahon's order], those agents had given me several indications that they were not succeeding in the mission I had given them, so I had them notified in that dispatch to return.

Rivières: I must observe that you must have been alerted to the arrival of that first dispatch by the two telegrams subsequently sent by the commandant at Longwy to Marshal de MacMahon on 23 August, one at 4 a.m., the second at 10 p.m. (He then read both of Massaroli's telegrams to Stoffel.)

Stoffel: Marshal de MacMahon did not tell me of the arrival of the two telegrams in question.

Rivières: When you settled with the two agents, they must have turned over to you the two original dispatches which they had said they had in their possession, notably the dispatch destined for MacMahon, which had been addressed to you by telegraph from Longwy, 22 August, 4:50 p.m.

Stoffel: When I settled with the agents, they gave me no dispatches coming from Marshal Bazaine, notably the one meant for Marshal de MacMahon.

Rivières: Did they not make known to you the transmission of the dispatches made to you on 22 August? This circumstance was too important for them not to have mentioned it at the moment when it came to settling their compensation.

Stoffel: As they had not fulfilled their mission to its full extent, I believe to remember that the discussion only bore upon the difficulty in getting into Metz, but did not involve at all the details on which you are questioning me.

In summing up this particular issue in his report, General de Rivières stated that Stoffel unquestionably had received the dispatch of 20 August from Bazaine to MacMahon. Stoffel's two agents had been given orders to send all information gathered to him personally. By his own admission, he had had the two agents sent an order to return to headquarters. He had then attempted to conceal the reception of the dispatch by expressing to Colonel d'Abzac his dissatisfaction with the agents' mission, complaining that they had brought him no information. Finally, his formal denials about the existence of the dispatch revealed that he had suppressed it. But for what purpose? The incident revealed, in Rivières opinion, that the emperor at that point in the campaign had still been endeavoring to undermine Marshal de MacMahon's direction of military affairs while leaving him formally responsible. And that Stoffel had been loyal to, and cooperating with, the emperor.[30]

While the political implications of the latter charges were clear enough, and quite believable for those eager to pin the guilt for Sedan upon both Bazaine and the deposed emperor, there remained a fatal flaw in Rivières' reasoning. Had the emperor really meant to subvert Marshal de MacMahon's direction of the campaign, it would have been for the purpose of countermanding the march toward Bazaine in favor of a retirement upon Paris. Bazaine's dispatch of 20 August, by raising the possibility that he might not leave the protection of Metz, provided the best possible argument for reverting to the emperor's preferred strategy. In time, Stoffel's enemies would recognize the feebleness of Rivières' explanation and deduce others.

Napoleon III's own account of the Sedan campaign, completed in exile in

1872, had been seemingly written without any realization that a second dispatch from Bazaine had reached MacMahon's headquarters on 22 August 1870, that is, after reception of the dispatch of 19 August.[31] The matter did not become a public issue until later in 1873, to be sure, with the preparation of the Bazaine court-martial. There remain two possible explanations: that he actually had not known of the dispatch of 20 August, or that he meant to conceal the existence of a document he had ordered Stoffel to suppress.

Testimony by Witnesses at the Court-Martial

Witnesses called to testify about the contested dispatch of 20 August were heard beginning with the audience of 1 November 1873, more than two weeks after the reading of the report had been concluded. Augustin Guyard, the commissaire de police at Longwy, was the first to be called. He had been summoned at 6 a.m. on 20 August 1870, he began, by Colonel Massaroli, the commandant at Longwy, to be informed that a dispatch had just arrived from Marshal de MacMahon. The marshal and the emperor were asking that news about Bazaine be obtained no matter the price. Massaroli asked Guyard to find several men who were willing to find their way into Metz; but Guyard, given the importance of the mission, volunteered to go himself.

Guyard: I proceeded immediately to see Colonel Turnier, the commandant at Thionville [about 40 kilometers], carrying the marshal's dispatch in a sealed envelope. Colonel Turnier read the dispatch, then replaced it in the envelope. I took the envelope and proceeded [southward] toward Metz, reaching Moulins [a village on the southwest edge of Metz] where I found a staff officer. After giving him the envelope, I waited between two and three hours until he returned with an envelope for me to carry back. I walked all night to reach the railway station in Thionville at an early hour, having been stopped twice by the Prussians, at Briey and at Fontoy, but let go. I arrived back in Longwy about 2 p.m. [22 August]. There I met an employee of the Paris prefecture of police whom I had known before becoming commissaire de police in Longwy. I was able to confirm that he was Rabasse, a government employee, and that it was safe to entrust him with the envelope I had given to Colonel Massaroli. The latter opened the envelope and put four dispatches on his table, copying them all or in part. I do not know whether Rabasse was given the originals or the copies, but he left with them sometime after 2 p.m.

Aumale: Did you report to Colonel Turnier in Thionville on your return trip?

Guyard: Yes. Colonel Turnier had opened and resealed the envelope I carried before I went on to Longwy.[32]

Guyard's testimony had differed from General Rivières' account in one respect. Whereas Guyard had indicated he had reached the outskirts of Metz to bring back an envelope, taking it first to Colonel Turnier in Thionville and then to Colonel Massaroli in Longwy, the report indicated that the dispatches had been carried from Metz to Thionville by Louise Imbert, and that duplicates had been carried there by Flahaut; after which Turnier had had them taken to Longwy by Guyard for transmission. The copies Turnier had made of them were given to young Bazelaire, the engineering student bound for Paris. Bazelaire, from a noble Lorrainese family and by then a 2nd lieutenant, was called to testify.

Bazelaire: I left Thionville on 21 August and reached Givet near noon on the 22nd. I went to the telegraph office at the railway station and asked that my dispatches be transmitted. The sealed envelope was opened in my presence, and one dispatch was transmitted in my presence. At that point, as a train was about to depart for Paris, I got on board.

Aumale: Do you know how many dispatches there were?

Bazelaire: I recall seeing only two separate sheets, one of which was telegraphed in my presence. Colonel Turnier did not tell me how many dispatches I would be carrying.

Pourcet: I must call your attention to your earlier deposition in which you said that the telegraph operator opened the envelope in your presence and removed four dispatches in cipher.

Bazelaire: I now remember having seen two sheets.

Aumale: Who led you to say during the *instruction* that there had been four?

Bazelaire: I discussed my adventure with my father shortly after completing my mission, and once again with him just before making my deposition.

The error must have been the result of those discussions. But I now affirm that there were only two sheets. Each sheet bore only one heading, implying one dispatch on each sheet.

Massaroli: On 20 August at 12:30 a.m. I received a dispatch from the minister of war addressed to Marshal Bazaine and to all the commandants of frontier posts. We were instructed to get the message to Marshal Bazaine using all possible means, to obtain news from him, and to spare no cost in keeping open communication. I called in the local commissaire de police, Guyard, whom I knew to be a former non-commissioned officer in the Zouaves, intelligent and resolute. He volunteered for the mission, not for the money, but for the honor of serving his country; and he left on the morning of 20 August. I know that he reached Thionville where he saw Colonel Turnier, and that he went on to Moulins-lès-Metz where he delivered the dispatch to a staff officer. He arrived back in Longwy on the 22nd, in the morning, with an envelope containing four dispatches. One, signed Coffinières, was quite long and not in code. A second dispatch, half in cipher and half in clear, came from Ban-Saint-Martin [Metz], dated either 19 or 20 August, was signed by Marshal Bazaine. The two remaining dispatches were in cipher and were addressed to Marshal de MacMahon.

Massaroli, continuing: At that point Rabasse and Miès reached Longwy, indicating that they represented Colonel Stoffel, "chief-of-staff" for Marshal de MacMahon, and had been sent to obtain news. I sent for M. Guyard who recognized Rabasse. Therefore, I confided these dispatches to him, showing him that they were addressed to the emperor, to the ministry of war, and to Marshal de MacMahon. I also wrote a short note to Colonel Stoffel, explaining that I had confided the dispatches to his delegates, and I took the opportunity to recommend some recognition for M. Guyard's service. The next day, about 3 o'clock at night, I received a telegraphic dispatch from Marshal de MacMahon: "Please have my two telegraphic inspectors come back immediately to Bétheniville-sur-la Suippe where I shall be tomorrow." I notified him at once that the agents had departed carrying four dispatches, two of which were in cipher. As I subsequently learned that the two agents had found it necessary to make a detour through Belgium to get back, I telegraphed MacMahon a second time to advise him of their route through Arlon, Namur, and Givet.

The court then ascertained for the record—as Massaroli's testimony had been somewhat confusing—that Guyard had brought four dispatches to him: three of them from Marshal Bazaine, the fourth signed by Coffinières had been sent by Colonel Turnier.

Massaroli: I forgot an essential point. Miès and Rabasse, having found the need to detour through Belgium to get back to France, took advantage of the fact that the Longwy-Bas to Longuyon telegraph line was still operating. Thus, on the same day [22 August], they had the contents of these dispatches telegraphed to Colonel Stoffel.

Aumale: Did not you, yourself, transmit any dispatch on the 22nd?

Massaroli: No, not the 22nd, but the following day.

Aumale: Which dispatch did you transmit the next day?

Massaroli: I sent two dispatches to the ministry of war: the one from General Coffinières, and the one addressed to Marshal de MacMahon which was half cipher, half clear.

Aumale: Did you order the agents to remit the dispatches by telegraph?

Massaroli: No. I believed them to be on their way back, and it was they who had the good idea to transmit the dispatches once they realized the impending delay.[33]

The court had become aware that the testimony by Bazelaire, Guyard, and Massaroli had not resolved the confusion over how the three critical dispatches had been brought from Marshal Bazaine to Colonel Turnier in Thionville. Nor was it clear which of the dispatches had been transmitted thereafter by Bazelaire, Rabasse, and Massaroli, or which of the transmissions had reached the intended destinations. Grasping for some clarification, the duc d'Aumale asked Colonel Massaroli whether the dispatches reaching him from Colonel Turnier had been on a single sheet of paper or on separate sheets. Massaroli said he could not be sure. The prosecutor then noted that the information Massaroli had been giving did not conform with what he had said during the *instruction*.

The duc d'Aumale next called Jules-Armand-Gustave Amiot, an official of the telegraphic service, who had been in charge of the telegraph office at the camp de Châlons in 1870. He endeavored to explain the organization of his telegraphic service once the army had left Châlons on 21 August, as well as the classification of dispatches. But he began by indicating that, on 17 August, when this particular service had been inaugurated, the emperor had ordered that all dispatches bearing on military events, if addressed to the emperor, should be communicated to Marshal de MacMahon. Amiot's resources were feeble (a staff of four men), another indication that Colonel Stoffel's advice before the war had been ignored.

Amiot: When army headquarters reached Courcelles-lès-Reims on 22 August, I was able to establish a direct wire between Courcelles and Paris. When headquarters moved to Bethenville on the 25th, no local line was available. I had a short line laid to Isles-sur-Suippe, where there was a line to Paris. Headquarters moved next to Rethel. There I found the telegraph line which stopped at Mézières; but by having it extended a bit, I got direct communication with Paris. [His improvisations continued until Sedan.]

We divided dispatches into two categories. The first we called *direct* dispatches: those sent to someone within the building where my service operated; in this case, dispatches sent directly to Marshal de MacMahon, to the general commanding army artillery, and to the heads of the various services. This category could also include *informational* dispatches coming from all parts of France: from commanders of the military divisions (regions), prefects, subprefects, mayors and so on—communications always addressed to the emperor, but, thanks to his authorization, directed to the marshal as well. The direct dispatches were carried immediately to their destination. Among the informational dispatches, those I judged to be of immediate importance were also taken at once to the emperor and the marshal. The remaining informational dispatches were simply grouped in the order of reception and sent every two or three hours to the emperor and the marshal.

Aumale: Did you also send dispatches you had received to Paris?

Amiot: Yes, for the most part; but let me note that during those days we were still at the camp de Châlons, between 17 and 20 August, I had no communication lines except the one with Paris. Consequently, all dispatches reaching me came through Paris.

Aumale: Let us say that a dispatch is sent to Marshal de MacMahon, who is at Reims or some other place, the dispatch coming from some point on the frontier. It is sent to the telegraph office closest to his headquarters and is then carried at once to his headquarters.

Amiot: I beg your pardon, it can be sent either to Paris or be sent to me.

Aumale: As for the four dispatches in question coming from Metz through Thionville, we may now assume that they were carried on both to Longwy and to Givet. The Givet office states that two dispatches were then transmitted from Givet, one destined for the emperor, the other for Marshal de MacMahon. But another dispatch from Givet to the ministry of war has also been found which the office in Givet did not record. For the same date, we find three dispatches sent from Longwy and reaching Paris, whether by direct or indirect transmission.

Amiot: To know which, we would have to know what direction the dispatches took. These evidently went through Mézières.

Aumale: They all passed through Mézières, but Mézières had direct communication with both Paris and Reims. The agent in Mézières would have had to exercise his judgment as to whether to send a message by direct wire to the ministry of war in Paris, or to send it to Reims to reduce the distance. In this instance, did he find it better to send those messages meant for army headquarters directly to Reims? unaware that there was no direct wire between Reims and headquarters in nearby Courcelles? It was possible, therefore, that a message from Mézières to Reims could have been sent on to Paris for retransmission to Courcelles.[34]

The testimony, in sum, failed to establish the route taken by the dispatches signed by Marshal Bazaine on 20 August, but revealed inadvertently some of the joys of improvisation while on campaign. To determine the disposition of the dispatch to Marshal de MacMahon, once it had reached his headquarters, the duc d'Aumale first called Colonel marquis d'Abzac, the descendant of an ancient noble family, who had served as one of MacMahon's aides during the campaign.

Aumale: Did you have knowledge of all dispatches received at the headquarters of Marshal de MacMahon, whether at Châlons, at Reims, or at Sedan?

Abzac: Most of the dispatches passed across my desk. I did not see all of them, but, certainly, none that were important were hidden from me.

Aumale: On 22 August did you receive a certain dispatch from Marshal Bazaine dated the 20th?

Abzac: No.

Aumale: Did you have any knowledge that it had reached the marshal?

Abzac: No, I am sure that it had not arrived.

Aumale: Did you know about a mission confided by a special staff intelligence officer to two police inspectors?

Abzac: Yes.

Aumale: Did you learn the result of their mission?

Abzac: Colonel Stoffel told me that those two agents had been charged with gathering information, but that, as they were not sending him any, he had given them the order to return.

Pourcet: Was any special officer designated to open dispatches?

Abzac: No. Opening dispatches was a duty of the officer of the day.

Lachaud: Did not all important dispatches go out in cipher?

Abzac: All were coded.

The second of MacMahon's aides, Colonel Louis de Broyé, was then called.

Aumale: To your knowledge, did Marshal de MacMahon receive any dispatches from Marshal Bazaine dated after 19 August?

Broyé: He received no other dispatch after the one dated the 19th.

Aumale: Were dispatches always remitted directly to the officer of the day?

Broyé: They sometimes passed through the emperor's quarters.

Aumale: You have no knowledge of any dispatch later than the one dated the 19th?

Broyé: None.

Aumale: Were you the officer of the day on the 22nd?

Broyé: We were nearly all on duty that day.

Aumale: You would have been struck by so important a dispatch if it had been remitted to Marshal de MacMahon?

Broyé: Certainly, especially if it had been a dispatch from Metz.

Pourcet: I should like to know whether a dispatch addressed to an officer who was not on duty would have been opened by the officer of the day.

Broyé: Yes, when a dispatch was urgent. In that case, the first of us who received it would open it and give it to the marshal.

Aumale: Did Colonel Stoffel have particular responsibilities at army headquarters?

Broyé: He was charged with intelligence.

Aumale: But was there any reason that a dispatch addressed to the marshal should have been sent to either Colonel Stoffel or to another officer?

Broyé: No, monsieur le président.

Aumale: But he alone was responsible for communications with those agents whom he had employed?

Broyé: He alone. I did not know of their existence.[35]

During the *instruction*, Marshal de MacMahon had made a deposition which had been reflected in Rivières' report. The *instruction* had been completed and signed (6 March 1873) a few weeks before MacMahon's election to the presidency of the Republic (24 May 1873). The duc d'Aumale had come to believe that additional testimony from the marshal was essential in resolving some of the contradictory evidence faced by the court. Assuming that the dispatch of 20 August had reached MacMahon's headquarters, why would no one admit to having seen it? Aumale had a high stake in the integrity of MacMahon's reputation and his presidency. The need to resolve the mystery of the dispatch, or the failure to heed it, was a political as well as a judicial necessity. But, as the duc d'Aumale observed, the president's high functions offered a difficulty in requiring his appearance in court.

Aumale resolved the difficulty by addressing an ordinance to the president of the civil tribunal of Versailles. It contained six questions relating to the dispatches of 19 and 20 August for transmission to the president of the Republic, who responded to the civil tribunal. The key question was the sixth: Had MacMahon received a dispatch from Marshal Bazaine dated 20 August? (A copy of that dispatch was provided with the question.) The response, different from the one he had given during the *instruction*, was the one sought by the prosecution:

MacMahon: I do not recall having received this dispatch, and I find it impossible that I could have overlooked it as it would have justified halting my movement toward the east if circumstances seemed to require it.[36]

The testimony from Colonels d'Abzac and de Broyé and Marshal de MacMahon had occupied the first part of the audience of 3 November 1873.

After an intermission, the court returned to hear testimony from Stoffel's two police agents, Achille-Napoléon Rabasse and Frédéric Miès, and in that order. Until that moment, the trial had been conducted with all the solemnity and decorum appropriate to a court-martial. Their testimony greatly enlivened the proceedings, not only because they would provide details which had not figured in General Rivières' report, but because they were characters who could have been the invention of a Balzac. Rabasse proved to have a pronounced ability to mimic the voices of the various individuals he named during his testimony, a natural clown who drew explosions of laughter from the delighted gallery; Miès was archly debonair.[37]

Rabasse: Just before noon on 20 August, Colonel Stoffel provided each of us with a requisition giving us free access to railway service. He told us that we were to get into the neighborhood of Metz. He needed news about Marshal Bazaine, saying "we have not had any for two or three days." The requisitions were signed by Stoffel and initialed in the margin by Marshal de MacMahon. We got to Carignan by train where we were given a private locomotive by the stationmaster, enabling us to reach Montmédy. We proceeded to Longuyon where we were warned to turn back because of the proximity of Prussian forces. Therefore, we headed for Longwy. Once there, we heard a story at the railway station that the local commandant had already sent an agent to the vicinity of Metz and that he had returned.

Consequently, we sought an interview with the commandant, but I alone was received. Guyard was present and identified me as reliable. Thus, Colonel Massaroli turned the four dispatches over to me. They had been removed from the envelope. Two were entirely coded, one partly coded, and one entirely free. I put them in my pocket and rejoined Miès. We next went to the telegraph office to see if the dispatches could be telegraphed. That way, we could fulfill our mission; and, if we should later be captured by the enemy, we could destroy the originals. The telegraphic employee at Longwy took down the dispatches from my dictation, after which we compared the texts for accuracy. Then the telegrapher asked several telegraphic centers if it were still possible to communicate with Marshal de MacMahon or with headquarters. After a forty to fifty minute wait, the information came that the dispatches could be sent via Reims or Bétheniville. The dispatches were then sent out along with these words to Colonel Stoffel: We possess the originals. Should we return? Await response.

Rabasse continuing: These messages were sent from Longwy between 4 and 4:50 that afternoon. The answer ordering us to return did not reach us until about 4 o'clock the following morning. With Prussians in the neighborhood, we thought it wise to return via Belgium. We had to go to Namur, then all the way back to Paris, then to Reims, and finally to Rethel, which we reached about 1 o'clock in the morning on the night of 25-26 August. We found Marshal de MacMahon's headquarters, but were warned to be quiet as the marshal was working. A servant directed us to the officer on duty, who came out of his room in nightclothes. He said, "You must be the two we are expecting." He went to another door and knocked, saying, "Colonel, here must be the two we are expecting." The door opened. The colonel, whom I did not recognize, was also in nightclothes. We entered the room and were asked for the dispatches. The colonel looked through them, then gave them back to Miès, saying, "We have had knowledge of that for two days." We were given sleeping space in the building after being told that Colonel Stoffel was lodged nearby, and that we could see him in the morning.

Rabasse continuing: We were summoned to see Colonel Stoffel at 8 a.m. All the dispatches given us by Colonel Massaroli were then delivered to Colonel Stoffel. After looking at them, he said, "Very well, there is nothing new." We then gave him the letter from Massaroli recommending favorable recognition of Guyard, which drew from Stoffel the remark that the marshal had many other fish to fry at that moment. He said that he was going to see the marshal, but asked us to be available at noon. We were on the spot at noon. Stoffel talked to Miès alone, and I only heard a concluding remark to the effect that the colonel would see us later in the day. About 6 p.m., when we were eating in the kitchen of the marshal's headquarters, Colonel Stoffel came in and spoke to Miès alone. When we left the next day, the 27th, our mission had been completed.

The court was quite aware that Rabasse, during the *instruction*, had not mentioned the unidentified colonel in nightclothes to whom the agents had shown the dispatches on the night of 25-26 August. The duc d'Aumale pointed out the discrepancy to Rabasse, who readily agreed that he had not thought of that incident until later. Aumale obviously suspected the validity of such belated memories; but Rabasse insisted that, only after Miès and he had had the opportunity to compare their individual recollections, had they found reason to alter their testimony after the *instruction*.[38] As Marshal de MacMahon had altered *his* testimony after further recollection, the court could hardly deny other witnesses that opportunity. Miès, who took the stand next, discomfited the prosecution even more, not merely by corroborating the gist of Rabasse's testimony, but by adding details of his own which undermined the integrity of Rivières' report. The critical part of his testimony concerned the night of 25-26 August when the two agents had reached MacMahon's headquarters bearing the originals of the four dispatches.

Miès: We went upstairs where the officer of the day was awakened. He took us to the room of the colonel on duty. I stood in front of Rabasse at that door. The colonel opened the door: a tall, bald man with a dark moustache, holding a candle. At my request, Rabasse handed over the dispatches, while I took the candle and held it so that the colonel could look at them. After reading them, he said, "we have known these things for two days; that's what you telegraphed." I begged his pardon for having inconvenienced him. I saw that officer again here. I recognized him easily the first day we were in the witnesses' room. He is Colonel d'Abzac. We saw Colonel Stoffel about 8 o'clock the following morning, 26 August, while he was breakfasting with other officers. I sat on his left, and Rabasse was to my left. He asked for the originals of what we had transmitted by telegraph. Rabasse also gave him the letter from Colonel Massaroli recommending Guyard. Stoffel was in uniform. He put both the letter and the dispatches in his pocket and said that he was going to take them to the marshal. He asked us to return at noon. As he still did not have any orders for us at noon, we waited until evening. After we had finished eating, Colonel Stoffel took me aside into the corridor near the dining room. He told me that the headquarters would be moving to Tourteron the next day and asked us to be there. We did go to Tourteron on the 27th and were in Le Chêne-Populeux on the 28th.[39]

In the subsequent cross-examination, the duc d'Aumale pressed Miès about the night of 25-26 August at Bétheniville at the headquarters of Marshal de MacMahon and about his claim to have shown the dispatches to Colonel d'Abzac. Miès corrected him by saying that it had been at Rethel, and he repeated what he had said in his testimony. Aumale then asked why Miès had not so deposed during the *instruction*, and Miès replied that he had not been questioned on the matter. In fact, he added, he had only been asked if he had remitted the dispatches to Colonel Stoffel, but had not been asked for any details. Under direct questioning, Miès repeated that he had shown the dispatches to Colonel d'Abzac, and that they had been read and then returned to him. He also reiterated his conversation with Colonel Stoffel, including Stoffel's statement that he would carry the originals to Marshal de MacMahon.

Miès was then asked to leave the courtroom, and Colonel d'Abzac was recalled. Aumale pressed him hard about his memory of the incident, but he would give no ground. He denied having received any dispatch at all from Bazaine while at Rethel. Both Rabasse and Miès were then recalled in the presence of Colonel d'Abzac. Under interrogation, both sides in the dispute held fast to their prior testimony. On rereading the verbal exchanges today, one is struck by the duc d'Aumale's evident belief that Abzac was telling the truth, and by Aumale's repeated attempts to undermine Miès' testimony. Was it simply a matter of caste: the instinctive preference for the word of a superior officer of noble origin? Or was Aumale determined to have Abzac's version of events prevail? Aumale's evident suspicion led Miès to volunteer a description of the officer of the day who had led the agents to Abzac's door, a lieutenant who Miès had again seen the following day in uniform—which he described.

Colonel Abzac admitted that it was a description of Marescalchi, since become a captain. General Guiod, a substitute judge and the same Guiod under whom Stoffel had served during the siege of Paris, then asked Aumale to ask Miès for a description of the house in which he had found Colonel d'Abzac. Miès readily provided a general description, including the arrangements he had encountered on the second floor where the officers in question had been sleeping. Colonel Abzac had to agree that the description of the second floor was accurate. Aumale then indicated he would summon Marescalchi for the following day if he were available. Replied Abzac, "He is in Burma."[40]

Not the least of the damage done to the prosecutor's case by the testimony of Rabasse and Miès was the nearly inadvertent revelation that their interrogation during the *instruction* had been grossly inadequate whether by accident or design. Colonel Stoffel, the first witness to be called on the following day, 4 November, was thereby strengthened in his determination to gut the charge formulated against him in the *instruction*.

Stoffel: At the outset of the war, I was attached to the personal staff of the major-general [Marshal Leboeuf]. After the emperor turned over the supreme command to Marshal Bazaine on 13 August, adjustments in Leboeuf's staff had to be made. Beginning 14 August I remained with the emperor's *maison militaire* until the 17th when I was attached to Marshal de MacMahon's headquarters for a special mission: to provide him with intelligence on the advance of the Prince Royal. The significance of my service ought not to be overstated. Dispatches assigned to the marshal's personal headquarters were not directed to me. If I saw them, it was only after they had been opened within that personal staff. Our constant preoccupation at that moment at Châlons was to obtain news from Marshal Bazaine. I conceived the idea of asking the prefecture of police for agents to use their talents in getting information. As the marshal approved the idea, I telegraphed the prefect of police in Paris to that effect. I believe that they, Rabasse and Miès, reached the camp de Châlons on 19 August. I explained to them what I hoped they would get for me, and they left on the 20th. I also promised them a large compensation if they succeeded, 20,000 or 25,000 francs if my memory serves me well. Not long after their departure, they sent me a message indicating they feared they would not succeed. On 22 August, they received a dispatch from Reims recalling them to the army.

Aumale: When you sent off these agents, had you directed them to Longwy?

Stoffel: No, monsieur le président.

Aumale: You simply told them to try to get into Metz, or to bring back some news from there?

Stoffel: Nothing more. They were free to take any direction and to employ any means they saw fit.

Aumale: You telegraphed them to return?

Stoffel: I cannot say for sure whether it was from me or not. As nearly as I can recall, it had been addressed from Marshal de MacMahon to the telegraphic agents from headquarters. For various reasons, but most notably the absence of a signature which I customarily used to sign my dispatches, I believe that it was not from me.

Aumale: If you did not sent it, how did you know that it had been sent?

Stoffel: Once again my recollection is unsure. I think that an officer from either Marshal de MacMahon's general or personal headquarters staff told me that a dispatch had arrived from my agents requesting an order to return. Let me add a detail of some importance, namely, that I was billeted about a quarter of a league [roughly three-quarters of a mile] from headquarters, so that it is possible that an officer at headquarters sent a dispatch for me during my absence. In any case, I did know that my agents had received an order to return and was not surprised when I saw them again in camp on the 25th or the 26th.

Aumale: Here were agents who had received the promise of 25,000 francs from you; who had dealt, I believe, only with you; who had seen you alone at their departure. Yet, any officer from either the general or the personal staff headquarters could have sent them the order to return?

Stoffel: Monsieur le président, it is the sort of service that one renders fellow officers. I was not there, and every officer in those headquarters knew perfectly well that I was employing two agents.

Aumale: An intelligence service does not generally operate publicly. Now, do you know to what place this order to return was sent? You probably had occasion to learn it subsequently.

Stoffel: It was Longwy as I subsequently learned.

Aumale: How was it known that they were at Longwy, as you had given them orders to get into Metz?

Stoffel: That is one of the circumstances which makes me think, as I said earlier, that the dispatch was not from me. It had to have been sent by some officer who knew of the agents' presence in Longwy.

Aumale: How could one of them have known that the agents were in Longwy?

Stoffel: I do not know, monsieur le président.

Aumale: But if all officers at headquarters were privy to the most secret missions—or to these at least—which one ordinarily supposes are most secret; and if anyone among them could give orders, they also must have been more or less aware of incoming dispatches. If these agents were recalled, there must have been some motive. No doubt some information had arrived from them, directly or through an intermediary. Did neither the officers who learned the results of the mission, nor the officer who had your own agents return, have anything to say about the motives which led to the recall?

Stoffel: No, for I cannot even say who the officer was, nor can I claim that I had given them a *secret* mission.

Aumale: They were responsible only to you! You have just said that some other officer could have recalled them. Thus, were they a bit responsible to everyone? But to another question. Do you think that dispatches, addressed nominally to Colonel Stoffel, could have been remitted to another officer without you being informed?

Stoffel: That could very well have happened.

Aumale: Do you remember the date on which your agents rejoined you?

Stoffel: That date had dropped from my memory. Only recently did I remember that they had rejoined me at Rethel on the morning of the 26th.

Aumale: Do you remember the conversation you had with them?

Stoffel: Not at all.

Aumale: Do you not recall that they gave you any document?

Stoffel: Excuse me, they did give me papers. When I saw the two agents (and I cannot remember the exact circumstances), they gave me a folder of papers and, at the same time, a letter. I cannot say whether or not I opened it. They told me it was a letter of recommendation from Colonel Massaroli on behalf (I believe) of someone named Guyard, who had done such and such a thing. In any case, I dismissed the matter, telling them that the marshal had no time at the moment for letters of recommendation. As for the other sheets that they gave me, I cannot say what they were. My agents could only have supposed that I had seen certain dispatches that they had earlier sent to me, and I did not even glance at the papers they gave me. As they had not attained the goal set for them, their return was of no significance to me. Therefore, the papers they gave me had no particular significance; and as these men did not know that I had not received their earlier dispatch, they did not indicate their significance to me [at that moment]. Did I stuff them into my coat? I do not remember. Whatever the case, I would have put them in my field locker and do not know what became of them, as it was taken at Sedan.

Aumale: We are to understand that you accepted in silence, without explanations, without comments, dispatches bearing the names of Marshal Bazaine and General Coffinières! That you did not even glance at the papers nor require any explanation from these agents! These men returned assuming that the mission you had given them had been accomplished, not knowing whether their telegraphic messages had been received. They sought out the officer who had sent them off, the one who had promised them 25,000 francs. They delivered those papers to him without saying anything to him! without even calling his attention to the papers! And this officer, for his part, did not think to look at the papers! He did not look at them, did not ask for an explanation, but put them in his locker:

Stoffel: I did not assert that they said nothing to me. Obviously they said something to me in turning over the papers they carried. Indeed, it would be unbelievable that they had said nothing to me in delivering four or five sheets of paper. But to testify, today, what they had to say to me, that is quite impossible. Whatever they said to me could not have seemed important to me or to have struck me in particular. It appears that I put those papers aside, meaning to look at them later. But one should not forget that we were then fully engaged in war, and everyone here knows what war really is. At Rethel, sixteen hours in a day were not enough to interrogate the spies of all sorts who were brought in to me.

Aumale: So, the names of Marshal Bazaine and General Coffinières were not mentioned by the agents—names that surely would have struck you?

Stoffel: Those names were not mentioned.

It may help the reader to proceed through this testimony if several plausible circumstances are interjected at this point. The tone of the duc d'Aumale's questions suggested that he had been convinced of Colonel Stoffel's guilt in suppressing a critical document: convinced either by Rivières' report or by the political profit to be made from establishing that guilt. But what if Colonel Stoffel, having not been the officer who opened the dispatch from the two agents, had not known for sure which officer had sent the order for them to return? The dispatch had arrived during the night, and Stoffel slept some distance from headquarters. Note, too, that the duc d'Aumale, by preferring the word of Colonel d'Abzac to that of Miès and Rabasse, ignored the possibility that their dispatch had become known at headquarters. And that Miès and Rabasse, having learned from Abzac that their dispatch had been received several days earlier, assumed they had fulfilled their mission and commented only on the new document (the letter from Colonel Massaroli) when they handed their papers to Stoffel.

Aumale's questions, in fact, betrayed not only his want of experience in modern warfare but a peculiar insensitivity to the uncertainty and confusion which had pervaded the Army of Châlons in its struggle to regroup after defeat. Aumale's remark to Stoffel that his recollections seemed to be quite vague about very serious matters drew from Stoffel the sober observation that we must think about the circumstances, the context, if we are to understand that one's memory can be unreliable. It had no effect upon Aumale.

Aumale: On the 22 August, or any other day, were you not given any dispatch coming from your agents and containing news from Metz?

Stoffel: No, monsieur le président.

Aumale: You are positive you received none?

Stoffel: None.

Aumale: You knew of no person in Marshal de MacMahon's headquarters, whether on 22 August or the next day, who accepted a dispatch from Metz transmitted by the two agents whom you had sent out?

Stoffel: I am unable to reply peremptorily to that question, because, as I had the honor to say earlier, I only seem to recall that others responded on my behalf to their request to return. It must follow from this that the dispatches had arrived, but I cannot state anything positively on that matter.

Pourcet: [After having asked for a reading of the deposition Stoffel had made to General Rivières during the *instruction*]: This is the matter that must be clarified. The colonel indicated in his written deposition that he had sent the message to the agents to have them return. That would lead us to believe that he had received the dispatch requesting authorization to return, sent by telegraph by the two agents. I should like to know whether the colonel, having just heard the deposition he made to the general during the *instruction*, believes that the statement made to the court should be altered?

Stoffel: When I underwent the interrogation during the *instruction*, I was quite unable to anticipate that anyone would make such an issue, such a stir, about this dispatch. The dispatch from Bétheniville, recalling the two agents, was shown to me during the *instruction* but without a careful examination of it. I was simply asked: "Did you give your agents word to return? Here is the dispatch through which you sent them the order." Owing to the uncertainty of my recollections at that moment, I assumed that the dispatch had gone out from me. Since then, I have had time to rethink the matter and now believe, as I had the honor to explain to monsieur le président, that the dispatch was not mine.

Pourcet: When the agents departed—when you sent them back to the prefect of police—what payment did you have allocated to them?

Stoffel: I am glad you have offered me opportunity to explain myself, as I have been accused of dishonorable behavior, portrayed as having promised those people a reward and giving them nothing. I had told them that, if they got into Metz, and if they brought back news of Marshal Bazaine, there would be a reward of 20,000 to 25,000 francs. I do not recall precisely which of those figures I used. But given the circumstances, I doubted that I owed them that reward. They had gone to Longwy peacefully, from where they sent off dispatches brought to Colonel Massaroli by Guyard. Had they fulfilled their mission? No. Yet, during their interrogation, they said that I had not given them the promised reward, and that perfidy was inserted into the indictment. I had given those agents money to enable them to go on the mission at the time of their departure from Châlons, either 500 or 1,000 francs, I cannot remember which. When I saw them again at Rethel, I believe that I gave them an additional 1,000 francs. But as for giving them a sum of 20,000 or 25,000 francs, it was not due them as they had not fulfilled their mission.

Pourcet: Commandant Massaroli telegraphed Marshal de MacMahon twice on 23 August to inform on the agents' trip. Did you receive those dispatches, or even one of them?

Stoffel: Not only did I not receive them, but I did not have knowledge of them. That can be explained by the fact that all dispatches came to the office, whereas I was lodged a quarter of a league from headquarters.

Chabaud-Latour: Colonel Stoffel has just said, I believe, that he gave the agents a sum of money as they were leaving Châlons, either 500 or 1,000 francs. When the agents handed him their papers they received a supplementary sum. On what day was that supplement given?

Stoffel: It was 26 August, at Rethel, where the agents rejoined me, and from where, after giving them the supplement, I definitely sent them back to Paris to the prefect of police.

Chabaud-Latour: And they accepted the supplement without discussion? They did not claim that their services were worth more?

Stoffel: No discussion.

This lengthy exchange about Stoffel's management of his two agents, if introduced by the prosecution for the purpose of raising doubt about his integrity, had the inadvertent result of revealing that the agents had not been satisfied with their financial settlement. At least that is what General Rivières had drawn from them during the *instruction*. If the prosecution had had any expectation of insinuating that alterations in the agents' testimony in the months between the *instruction* and the commencement of the court-martial were the result of collusion with Stoffel, the tactic was no longer viable. The duc d'Aumale told Stoffel at that point that he might retire to the witnesses' room, subject to recall.

Stoffel: I am counting on your benevolence and your fairness, which are universally appreciated, to ask to add a few words before retiring. I know that I have been summoned only as a witness, and I shall not cease to be a respectful witness and deferential to Monsieur le président and the court. But may I present a few additional explanations? May I put myself in a different situation other than the one I have been put in despite myself?

Aumale: A witness may neither plead nor discuss. He makes a deposition, and he answers questions put to him. In making your deposition, you had the opportunity to say all that you had to say.

Stoffel: I have additional explanations to give.

Aumale: I shall stop you if necessary.

Stoffel: I am accused of having suppressed a dispatch.

Aumale: You are accused of nothing before this court. You have made your deposition, and you have spoken as you intended. I have questioned you about the location of a certain dispatch, and you have answered in the manner you have judged to be proper. No doubt you will be able, in the course of the proceedings, to supply further explanations, as you will probably have occasion to reappear before the court. I do not believe that I can allow you to broach a discussion beginning with the phrase, "I am accused of having suppressed a dispatch."

Stoffel: I have no intention of attacking either the report or the reporter. I share the entire army's opinion of the reporter . . . .

Aumale: You are not attacking anyone. You began by saying, "I have been accused . . . ," and I stopped you then to say that you are not accused.

Stoffel: Will the court not permit me to wash these slanders and insults?

Aumale: You are out of order.

Stoffel: And to say, in regard to the reporter, that I share the sentiments of the entire army and feel for him only contempt and disdain.

Aumale: You are out of order, Colonel. You have made a deposition, and you have responded to the questions put to you. If you still have a deposition to make, you will have the opportunity when you are recalled later on.[41]

Unfortunately for him, Stoffel's slanderous words were heard not only by the court but by the packed gallery. The earlier contradictory debate between Colonel d'Abzac and the two agents had finally aroused public interest in the trial, and a large number of people had come out to the Grand Trianon in the hope of seeing how Colonel Stoffel would resolve the mystery of the critical dispatch. The room had never been so full since the opening of the trial, and this was its twenty-fourth session. Stoffel, moreover, had been something of a celebrity after the publication of his book on his mission to Berlin. At fifty-two, he was a man of imposing stature, his severe appearance giving a hint of harshness, of the bluntness that had always been characteristic.[42]

Although several members of the court had heard his thrust at General de Rivières, the duc d'Aumale had somehow missed it. Consequently, he proceeded with his plan to recall Rabasse and ordered that his deposition be read aloud in order to compare it with the testimony he had given in court. How could it happen, he asked Rabasse, that someone like you, obviously familiar with legal practices and aware of what constitutes significant evidence, failed to note in your first deposition the delivery of dispatches to a colonel [Abzac] during the night of 25-26 August? You have said that your memory of it only came later. When did that memory come to you?

Rabasse: Only when Miès spoke of it to me in recalling the events of that night.

Aumale: If you had not talked to Miès, would you have remembered the circumstances by yourself? [Aumale was clearly suspicious of Rabasse's story. He had given considerable detail in his written deposition, but now claimed to have forgotten an obviously important detail.] In your deposition you indicated having given the originals of the dispatches you were carrying to Colonel Stoffel. You gave them to him the morning of the 26th—and into his own hands? The answer being affirmative, Aumale asked whether Stoffel had settled financially with them at that point. The answer was *no*.

Aumale: What had he promised you when you left on your mission?

Rabasse: He did not promise us anything.

Aumale: No sum of money?

Rabasse: Nothing. At the time of our departure, he gave Miès 500 francs for us both. But he gave us nothing upon our return. The following day Miès told him that, because of the detours we had made in returning, we had run out of money. The colonel then gave Miès an additional 200 francs.

Chabaud-Latour: Did the witness speak to Colonel Stoffel about the importance of the dispatches he was carrying? Did you indicate that among them he would find dispatches coming from Bazaine?

Rabasse: I gave them to him in a military fashion, simply saying to him, "Here are the dispatches given to me by Colonel Massaroli." I did not indicate that one was for the emperor, or for Marshal de MacMahon, or for the minister of war. Colonel Stoffel acknowledged them, glanced at them, and then said, "This is what you sent to me." Then I gave him the letter from Colonel Massaroli which he read, then pronouncing the words I have earlier indicated.[43]

Miès was next recalled, and the duc d'Aumale pursued the same line of questioning as he had with Rabasse. Why, in the original deposition, had Miès not mentioned showing the dispatches to a colonel in headquarters on the night of 25-26 August?

Miès: My report was not written for submission to General de Rivières, but was only an accounting of my time as requested by Monsieur Claude for the records of the municipal police.

Aumale: But you could well have said—as it seems to me that it was a matter of some importance—that before delivering the dispatch to Colonel Stoffel you had had the originals seen by another person.

Miès: I did not see the significance of the incident at that time.

Aumale: This becomes even more serious. In your written deposition, you stated that Colonel Stoffel said to you, "There is nothing new here; these are the dispatches that you telegraphed to me." In your testimony yesterday, you said that is was Colonel d'Abzac who pronounced those words.

Miès: Colonel d'Abzac said to us, "We have known that for two days. These are the dispatches that you telegraphed to us." When we gave the dispatches to Colonel Stoffel the following morning, he said, "There is nothing new here; these are the same that you sent us."

The duc d'Aumale, increasingly frustrated by his inability to eliminate Colonel d'Abzac from the history of the controversial dispatch, and seemingly unable to accept the possibility that memories can be honestly imprecise after the passage of three years, continued to see discrepancies in Miès' testimony that he thought to be disingenuous. Whether he had also come to suspect that these difficulties ought to have been resolved during the *instruction* we cannot know. He did not say so, nor could he have said so without jeopardizing the integrity of the indictment of Marshal Bazaine. When Aumale learned from his fellow judges about Stoffel's expression of contempt for Rivières, the matter had to be addressed at once; for much more than a case of slander as at stake. Meanwhile, he finished with Miès by asking the same questions about money he had asked Rabasse, receiving essentially the same responses.[44]

The court announced a twenty-minute recess at the end of Miès' testimony, a common practice to relieve the long sessions. When the recess became prolonged without explanation, the audience, which had heard Stoffel's remark, soon concluded that the court was deliberating on what punitive measures ought to be taken. When the judges returned at 4:50, after a recess of an hour and five minutes, Colonel Stoffel was recalled. His slanderous words were read to him: "In regard to the reporter, I share the sentiments of the entire army, and I feel for him only contempt and disdain."

Aumale: I ask you if you said those words, if, having said them, you maintain them; or if, in the circumstances that they did come from you, you are ready to retract them before the court?

Stoffel: I said them, monsieur le président.

Aumale: You stand by them?

Stoffel: I cannot refuse to stand by words that I have pronounced.

Aumale: You do not retract them?

Stoffel: I have been abused and insulted!

The duc d'Aumale then read from articles 116 and 222 of the Code of Military Justice and the Penal Code respectively, defining both the offense and its punishment, after which he once again endeavored to get Stoffel to retract his words. The issue was an embarrassment for all parties. As Stoffel repeatedly insisted, his honor had been attacked by the charge of having deliberately suppressed a dispatch. The president, quite correctly, continued to insist that Stoffel was not on trial, but he could not allow Stoffel's protest to stand as it threatened to compromise the integrity of the *instruction* and the entire trial. Even Marshal Bazaine's defense attorney, Lachaud, faced a dilemma. He could have exploited the issue to mitigate Bazaine's culpability in having failed to communicate succinctly with MacMahon before Sedan. Yet, Stoffel was a loyal Bonapartist who could not easily be abandoned in a trial where a political attempt was being made to equate Bonapartism with betrayal.

Lachaud endeavored to intervene, not by criticizing the president's threat to bring criminal action, but by advising Stoffel publicly to retract his excessive language. A gallant man had been pushed too far, Lauchaud observed; but he must nevertheless remember that a magistrate has the obligation to maintain legal propriety, and his rulings must be observed. In response, Aumale once again gave Stoffel the opportunity to retract, and once again Stoffel refused. The written charge against him was then read aloud in court, and Stoffel became liable to a later trial for his offense.[45]

The prosecutor, General Pourcet, was not ready to settle for a simple charge of contempt of court or slander, but meant to seize the opportunity to pursue Stoffel for the criminal suppression of the dispatch. He asked to have Miès recalled, to be followed by Stoffel.

Pourcet: When you gave Colonel Stoffel the papers, you told him they were the dispatches you had been given at Longwy. The colonel took them, leafed through them and said, "Nothing new." What was the size of those dispatches?

Miès: About the size of an ordinary sheet of school paper. He said to us, "These are the dispatches that you telegraphed to me." Rabasse then said to him, "There is a letter from Colonel Massaroli which recommends M. Guyard to the attention of Marshal de MacMahon." Colonel Stoffel took the letter, broke open its cover, then crumpled it, saying that the marshal had other fish to fry. That is all.

Aumale: [To Stoffel] I must ask you to be more precise about several points on which you have already been questioned. On 22 August, at Courcelles-lès-Reims, about 10:30 in the evening or later during the night, did you receive a dispatch addressed to you from Longwy by the agents Rabasse and Miès, a dispatch where the message from those agents was not in cipher, which enclosed a ciphered dispatch from Marshal Bazaine to Marshal de MacMahon?

Stoffel: No.

Aumale: You attest that you did not receive it?

Stoffel: I attest to that.

Aumale: You had no knowledge of it, either that day or later? You did not see any dispatch coming in that manner, that same day, the 22nd?

Stoffel: I had no knowledge of any.

Aumale: On 26 August, in the morning at Rethel, Rabasse and Miès appeared at your residence. They gave you a packet of letters and a letter from Colonel Massaroli. Did you read that last letter?

Stoffel: My memory is uncertain. I do not know whether I read it.

Pourcet: Did not Colonel Stoffel learn from agent Miès that these were dispatches sent by Marshal Bazaine that were being given to him?

Stoffel: No. I have already responded earlier to that question. I cannot recall what those agents said to me. But they certainly did not say that they were from Marshal Bazaine; for that would have struck me, and I have no memory of such information.

Pourcet: [To the court] You have heard the depositions of Rabasse and Miès about the dispatches they carried, which they were charged to get to the emperor, to Marshal de MacMahon, and to the minister of war. The evidence from these witnesses, as well as from others, is sufficient to charge that, between the 22nd and the 27th of August, Colonel Stoffel, *chief of the intelligence service* at the headquarters of Marshal de MacMahon, either destroyed, burned, or tore up said dispatches which, in consequence, did not reach Marshal de MacMahon, a crime specifically defined and punished under article 255 of the Code of Military Justice. Accordingly, we ask to reserve the right to proceed with suitable prosecution of Colonel Stoffel at the proper time and under competent authority.

Lachaud: I have nothing to say about the reservation the prosecutor has requested. He has the right to ask for it. But this is an incident about which I have the right to be heard. One ought not to require more of human memory that it can provide. I have determined not to say a word about this serious incident; and everyone here, I believe, will understand the motives behind my silence. But is *he* the only person who has forgotten? And, since you think that a defect in memory is a crime, does that mean that all those who have not remembered should be prosecuted? I have nothing else to say.

Pourcet's statement to the court contained such a gross error as to suggest that he was either unequal to his task or determined to stick to the information provided in Rivières' report no matter what had emerged during the court-martial. Even the court took no notice of the error.

Aumale: The court, having heard both the commissaire du gouvernement and the attorney for the accused, approves the reservation in regard to Colonel Stoffel, colonel in retirement, and discharges him from further participation in this trial.[46]

So ended the session of 4 November 1873. The incident had considerably overshadowed anything to date in the Bazaine trial, and groups from the audience remained to talk and argue about it long after the end of the session. As for Colonel Stoffel, he wrote an open letter to Parisian newspapers, dated 5 November, to the effect that he had been charged by the commissaire du gouvernement as having knowingly intercepted or destroyed dispatches addressed to Marshal de MacMahon, which warranted bringing charges against Stoffel as the prosecutor should deem suitable. "I do not accept the commissaire's reservation," Stoffel concluded, "and I am herein addressing a request to be brought before a court-martial."[47]

Stoffel may have departed from the trial in person, but the issue was not so easily banished. Its memory haunted the courtroom during the session of 7 November when the mysterious fate of another dispatch from Bazaine came under scrutiny. This dispatch, also directed to Marshal de MacMahon, had also reached Colonel Turnier at Thionville. Neither the date of its departure from Metz nor its emissary had been established during the *instruction*, but the message had struck Colonel Turnier as important: "We are cut off, but only weakly. We can break through when we want. We shall await you."[48] As Colonel Turnier transmitted that message on 27 August, it had to have been sent before Bazaine had had any news that MacMahon had begun his march to the east. Turnier entrusted the dispatch, which was not in cipher, to M. Lallement, the imperial prosecutor at Sarreguemines who happened to be passing through Thionville, with instructions to deliver it to the first general officer he met. On 29 August, Lallement reached Sedan where General de Beurmann had just relieved Colonel Melcion d'Arc as commandant of the post. As Lallement knew both Melcion d'Arc and the local substitute imperial prosecutor, Bouchon-Garner, it was an easy matter for Lallement to be identified to Beurmann's satisfaction. He immediately sensed the importance of the message and discussed it with Melcion d'Arc.

A Monsieur Hulme, the owner of a spinning mill in Mouzon (just southeast of Sedan) where he was deputy-mayor, was also present; and Melcion d'Arc recommended him for the task of taking the dispatch to Marshal de MacMahon. Hulme told the court during the session of 7 November that he had accepted the mission as he had had some information about the movements of MacMahon's army and knew him to be near Raucourt. He took a carriage from Sedan to Mouzon where he obtained a fresh horse, reaching Raucourt about the time the emperor arrived there.

Hulme: I indicated that I was carrying a dispatch and was directed to where the emperor was. But a general prevented me from entering the door, saying that he would deliver the dispatch to the emperor. I responded that I had been instructed to deliver the message in person either to the emperor or to Marshal de MacMahon. I was then allowed to enter. After the emperor read the dispatch, he told me to take it to the marshal. I was able to enter the house where the marshal was without difficulty and found him on the second floor in a small room. I gave him the dispatch, but he did not appear to be much struck by it. He did ask me for information about the roads near Montmédy—their size—as well as about rivers and bridges. I told him I had just seen a coachdriver from Sedan, named Gillet, drive into Raucourt with a military doctor. As Gillet's information on such matters was more current than mine, I went out to find him. I found him only after some searching and took him back to be questioned by Marshal de MacMahon. Then we both went out. The emperor had me called for further discussion, and I took the dispatch to him.

Hulme continuing: After leaving the emperor for the second time, I had nothing more to do; but I had to return to Marshal de MacMahon [his third visit] to obtain a requisition for a horse to get back to Mouzon. The marshal talked to me about provisions for the army. I told him that, as deputy-mayor of Mouzon, I could probably requisition some supplies for the following day. He authorized me to get what I could, signing his name for the provisions. I reached home about six o'clock and immediately sent out messengers and forest guards in search of supplies. General de Beurmann even assigned six cuirassiers to help me. By the next day, we had gathered substantial supplies.

Aumale: Are you sure you talked to the marshal himself?

Hulme: Yes, quite sure. I saw him again the next day at Mouzon. I had sent out several men into the area to seek intelligence, and the marshal summoned me.

Aumale: He had knowledge of the dispatch, and you had given it to him?

Hulme: Yes.

Aumale: He had then questioned you about the roads around Montmédy?

Hulme: Yes, about the roads between Raucourt, Mouzon, and Montmédy.

Aumale: What was the shape of the paper on which that dispatch had been written?

Hulme: On a sheet of letter-paper, folded in quarters; and it had been put in an envelope.

Aumale: Did you see the dispatch put into the envelope?

Hulme: No, monsieur le président.

Aumale: Do you know whether it had been signed and by whom?

Hulme: Yes, it was signed by Colonel Turnier.

Aumale: Did it say that he was sending it in the name of Marshal Bazaine?

Hulme: Yes, monsieur le président.

Aumale: Do you recall the words in the dispatch?

Hulme: Not precisely, but the sense of it very well: "We are surrounded, but weakly. We can break out. We await you."[49]

The foxy Lachaud, who knew very well that Marshal de MacMahon, during the *instruction*, had denied seeing this particular dispatch, had seen in this incident the opportunity to score a point for Colonel Stoffel. He now asked the duc d'Aumale for the privilege of having that portion of MacMahon's deposition germane to Hulme's testimony read in court. General de Rivières' report indicated that, by the time MacMahon had been shown the depositions of Lallement, Melcion d'Arc, and Hulme, the *instruction* had already concluded that testimony given by a remarkable number of additional witnesses from Sedan, Mouzon, and Raucourt confirmed Hulme's testimony in virtually every detail. Yet, MacMahon could not recall having been given such a dispatch at Raucourt, noting that such a message, had it reached him after he had made his decision to move in the direction of Metz—and despite the emperor's reservations—would surely have struck him. As Hulme had been recalled for a confrontation with the marshal, MacMahon had turned to him to say, "I am astonished that you did not believe yourself obliged to give the dispatch to me as head of the army." And then to General de Rivières he had said, "Had Monsieur Hulme spoken to me about that dispatch, I would have ordered him to give it to me."

"The reason I did not leave it with you," Hulme had replied, "is that, while I was with you, I was called back to see the emperor, and I returned with the dispatch." When Hulme was asked in the presence of the marshal whether, in view of the marshal's denial, he still persisted in declaring he had communicated the dispatch to MacMahon, he answered, "I hold to my declaration." The evidence was overwhelming, beyond any doubt, especially in view of Hulme's activity in obtaining provisions for the army in MacMahon's name. Not only had the dispatch existed, but Hulme had surely given it to the marshal to read.[50]

The court tried rather too transparently to shield MacMahon in this damaging business by falling upon testimony which indicated that Hulme had sometimes worn his beard closely-trimmed, sometimes very full and long. It happened to have been well-trimmed in August of 1870, as it was at the time of the court-martial. But it had been very long at the time of the *instruction*. The lengthy testimony about this factor was meant to suggest that MacMahon had been misled during the *instruction*[51] by his inability to recognize Hulme. The audience, which followed Hulme's testimony closely, quite understood that Hulme's person was of little import. The analogy in the Hulme and Stoffel incidents *was* perceived. In each case, an important dispatch, whose departure and reception had been affirmed by depositions, but whose reception was denied by the marshal himself.

In the case of the dispatch brought to him by Hulme, the evidence that MacMahon *had* seen it was conclusive. Had he failed to perceive the implications of the dispatch? Or had he become so reconciled to the government's insistence that he attempt Bazaine's rescue that—once he had given the order to advance toward Metz—he became indifferent to any information which suggested the wisdom of retreat? A journalist who had followed the testimony, and who had watched the reaction of the audience, reported that, if Colonel Stoffel should be brought before a court-martial on the charge of having suppressed a dispatch addressed to Marshal de MacMahon, his defense attorney would certainly find more than one useful argument in Stoffel's favor emerging from the Hulme affair.[52]

Lachaud's intervention, in sum, was no small service to Colonel Stoffel. But Lachaud's greater task was not only to defend Bazaine's conduct at Metz, but to remove the charge that his equivocal message to MacMahon, the dispatch of 20 August, had led directly to the surrender at Sedan. In the later days of the trial, he would argue that the phrase, "And I shall inform you of my march, if, that is, I can undertake it without compromising the army," was not an equivocation. It had been, rather, an instruction to move only when word of the actual march should be received. In other words, "I shall inform you if I can undertake my march without compromising the army. Until then, do not move."[53] Lachaud argued, in fact, that had Marshal de MacMahon received the dispatch, he most assuredly would not have moved, an interpretation at odds with the marshal's initial deposition but in agreement with his later testimony.

Lachaud: What, then, became of that critical dispatch? I do not know; and you, Monsieur le commissaire du gouvernement, know no more than I do on the matter. I only know one thing: a dispatch was sent by Marshal Bazaine. You have shown me that it arrived by telegraph on 22 August at Marshal de MacMahon's headquarters. That is certain. M. Stoffel has said that he did not receive it, hardly surprising as he lived a certain distance from headquarters. It has been established that it could have been opened for him; that, in general, when dispatches arrived, they were opened in the common interest. It cannot be proved that Colonel Stoffel received that dispatch; nor, if he had received it, that he did not notify Marshal de MacMahon.[54]

The commissaire du gouvernment, however, saw no reason to retract his charges against Stoffel, especially as a retraction could have undermined the authority of the indictment of Bazaine. As Stoffel had asked to be brought before a court-martial, there was no turning back.

Notes

1. See especially Generals Edmond Ruby and Jean Regnault, *Bazaine, coupable ou victime.*
2. Boreau-Lajanadie, *Rapport fait au nom de la Commission d'Enquête sur les actes du Gouvernment de la Défense Nationale. Actes de la délégation de Tours et de Bordeaux*, pp. 104–105.
3. J. P. T. Bury, *Gambetta and the National Defense*, pp. 170–73, 322.
4. François-Charles Du Barail, *Mes Souvenirs* 3: 200–18, 297.
5. Ibid. 3: 305, 443–44.
6. Maurice Garçon, *Histoire de la justice sous la IIIe république* 1: 121.
7. Ibid. 1: 122; Du Barail, *Mes Souvenirs* 3: 352.
8. Du Barail, *Mes Souvenirs* 3: 301–302.
9. Amédée Le Faure, *Procès du Maréchal Bazaine* 1: 3.
10. Louis-Adolphe Thiers, *Memoirs of M. Thiers 1870–1873*, pp. 168–69.
11. Raymond Cazelles, *Le Duc d'Aumale, prince aux dix visages*, p. 299.
12. *Le Procès Bazaine: Conseil de guerre du Grand Trianon. Compte-rendu sténographique quotidien*, p. 8.
13. Cazelles, *Le Duc d'Aumale*, pp. 354–55.
14. Maurice d'Irisson, comte d'Hérisson de Saulnier, *La Légende de Metz*, pp. 224–33.
15. Du Barail, *Mes Souvenirs* 3: 446–48.
16. The first fraction: La Motte, comte de La Motte-Rouge, baron Chabaud-Latour, and Tripier. The second fraction: Princeteau, Ressayre, and baron Martineau-Deschenez. The substitutes: Susleau de Malroy, Lallemand, and Guiod. *Le Procès Bazaine*, pp. 6, 8, 24; Le Faure, *Proces du Maréchal Bazaine* 1: 34.
17. Cazelles, *Le Duc d'Aumale*, p. 354.
18. General de La Motte-Rouge to Commandant Multzer, 16 August 1873. Joseph-Edouard de La Motte-Rouge, *Souvenirs et campagnes* 3: 575–76.
19. Hérrison, *La Légende de Metz*, pp. 70–73.
20. Bury, Gambetta and the National Defense, pp. 228–30; Raymond Manevy, *La Presse de la IIIe République*, pp. 73–74. For Challemel-Lacour's troubled administration in Lyon, see Louis M. Greenberg, *Sisters of Liberty: Marseille, Lyon, Paris and the Reaction to a Centralized State, 1868–1871*, pp. 214–61.
21. Le Faure, *Procès du Marechal Bazaine* 1: 3–6, 32; Du Barail, *Mes Souvenirs* 3: 444–46.
22. Raymond-Adolphe Séré de Rivières, *Rapport complet. Procès du Maréchal Bazaine*, p. 30.
23. Ibid., p. 31.
24. Ibid., pp. 31–32. MacMahon's early and partisan biographer, Léon Laforge, contributed to the confusion by asserting that, had the marshal received the dispatch of 20 August, he *probably* would have renounced the march toward Bazaine, no matter the orders from Paris, or at least held back. *Histoire complète de MacMahon* 1: 256.
25. *Le Procès Bazaine*, pp. 9–15.

26. Stoffel to *Le Bien Public*, 10 October 1873. Jules Claretie, *Histoire de la Révolution de 1870–1871* 2: 757–63.

27. Léonce Rousset, *La Second campagne de France* 2: 155.

28. Michael Howard, *The Franco-Prussian War*, pp. 185–87.

29. Rivières, *Rapport complet*, pp. 127–29.

30. Ibid., pp. 129–31, 135.

31. Alfred, comte de La Chapelle, *Oeuvres posthumes et autographes inédits de Napoléon III en exil* 2: 109-10.

32. La Faure, *Procès du Maréchal Bazaine* 1: 197–99; *Le Procès Bazaine*, p. 209.

33. Le Faure, *Procès du Maréchal Bazaine* 1: 199–202.

34. Ibid. 1: 203–205.

35. Ibid. 1: 205–206.

36. Ibid. 1: 208–10.

37. *Le Procès Bazaine*, p. 228; Maurice Baumont, *Bazaine, les secrets d'un maréchal (1811–1888)*, pp. 251–52.

38. Le Faure, *Procès du Maréchal Bazaine* 1: 214–19.

39. Ibid. 1: 219–20.

40. Ibid. 1: 220–26; Baumont, *Bazaine*, p. 252.

41. Le Faure, *Procès du Maréchal Bazaine* 1: 226–31.

42. *Le Procès Bazaine*, p. 233.

43. Le Faure, *Procès du Maréchal Bazaine* 1: 231–34.

44. Ibid. 1: 234–35.

45. Ibid. 1: 236–38; *Le Procès Bazaine*, pp. 236–37.

46. Le Faure, *Procès du Maréchal Bazaine* 1: 238–40.

47. *Le Procès Bazaine*, p. 241.

48. Rivières, *Rapport complet*, p. 34.

49. Le Faure, *Procès du Maréchal Bazaine* 1: 250–54.

50. Rivières, *Rapport complet*, p. 147.

51. Le Faure, *Procès du Maréchal Bazaine* 1: 254–59.

52. *Le Procès Bazaine*, p. 273.

53. Session of 8 December 1873, Ibid., p. 568.

54. Ibid., pp. 569–70.

Part VII

Judicial Equivocation

The unsatisfactory outcome of the lengthy judicial procedure against Colonel Stoffel in 1874 had its precedent: the equivocal consequences of the Bazaine court-martial. On 10 December 1873, the court found Bazaine guilty of having treated with the enemy, and of having surrendered the post of Metz without having first exhausted all means of defense, and without having done all that duty and honor required. He was sentenced to death with military degradation.[1] Certain politicians may have secured their immediate goal, the general public had no doubt that justice had been served, but more dispassionate observers, such as the British journalist Archibald Forbes, recognized that a conspiracy to betray had not been proved. The army, whose command he had assumed on 13 August 1870, had been inferior in all respects, except for its infantry rifle, to that of the enemy; and Bazaine had succumbed to the difficulties of the task and to the magnitude of his command, having had no prior experience with a command on that scale.[2]

Immediately following the pronouncement of its verdict, the court addressed a letter to the minister of war asking him not to have the sentence carried out. "As judges in this case, we have had to apply an inflexible law which does not provide for any circumstances to be taken into consideration to attenuate a crime against military duty. But at least we have the right to call those circumstances to your attention: that Marshal Bazaine took and exercised command of the Army of the Rhine in the midst of unusual difficulties; that he was not responsible for the disastrous beginning of the campaign nor for the choice of the plans of operation. We remind you that under fire he was always master of himself—at Borny, at Gravelotte—and at Noisseville no one surpassed him in valiance; and that his military career, beginning in 1831, was of such merit as to justify the baton of a marshal of France. Consider his long detention, the agony of having had to endure two months during which he listened every day to debate about his honor. We ask you to join us in begging the president of the Republic not to allow the sentence we have just pronounced to be carried out."[3]

As a consequence, the court opened a breach which has never been adequately closed. Did the judges mean that the law had not permitted the consideration of mitigating factors which they, as fellow officers, believed should weigh in the balance? Or had the judges tacitly believed they had rendered the verdict that was politically necessary for the nation, but which they, as soldiers, knew was unfounded? As we know that the trial would not have taken place had Bazaine not demanded it, and as most officers thought poorly of the idea of a trial, the likelihood of the second alternative looms large. The verdict was rendered "in the name of the French people," a statement true in both law and spirit. The people in general had seized upon the charge of treason from the moment Gambetta had uttered it; and, in a nation where attorneys were known not only by name but by political affiliation, the politization of trials was accepted as a fact of legal life. Because the army was supposedly nonpolitical, some may have supposed that military justice was untainted by politics. Had the Bazaine trial been more widely studied, or had the Stoffel affair become more widely known in detail, that confidence would have been laid to rest.

Two days after the pronouncement of the death sentence, as Bazaine had not lodged an appeal for revision within the required twenty-four hours, the government announced that his sentence had been commuted by the president to twenty years of detention without the loss of military rank. MacMahon's leniency has been attributed to a pronounced instinct for military comradery by those who believed he had pushed indulgence too far.[4] For the few who believed that Bazaine's guilt had not been proved, the most grotesque aspect of the case was that the penalty had been commuted thanks to the clemency of a man who, himself, had led another French army into a position where it had been obliged to capitulate. And the recompense for that exploit had been his elevation to the presidency of the Republic.[5] But that fact perhaps accounted for MacMahon's leniency.

Bazaine was then confined in the prison-fortress of Ste. Marguerite on the island off Cannes. He managed to escape from it on the night of 9 August 1874, a moment when General de Cissey, who had never favored bringing Bazaine to trial, headed the cabinet. In view of the commutation of the sentence, the government was immediately suspected of having connived in the escape. Recent access to a journal kept by Bazaine's aide, Lt. Col. Willette, has made it evident that Bazaine had had no official assistance in his escape. In truth, the incident was an embarrassment, coming only several months after Henri Rochefort's flight from New Caledonia; and the regime forced the resignation of the prefect of Alpes-Maritimes, the marquis de Villeneuve-Bargemon, for his inattention to security.[6]

These events—between 10 December 1873 and 9 August 1874—coincided with Colonel Stoffel's judicial crisis. Having refused to retract his insulting remark about General de Rivières, he was brought before the tribunal correctionel de Versailles on 13 November, really a police court, and charged with having insulted a magistrate in the exercise of his duties. He was accompanied by Bazaine's attorney, Lachaud. The penalty provided for such a charge under article 222 of the Penal Code was two to five years imprisonment. The judge, citing extenuating circumstances which had aroused Stoffel's passions and left him without full understanding of his words, condemned him only to three months in prison. He was not immediately incarcerated, having indicated his intention to seek official postponement of his prison term.[7] He wanted, in particular, to await the outcome of his request for a court-martial.

On the very evening of the day that Bazaine's sentence was commuted, Stoffel joined Edouard Lefebvre de Béhaine and Edmond de Goncourt for dinner. Lefebvre had been secretary in the French embassy in Berlin during Stoffel's years there, and he would keep up his friendship with Stoffel in later years, convinced that he was honorable. Lefebvre had also been an intimate of the Goncourts, especially of Edmond after 1870, who did not share Lefebvre's favorable opinion of Stoffel. "I know not why the appearance of this man seems to give credence to the rumors which are circulating about him. He does not have a loyal appearance."[8]

A month later, Lefebvre read Goncourt a letter from Stoffel to the effect that his request for postponement of his prison term until May had been rejected by the garde des sceaux. Consequently, he had requested an audience with MacMahon, whom he called "the timorous", but had been refused. "And yet it is I," he added, "when he was wounded at Sedan, who carried him in my arms amidst shot and shell."[9] Nevertheless, for reasons unclear, Stoffel was permitted to postpone his prison term, and the record shows that he turned himself in to the Maison de Justice in Versailles on 29 May 1874.[10]

The first thirteen days of Stoffel's three-month sentence were spent in the Maison de Justice, which was actually a house for temporary detention until the inmates could be assigned to prisons suitable for their crimes. As a consequence, Stoffel found himself lumped with swindlers, murderers, and thieves for a few days, and he was still steaming about that indignity when he was finally released in late August. The detention center happened to be in the rue Saint-Pierre, across the street from military headquarters. But none of his former associates bothered to cross the street to visit him. It is evident that Stoffel had seen a gradual change in his fellow officers' attitudes. Initially, they had believed that the charge of suppressing a document had been preposterous; as time went on, they gradually became more reserved, perhaps uncertain about the outcome of the *instruction* for his possible court-martial. His real friends proved to be outside the military service, and they were highly critical of MacMahon's failure to intervene. Imprisonment did afford Stoffel the opportunity to collect his thoughts and to prepare his own version of events for publication after his release. He would defend MacMahon's inaction on the grounds that the chief-of-state was encumbered by too many duties and expressed the confidence that, if MacMahon had held any other position, he would not have failed to defend him openly. But he would not have welcomed a pardon, for to have accepted it would have been an admission of guilt. One cannot, indeed, read those pages he prepared without sensing his conviction of innocence and his confidence of exoneration.[11] That conviction may have been soundly grounded, but the confidence was misplaced.

The preparations to bring Stoffel before a court-martial began on 28 December 1873 when the minister of war appointed Colonel Alexandre-Victor-Edmond Clappier to be the commissaire du gouvernement for the case, thus technically in charge of the *instruction*. The minister also nominated Captain Paul-Joseph-Louis Janicot to be the reporter assigned to the investigation. This meant, in effect, that Captain Janicot would prepare the indictment, if one should be warranted; and Colonel Clappier would prosecute the case. The two men, both of whom had been commissioned as infantry officers, were roughly the same age, and neither one had had formal legal training. Each officer had had, however, a singular record of service over many years, suggesting why they would have been recommended for their respective tasks by the director of personnel in the ministry of war.

Captain Janicot had requested retirement late in 1868 at the end of thirty years of active service. His request had been granted at the outset of 1869 with a pension of 1,770 francs. The only remarkable thing about his service was that, from the time he reached the rank of lieutenant—in 1852—he had been repeatedly detached from his regiment for military judicial service, either as a reporter or as an assistant prosecutor. One gets the impression that he became something of a specialist in the preparation of indictments. Then, although officially retired, he had accepted employment as a reporter within the First Military Division (region) in 1870: a commissioned bureaucrat, in other words, working for the military administration. His two decorations were not for valor in the field, but for dedicated service in the office.[12]

Colonel Clappier, who was still on active duty in 1873 (and who would retire as a brigadier general in 1881), had had a career characterized by two types of service. For the most part, he had either been an aide-de-camp to a general officer, or he had served on a headquarters staff. Perhaps the key to his character lies in a malicious remark made by an inspector-general in his review of Clappier's service in 1880: "An intelligent officer, but likes his comforts too much."[13] Otherwise, his superiors had regarded him to be a model officer, not only intelligent but well-instructed, and a student of German. In July of 1870, he was assigned to be chief-of-staff of the 1st Division of V Corps in the Army of the Rhine, one of the army corps later shunted into the Army of Châlons. Taken prisoner at Sedan, he was not released until April of 1871. He was then reemployed in the new Army of Versailles, formed under the command of Marshal de MacMahon for the destruction of the Commune of Paris. He served as assistant chief-of-staff of IV Corps, the chief-of-staff being General Renson.

When Thiers reorganized his cabinet that summer and began his moves to reform the army, he installed General de Cissey as his minister of war, and Cissey chose General Renson to be his director of personnel. We have already seen their collaboration in removing Colonel Stoffel permanently from the army, and the report on Stoffel's career made by Renson to Cissey was so obviously at odds with the facts in the case as to suggest Renson to be a man quite ready to subvert the truth in defense of the army. General de Cissey had, of course, since been removed from office at the request of President MacMahon. Renson had sought to resign because of his loyalty to Cissey, but MacMahon intervened personally to secure Renson's continuation as director of personnel.[14]

Administrators obviously make appointments to obtain anticipated results, and the appointment of Colonel Clappier as prosecutor in the Stoffel case was no exception to this rule of common sense. It seems quite probable, however, that General Du Barail, the incumbent minister of war, did not comprehend the implications of the appointment when the order was signed in his name. Although Du Barail has often been rated as nonpolitical because of his unquestioning service to whatever regime was in power, he was in principle and in spirit an authoritarian Bonapartist who gave no hint, in his memoirs, of antagonism to Stoffel. But the real measure of Du Barail is that he had always been an active soldier, not a desk chair officer. So inexperienced was he in administration that he sensed, on entering the ministry in the rue St. Dominique, that he was in alien corn. For the first time in his life, as he put it, he had as colleagues men who did not wear a sword, as he did. Not only did he like and trust Renson, he needed him as an experienced administrator wise in personnel matters. The need to destroy Stoffel's credibility had been only partially accomplished in 1872. By requesting his own court-martial, he opened the way for his enemies to complete their work in 1874; and Renson was quite equal to the task. By chance, the general then in command of the First Military Division (Region), the governor of Paris, was General de Cissey; and, if a court-martial were to be recommended, it would be within that administrative division.

Captain Janicot began his investigation of the fate of the dispatch of 20 August early in January of 1874. His report, which ran to sixteen handwritten pages, was not signed until 11 June 1874. He stated at the outset that he had endeavored to review the entire history of the incident; and he also repeated, at the outset, the critical and mistaken assertion that Stoffel had been chief of MacMahon's intelligence service. We learn for the first time, however, that Stoffel had been provided an assistant at Châlons, Lt. Paul Laurens de Waru, another officer who had originally been on the personal staff of Marshal Leboeuf and had become unemployed once Leboeuf gave up his command.[15] The revelation was seemingly unimportant in that Laurens de Waru had testified that, although Stoffel had been kind enough to him, he had not been communicative, working essentially alone. But Janicot made something of that fact as it could imply that Stoffel had had good reason to be secretive.

In view of the predispositions of those who had arranged this legal procedure, did the report, taken for the moment as a whole, give any indication that Colonel Clappier and Captain Janicot had undertaken the *instruction* without prejudice? Unfortunately for Colonel Stoffel, the answer seems to be *no*. Therein lay the irony of Janicot's product, a report highly damaging to Stoffel in its conclusion, but in too many respects inadequately conclusive for the hierarchy to risk a public trial. It would appear that the army had learned something from the experience gained during the Bazaine court-martial. General Rivières' report had been extensive, based upon much testimony, giving reason for confidence in its invulnerability. Yet, a practiced defense attorney had picked some embarrassing holes in it, and there was reason to believe that the same attorney would be engaged by Stoffel should the case come to trial. As there would be no trial after the conclusion of Janicot's *instruction*, the defense would never be given the opportunity to provide refutation of testimony.

Janicot obviously studied the Bazaine trial carefully; and as he took nearly six months before presenting his report, its shortcomings were not the product of slipshod work but of his too obvious determination to do whatever was necessary to prove Stoffel's guilt. He had depositions given by a few witnesses who had not been heard during the Bazaine trail, such as Laurens de Waru and Marescalchi. But in general he summoned as witnesses only those whose original testimony had strengthened the case for Stoffel's probable innocence of the charge against him. Theirs was the testimony that had to be shaken, weakened, and revised; the testimony of MacMahon and his staff officers went unquestioned, and the Hulme incident was entirely sidestepped.

Janicot also made an unqualified judgment about the dispatch of 20 August, which helped to magnify the gravity of Stoffel's alleged crime. Bazaine's dispatch of that date, he asserted, "essentially modified" the information which the dispatch of 19 August had contained; and MacMahon had testified during the trial that a message of such seriousness would certainly have aroused his attention had he seen it. Janicot ignored the possibility, raised earlier by the marshal himself, that the message, had he received it, would not have altered his line of march.[16] In the second place, Janicot's judgment about the character of the dispatch of 20 August failed to take into account the possibility that it had been read by officers on MacMahon's staff without anyone perceiving its significance. In fact, both of Bazaine's dispatches, those of 19 and 20 August 1870, had contained conditional clauses. The former had stated that Bazaine would follow the direction of the Nord in retreating toward Montmédy *if* that route should not be too strongly occupied by the enemy. The later dispatch said he would move in that direction *if* he could undertake the movement without compromising the army.

Those who would argue, in later years, that MacMahon, knowing Bazaine's character, would have immediately realized upon reading the dispatch of 20 August that Bazaine would not emerge from an entrenched camp, and would have understood that the march to the east was not only perilous but useless,[17] ignored the possibility that MacMahon had not recognized the conditional character of the earlier dispatch. The alternative view, in other words, would be that neither MacMahon nor his staff officers had seen the significance of Bazaine's hesitation in either of the two dispatches, therefore saw no reason to modify their plans to move to join Bazaine.[18] Emile Ollivier would deny that it had been a failure to perceive on their part, but rather that Bazaine's qualifications applied to *any* military operation planned: that any plan or intention becomes subordinate to unanticipated circumstances. And that explained why, for Ollivier, when MacMahon was asked if reception of the dispatch would have caused him to alter his decision to move forward, he had answered that it was probably he would have proceeded toward the Meuse.[19] Janicot's version of events contained no considerations of that genre. As all the officers on MacMahon's staff had testified during the trial that they had never seen the dispatch of 20 August, it followed that Colonel Stoffel was the author if its suppression.

To substantiate this conclusion, Janicot cited, first of all, information he gathered from the telegraphic personnel involved in the transmission of the critical dispatch. Amiot, who had been the director of the telegraphic service at imperial headquarters, gave absolute assurance that he had received the dispatches sent by Stoffel's police agents, and that they had been transmitted directly to the addressee, namely, Stoffel. The dispatch signed by Marshal de MacMahon ordering the agents to return further confirmed that their message had been received, and Janicot asserted that the order had to have been given by Stoffel.

This additional investigation turned up the name of the female servant who had admitted the two agents to MacMahon's personal headquarters and took them to the officer on duty, Lt. Marescalchi. (Her name was Duget.) Marescalchi, "who no doubt did not know where Stoffel was quartered," awoke Commandant de Vaulgrenant who slept in the same room. But neither officer knew where Stoffel was. Consequently, Marescalchi told Miès (the name was consistently spelled Niès in the report) that Stoffel would come in about eight o'clock in the morning, and that they could see him then. They did see him at breakfast and gave him the dispatches. This new version of events not only eliminated Colonel d'Abzac from the scene, but implied that none of the staff officers had seen the disputed dispatch. That is, when Rabasse handed the papers to Stoffel, he looked at them and said, "All very well, but there is nothing new here. It is what you already sent to me."

Janicot noted correctly that Stoffel had made a deposition to General de Rivières on 28 August 1872 concerning his order to the two agents to return, a version which Stoffel altered when called to testify on 4 November during the court-martial. He scoffed at Stoffel's explanations given at the trial: that he had not anticipated that this particular dispatch would generate such a furor, and that the dispatch ordering the return of the two agents had been shown to him during the *instruction* without him taking any real significance in it. He had merely been asked whether he had told the agents to return, and told "here is the dispatch by which you sent the order." Later he claimed that his memory had been faulty, and that he could only *suppose* that the agents could only have been recalled by him personally. After reconsideration, he had come to believe that he had not, in fact, sent the dispatch.

"It is difficult to accept the idea," commented Janicot, "that a man of such quality as Colonel Stoffel, an observer of such indisputable merit, should find himself reduced to such circumlocutions. Just as one will find it difficult to believe that a man, so much the master of himself under all circumstances, was able to misjudge to the point of being led to alter, not only his thought, but even more the truth, unless he was obedient to a pressure which would have dominated his will." Janicot cited all the confused, or confusing, exchanges between the duc d'Aumale and Stoffel as to whether, or when, Stoffel had received dispatches, or in what manner he had coped with his two agents, as proof that Stoffel had been concealing the truth about the suppression of the dispatch, because he had been under orders to conceal it. "It is also probable," Janicot added, "that at the time of Stoffel's initial deposition, he believed that the suppressed dispatch had disappeared without a trace."

One difficult point remained for Janicot in that context. The request from Stoffel's agents for instructions about returning had been recorded as arriving at 10:10 p.m. on 22 August. Stoffel had earlier testified that he had left headquarters that evening by 8 o'clock to account for why he could not have sent the responses. Janicot dismissed the alibi as worthless, stating that he had found that the dispatch received at 10:10 had only been a second edition of one received earlier at 7 p.m., a most curious belated discovery.

To the end of his questioning by Janicot, Stoffel stood by the version of events he had given during the Bazaine court-martial. He had not received the dispatch of 20 August, but that it had been received at the marshal's headquarters as the Abzac incident had brought to light. The critical information in it had been known for several days before the agents' return. When asked again which officer at headquarters had received the dispatch, he answered that there had been more than twenty officers assigned to the marshal's headquarters; and he could not say which one had opened it. But it had been received and deciphered. Janicot's interrogation of Stoffel concluded with a question about his treatment of the original dispatches when they were given to him by his agents at Rethel. As Colonel Massaroli's accompanying letter had been quite pointed about the importance of the papers, why had he simply put them away? According to Janicot, Stoffel retorted that he thought the question was improper, and that he had then refused to append his signature at the conclusion of his testimony.

In summing up the report at considerable length, Janicot disposed of the Abzac incident by attacking the reliability of both Rabasse and Miès as witnesses. He pointed correctly to testimony during the court-martial when they had said quite openly that they had reviewed together the events of the night of 22 August, which Janicot interpreted as private collaboration to avoid conflicting testimony. He interrogated each of them separately, inducing Rabasse to admit that he did not know whether he had actually spoken to Colonel d'Abzac, nor could he recognize him. Miès was told by Janicot that what he had reported could not have taken place. If Colonel d'Abzac had looked at the dispatch as Miès had testified, he could not have said after a glance that its contents were already known as it was in cipher. That point was well made, but it skirted an alternative possibility that Lachaud would have seized upon. The officers awakened on that fateful night had indicated that the agents' return had been anticipated, and it had to be known that they were bringing back the originals of dispatches that had already been received, deciphered, and read. Did not Abzac legitimately assume he knew what the dispatches were in his irritation at being awakened unnecessarily in the middle of the night? In any case, Janicot claimed that the agents' testimony had been unreliable, and that only two officers, Marescalchi and Vaulgrenant, had been awakened on the critical night. As for the motive which had induced the agents to give false testimony during the court-martial, the implication left by Janicot was that Colonel Stoffel had designed their testimony.

This new version of events did more than strengthen the case against Stoffel. It removed Colonel d'Abzac from any suspicion of negligence, no small matter as Abzac had survived Sedan to become an aide-de-camp to MacMahon during his presidential term.[20] MacMahon was also absolved by Janicot's report, which cited a letter from the marshal to the minister of war on 27 August, indicating he had had no word from Bazaine since the dispatch of 19 August.

Janicot's summary: "I believe that Colonel Stoffel received a dispatch about 7:00 p.m. on 22 August 1870 that he was charged to remit to Marshal de MacMahon; that he received the same dispatch by telegraph at the imperial headquarters that same evening; and that, finally, on 25 August at Rethel, the two agents brought him the original copy of the dispatch. As Marshal de MacMahon has affirmed that Colonel Stoffel never delivered that dispatch to him, it necessarily follows that Colonel Stoffel voluntarily suppressed it. Accordingly, I recommend that an indictment be prepared because of the particular function Stoffel exercised within MacMahon's headquarters, namely, charged with the intelligence service, for a crime under article 267 of the Code of Military Justice and under article 173 of the common Penal Code."[21] The report was dated 11 June 1874. The reference in it to imperial headquarters had to have been included to provide the occasion for the emperor to give Stoffel orders to suppress the dispatch. Janicot, no more than had Rivières, endeavored to provide an explanation for why the emperor would have ordered destroyed the very document that would have recommended the implementation of his favored strategy—the retreat upon Paris.

Janicot's report was then put in the hands of Colonel Clappier, the commissaire du gouvernement for the case. As the potential prosecutor, Clappier had had a number of months to ponder the ramifications of the Stoffel affair as he watched the case restructured by Captain Janicot; and he had taken part in the interrogation of witnesses. About four weeks before Janicot signed his report, the Broglie cabinet fell (16 May 1874), removing General Du Barail from the ministry of war. General de Cissey was then restored to his old position as well as named to the presidency of the new cabinet. Whatever may have been Cissey's antagonism to Stoffel, he had suddenly acquired a new responsibility for the reputation and the stability of the regime. He placed in command of the First Military Division, and as governor of Paris, his longtime colleague, General Paul de Ladmirault, within whose jurisdiction the Stoffel *instruction* was being completed. The speed with which the Stoffel affair was terminated, once Janicot had submitted his report, makes it reasonable to suppose that Colonel Clappier had consulted with his superiors before the paper work began.

His review of the issues in his formal recommendation to General Ladmirault was not a document hastily or casually penned, its very brevity suggesting careful preparation. Additional evidence had been brought to the surface during the *instruction*, Clappier asserted, on issues that had not been resolved during the Bazaine trial. There was now reason to believe that Colonel Stoffel's guilt had been properly established during those public debates: that he had knowingly destroyed and suppressed dispatches without bringing them to the attention of the commander-in-chief. "In considering the motive, however, which led Colonel Stoffel to his action, namely, to assure the application of a certain set of ideas to the direction of military operations, and which had to have been suggested to him, one is forced to recognize that, quite beyond the material fact, which devolves upon him entirely, one will run up against responsibilities at a higher level, difficult or impossible to reach, and which will in part absolve him."[22] Indeed, in Clappier's opinion, the condemnation of a relatively obscure, if guilty, man would hardly compensate the public for the pain and the scandal of reopening the memories of the national humiliation.

His letter still reads as having been artfully designed to reassure the army that military justice had been well-served in 1873, but to caution that it would be most impolitic to reopen the Stoffel aspect of the case. Both General de Rivières and Captain Janicot had pointed to Napoleon III as the ultimate villain, and he was unreachable; but the evidence for the crime was entirely circumstantial, and, in view of his repeated (and documented) recommendations to MacMahon against the march toward Bazaine, flimsy at best. Stoffel's faulty memory had several times been cited as the proof of his criminal action. Yet, would not the reopening of the Stoffel affair not merely recall the memories of the national humiliation, but run the risk of exposing again Marshal de MacMahon's own lapses of memory, not to speak of his judgment during those terrible days? And he, too, would now be "difficult or impossible to reach."

General Ladmirault at once forwarded Clappier's recommendation, along with Janicot's report, to the minister of war, noting that he *completely agreed* with the recommendation that an ordinance of *non-lieu* (nonsuit) be issued.[23] Said ordinance was issued the following month by the ministry of war, at which time Colonel Stoffel had served approximately half of his sentence for slander. General de Cissey signed the ordinance, which had clearly been prepared with the aid of legal counsel.

> Whereas the conclusions of the commissaire spécial du gouvernement recommend no further action in this affair, notwithstanding the contrary opinion of the reporter;
> Whereas the evidence reviewed to support the charge against Colonel Stoffel by the investigation does not establish that this officer destroyed, burned, or tore up the dispatches; and that, in consequence, article 255 of the Code of Military Justice is not applicable in his case;
> Whereas Colonel Stoffel being neither a functionary, agent, official, nor an administrative clerk of the government, the provisions of article 173 of the Penal Code are not legally applicable to him;
> Whereas in jurisprudence the silence of the law must be to the advantage of the accused;
> We declare that no indictment shall be pronounced and order said retired Colonel Stoffel to be set free immediately unless he is detained for other cause.[24]

Stoffel learned of the dismissal of charges in a letter from Colonel Clappier on 17 July 1874, four days after the ordinance of non-suit had been issued. The lack of any publicity surrounding the dismissal spurred Stoffel to write and publish a brochure on the dispatch of 20 August 1870. Having been denied the public platform a court-martial would have provided him, the publication, which ran to 117 pages, was his best alternative in his desire to clear the record. Some months before the court-martial of Marshal Bazaine, on 27 April 1873 to be precise, he had received the support of nearly 27,000 voters in his quest for a seat in the National Assembly, and he now believed that he owed his supporters the dignity of an explanation.[25]

He had seen neither Janicot's report on the *instruction* nor Clappier's letter to the governor of Paris, documents which necessarily had remained confidential. As is routine in French legal procedure, he *had* been permitted to hear a reading of the many depositions given by interrogated witnesses during the *instruction*. On the basis of what he had heard, the case against him had had to be dismissed for lack of evidence; and he wrote his brochure without the glimmer of a suspicion that he had been branded a criminal in the official report on the *instruction*. His brochure, albeit a personal account, became an essential document in the affair, reflecting what had actually transpired during the *instruction*, and written in the confidence that he would not be contradicted from above. To the best of his knowledge, he had been exonerated. Willy Schädler, our source on Stoffel genealogy, who saw Colonel Clappier's recommendation in the Stoffel dossier, believed in Stoffel's guilt and was astonished that he had dared to revive the issue with his brochure. But Schädler, who also stated that he had been unable to study the matter in any depth, seems not to have suspected that Stoffel had been made the scapegoat for an inexplicable lapse in MacMahon's headquarters, nor to realize what an attractive target Stoffel had been. Thus, it did not occur to him that Stoffel's confidence had been based upon his assurance of having done nothing wrong.[26]

The lengthy brochure reviewed the entire history of the dispatch of 20 August. Beyond its exposure of Stoffel's interpretation of events, critical matters were brought to the surface for the first time which go far to explain Stoffel's occasional outbursts of anger during the affair. He tackled first General de Rivières' determination to attribute to him functions that were not his by using titles in his report which were not Stoffel's ("chef de la section des renseignements à l'état-major du maréchal de MacMahon; chargé du service des renseignements; chef du service des renseignements de l'armée de Châlons; chef du bureau des renseignements à l'état-major du maréchal de MacMahon"). In fact, MacMahon's personal headquarters staff had already been constituted by the time he reached Châlons. Stoffel was taken on as a supernumerary to utilize his knowledge of the German armies. His orders were given to him orally by the marshal, namely, to inform him about the composition and the movements of the enemy forces. At first he had been alone, without an aide or a deputy, and had had to depend upon the telegraph to obtain information from those departmental authorities whose areas were about to be invaded. The section entitled Intelligence had been within army headquarters and had been subordinate to General Faure, the chief-of-staff, and Stoffel had had no connection with army headquarters. After working alone for a few days gathering information about enemy strength and movements, he had asked to have Laurens de Waru, a cavalry lieutenant, assigned to assist him.

Far from being responsible for the distribution of information, he had not even been kept current on news reaching the marshal or army headquarters, understandable in that Stoffel did not occupy an established position in the hierarchy. He had retained, moreover, a memory of the confusion and the anxiety which had blanketed Châlons, barriers to rational order and decision, and a sympathy for MacMahon's plight given the circumstances. The marshal had recognized that an army driven to retreat into a fortified place was probably an army already severely beaten. He knew that Bazaine, although commander-in-chief, did not expect to give him orders because of the distance between them, forcing MacMahon to acknowledge orders from the ministry of war. He was painfully aware of the unreadiness of his own improvised forces, not to speak of his certainty about what the consequences would be for Paris should he be crushed on an offensive to rescue Bazaine. The anxiety only intensified as additional news from Bazaine was awaited. The reason that the forces at Châlons were moved toward Reims on 21 August, despite no new word from Bazaine, was the approach of Prussian cavalry. Stoffel warned MacMahon that Prussian cavalry, because of its particular training, was quite capable of sweeping across the flat open plain of Châlons to cause a panic in the ill-prepared French army. The heights between Reims and Epernay provided a more defensible terrain.

The marshal's headquarters was installed in the château de Courcelles, three kilometers from Reims. Three of the staff officers, including Stoffel, had to be billeted in a house belonging to Monsieur Cliquot, five or six hundred steps from the chateau. That was the moment when Rouher arrived from the capital, and discussions began about the advisability of retiring upon Paris. Stoffel believed that MacMahon's decision to retreat had not only been the correct decision, but that it had been made firmly without any reservation, no matter what he would later say in his deposition, a firmness revealed in his orders. Yet, counter-orders were issued on 22 August after receiving the dispatch of 19 August from Bazaine (an unwise reversal in Stoffel's opinion) and maintained despite the later reception of the dispatch of 20 August.[27]

Stoffel also reiterated his version of his having engaged Miès and Rabasse for a mission to Metz, and how they had turned back from Longuyon upon hearing rumors that enemy forces were nearby. Once they had acquired the dispatch of 20 August meant for Marshal de MacMahon from Colonel Massaroli, "they addressed it to me at Reims conforming to the instructions I had given them. It was in code, dated from Longwy, 4:50 p.m., 22 August 1870, and reached Reims directly at 6:50 p.m., that is, without having passed through Paris. It was then brought from Reims to Courcelles and carried to the chateau occupied by the marshal and by both personal and army headquarters. I was at that moment in my quarters, so the dispatch was opened and deciphered in the personal headquarters of the marshal."

At the dinner hour, Stoffel returned to the marshal's headquarters where the staff members took their meals in common. "Hardly had I entered when I was told of the arrival of a dispatch from the police agents, addressed to me but containing a message from Bazaine to MacMahon. I cannot remember which officer or officers I talked to, but I immediately asked if the dispatch had been deciphered and given to the marshal. The response was affirmative; and, in fact, I then found a complete translation of the dispatch on my work table. Bazaine told us nothing more in it than he had in prior dispatches, namely, that he would advise us of his march in the event he could undertake it without compromising his army. And it was virtually a needless message, as it was understood that Marshal Bazaine would not undertake such an important operation, putting an army of 120,000 men on the march, without notifying his subordinate, the commander of the Army of Châlons. Accordingly, the dispatch did not impress any of the officers who had knowledge of it, and MacMahon did not consider for an instant modifying his intended operations, much less returning to those orders previously given. So the army moved on the following day to Bétheniville."[28] Stoffel's interpretation implied that MacMahon, under pressure from the government in Paris, believed he had no option except to march toward Metz so long as he had evidence that Bazaine meant to break out. Only long after the event did anyone see in Bazaine's messages evidence that, consciously or otherwise, he had decided against an active course.

Captain Janicot's report had specifically denied the credibility of the earlier testimony given by Rabasse and Miès, asserting that they had admitted during the *instruction* never having spoken to Colonel d'Abzac on the night of their arrival in Rethel. They had spoken only to Lt. Marescalchi, who had awakened a second officer, Commandant de Vaulgrenant, who had been sleeping in the same room. Stoffel, unaware of that assertion, claimed in his brochure that the most important new information produced during Janicot's *instruction* came from those who shed light on the conflicting testimony which had been given by Colonel d'Abzac, Miès, and Rabasse during the Bazaine court-martial. On two separate occasions, Colonel Clappier had taken the trouble to interview the servant woman in Rethel who had worked for ten years in the house occupied by Marshal de MacMahon in August of 1870. She had confirmed on all points the testimony of Miès and Rabasse: how she had admitted them to the house, taken them upstairs to the officer on duty, whom she had then seen awaken Colonel d'Abzac. Her testimony, in fact, had so squared with what the agents had claimed that Clappier had not bothered to confront Colonel Abzac with the servant.

He had also questioned Marescalchi, the lieutenant on duty that night. He recalled that two men bearing dispatches had been brought to his door on the second floor (although he could not identify them) and remembered that he, himself, had awakened Colonel d'Abzac. He had seen one of the men give the colonel a packet of papers, but recalled that they had been returned to him almost at once. Why, then, had Colonel d'Abzac denied having received the two agents? Stoffel thought it to be nothing more than a faulty memory when being interrogated in an improvised manner about events two years earlier.

Who, then, had actually deciphered the disputed dispatch when it arrived by wire? Stoffel never knew. All he could say was that the marshal's cipher for the entire campaign had been kept by Colonel d'Abzac and the marshal's personal secretary, Emmanuel d'Harcourt (a cousin of Mme de MacMahon). Not having a cipher, Stoffel could not have deciphered the dispatch had it reached him.[29]

Stoffel made no mention of Vaulgrenant in his brochure; but the latter was not a creation of Janicot's imagination, as he had been on MacMahon's personal staff. The rather gross misspelling of his name in Janicot's report suggests that he had not been called as a witness, and that either Clappier or Janicot had simply heard the name during Marescalchi's deposition. Vaulgrenant's opinion of the affair would not be made public until after the turn of the century.

Perhaps the most surprising passage in Stoffel's brochure was his account of Séré de Rivières' behavior during the *instruction* for the Bazaine court-martial: surprising not only for its revelations but for its candor, considering that the author was already in jail for slander. He called attention to the reasons behind the choice of Rivières as the reporter to prepare the indictment of Marshal Bazaine's, "an army engineer who had never before participated on a military court and lacking the required knowledge of proper procedure. He owed his promotion to the rank of brigadier general to Gambetta, the recommendation for promotion having been made by Challemel-Lacour."[30] The task he was given required the interrogation of a great number of witnesses; and Stoffel had been considerably surprised to be summoned on 28 August 1872, as he had not seen service in the Army of Metz, and as he had seen Marshal Bazaine only once in his life.

In Stoffel's opinion, his interrogation turned out to be highly singular, neither its character nor its actuality being reflected in the ultimate written deposition attributed to him. The reporter had asked a great number of preliminary questions which his clerk did not enter in the record when later writing up the deposition. He had been questioned about the progress of his career from its beginning to the period when he had joined the emperor's household; he was asked about his collaboration with the emperor on the *Histoire de Jules César*; he was asked about the degree of his closeness to the emperor. To the latter question, he had answered, "There can be no intimacy between a sovereign and his subjects."[31] These questions had served as a long prelude to an attempt to establish a continuing collaboration between the emperor and Stoffel at Châlons in August of 1870. Did he remember having had secret meetings with the emperor there? Stoffel had so bridled at this suggestion of secret meetings that Rivières had revised the question. Had he had private discussions on serious political and military matters with the emperor? Stoffel could not recall having had any private discussion with the emperor at Châlons.

The questions then turned to his function on the staff of Marshal de MacMahon and to his part in the mission given to Miès and Rabasse without Stoffel having yet divined the purpose of Rivières' line of questions. When pressed to account for a dispatch addressed to him personally from Marshal Bazaine, he could not remember ever having received a dispatch from Bazaine. At which point he was shown a true copy of the dispatch of 20 August, marked received from Longwy, 22 August 1870, Reims, addressed to Colonel Stoffel. He could vaguely remember that such a dispatch had reached Courcelles, but he had no recollection of the hour or the day of its arrival. Rivières had then urged him to think seriously about the incident, to make an effort to recall, as it was *a very grave matter*. Stoffel, astonished and caught short, could only say that he had not received the dispatch, but said he was certain that he had not deciphered a dispatch during the entirety of the campaign.

The latter observation seemed to surprise Rivières, who remarked that Marshal de MacMahon had already declared that he had not received the dispatch. At the end of the interrogation, as an explanation for the tone of the interview, Rivières said: "Before questioning you, I believed that you had suppressed the dispatch from Marshal Bazaine in connivance with the emperor. But I believe what you have told me, and I am going back to my earlier opinion that it was the emperor who received the dispatch, even though it had been addressed to you, and that it was he who retained it."[32] Listening to such an opinion, Stoffel noted, "I found it hard to believe that I was in the presence of a magistrate, a French general at that! I found the suspicion odious and said so before retiring. But at least I had learned the cause behind the highly unusual interview. It was now clear that the reporter, after his interview with Marshal de MacMahon, was determined to find an intrigue in the matter of the dispatch, rather than to see things, or such things, as they generally happen; and he had set out to find a guilty person."[33]

Despite this insight, Stoffel had remained untroubled for himself in the aftermath, in no way suspecting what would emerge during the court-martial. There had been no additional interrogation, no criminal charges had been brought against him, and he had been called to appear at the trial as a witness, not as a defendant. Only on 7 October 1873, when Rivières' report was being read in the courtroom, did he hear himself accused of suppressing the dispatch. Even then, he was confident that the truth about the dispatch would come out in the trial, and he stated in his brochure that the truth did emerge during the session of 3 November when Miès and Rabasse testified about their encounter with Colonel d'Abzac at Rethel.[34]

Faced with unanticipated conflicting testimony, the duc d'Aumale had reexamined the witnesses on the following day. But when both Abzac and Miès held fast to their stories, the court failed to summon additional witnesses such as the servant who had opened the door to the two agents, or other staff officers, or Lt. Marescalchi even though he was abroad at that moment. As Colonel d'Abzac was a man of recognized honor, the court had preferred his testimony to that of the police agents; and that left Stoffel and his honor exposed to public discussion. He had felt obliged to use the opportunity in court, whether wisely or not, to force the issue. In retrospect, he recognized that his exasperation had been fed by Thiers' arbitrary order to remove him from the army the previous year. The new action taken against him by the prosecutor, Pourcet, after his refusal to withdraw his remarks about General de Rivières, convinced Stoffel that the court had decided to let the Abzac incident be forgotten.[35]

Stoffel devoted the final section of his brochure to the ultimate enigma behind the Stoffel affair: why had a dispatch, which had not struck either Marshal de MacMahon or his staff officers in particular when it had been received, suddenly loomed so large two years later during the *instruction* for the court-martial of Marshal Bazaine? No one had concealed the dispatch of 20 August 1870, and no one among those who saw it had believed it contained critical new information. For that matter, the dispatch did not become an issue until Marshal de MacMahon, during the *instruction*, indicated he had never seen it. The answer to Stoffel's question lay in his formulation of it: "Why did a former colonel of engineers, appointed to be a general officer by the men of the 4th of September after only two years in grade, attribute so much importance to the phrase, 'I shall very probably follow the line of the . . . Nord, if, that is, I can undertake the movement without compromising the army,' an expression not to be found in either of Bazaine's other two dispatches of that date?"[36] Stoffel had discovered the answer thanks to his initial interrogation by Rivières. The republicans were bent upon demonstrating that Sedan would have been avoided had not the emperor meant to undermine MacMahon's control of the army and to direct the army eastward. The charge was risky. Accounts of the campaign had already been published which revealed that at Le Chesne, on 27-28 August, MacMahon had received messages from the minister of war urging him onward, which the emperor had pointed out were not worded as orders; and that, accordingly, MacMahon retained his freedom of judgment. The emperor had urged MacMahon to reflect further before abandoning his plans for a retreat. But the popular will to believe the worst is ever the politician's best ally. The charges made during the affair, Stoffel concluded, were simply the product of the hatreds and the internal discord then dividing France.[37]

Notes

1. Le Faure, *Procès du Maréchal Bazaine* 2: 370–72.
2. Edmond Ruby and Jean Regnault, *Bazaine, coupable ou victime*, pp. 355–56.
3. Henri d'Orléans to General Du Barail, 10 December 1873. Le Faure, *Procès du Maréchal Bazaine* 2: 373–74; Léon Laforge, *Histoire complète de MacMahon* 3: 389.
4. Jacques Chastenet, *L'Enfance de la Troisième*, p. 170.
5. Maurice d'Irisson, comte d'Hérisson de Saulnier, *La Légende de Metz*, pp. 145–46.
6. Louis Hastier, "L'Evasion de Bazaine," *Historia* 15 (February 1954): 244.
7. Jules Claretie, *Histoire de la Révolution de 1870–1871* 2: 762–63.
8. Edmond and Jules de Goncourt, *Journal, mémoires de la vie littéraire* 10: 151.
9. Ibid. 10: 157.
10. Commandant of the Gendarmerie of Seine et Oise to the Ministry of War, 29 May 1874. Dossiers Stoffel (dossier Lt20). Bibliothèque du service historique du ministère de la guerre, Vincennes.
11. Stoffel, *La Dépêche du 20 août, du maréchal Bazaine au maréchal de MacMahon*, pp. 111–17.
12. Etat des services. Certificat des services, 2 October 1888. Dossier Janicot, no. 40868–3è Série. Bibliothèque du service historique du ministere de la guerre, Vincennes.
13. Etat des services. Dossier Clappier, no. 4075 GB 2è Div. Ibid.
14. François-Charles Du Barail, *Mes Souvenirs, 1820–1879* 3: 361–64.
15. Laurens de Waru would enjoy rapid promotion under the Third Republic, retiring as a brigadier general. Etat des services. Dossier Laurens de Waru, no. 548 GB 3è Div. Bibliothèque du service historique du ministère de la guerre, Vincennes.
16. Paul-Joseph-Louis Janicot, *Rapport sur l'affaire de Monsieur Stoffel*, [p. 3]. Dossiers Stoffel (dossier Lt20).
17. Emile-Auguste-François-Thomas Zurlinden, "La Dépêche du 20 août 1870," *Le Gaulois*, 22 August 1907.
18. Henri Welschinger, *La Guerre de 1870, causes et responsabilités* 1: 279.
19. Emile Ollivier, *L'Empire libéral* 17: 337–38.
20. Laforge, *Histoire complète de MacMahon* 1: 256; 3: 144.
21. Janicot, *Rapport sur l'affaire de Monsieur Stoffel*. Dossiers Stoffel (dossier Lt20).
22. Colonel Edmond Clappier to the Governor of Paris [General Louis-René-Paul de Ladmirault], 15 June 1874. Ibid.
23. Governor of Paris [Ladmirault] to the Minister of War [Cissey], 15 June 1874. Ibid.
24. General de Cissey, "Ordonnance de non-lieu," 13 July 1874. Ibid.
25. Stoffel, *La Dépêche du 20 août 1870*, pp. 64–65, 95–97.
26. Willy Schädler, *Les Barons Stoffel* 1: 33–34, 42–43.
27. Stoffel, *La Dépêche du 20 août 1870*, pp. 7–29.
28. Ibid., pp. 17–19, 29–33.
29. Ibid., pp. 37–38, 97–101.

30. Ibid., pp. 41–42.
31. Ibid., p. 43.
32. Ibid., p. 46.
33. Ibid.
34. Ibid., pp. 47, 50, 54–55.
35. Ibid., pp. 58–63.
36. Ibid., pp. 68–69.
37. Ibid., pp. 81–86, 101.

Part VIII

Active Retirement

The years of retirement became the longest period in Colonel Stoffel's life: thirty-five years. In 1872, he had been required to leave the army at the age of 51 after thirty-one years of active service. During the final decade of that service, he had come to know Napoleon III, William I, Bismarck, Moltke, and MacMahon. His knowledge of the German army was thought to be unsurpassed, at least by some German officers; and as Stoffel and Trochu had been the most insightful critics of the imperial army before 1870, it could have been expected that either one or both of them might be chosen to advise on French military reform after 1871, a matter that preoccupied the French in general and Thiers in particular. Although Stoffel had not attained Trochu's military rank, his greater experience in the world of affairs, his facility with language, his sense of history, and his concern for honor (which guaranteed an indifference to popularity) ought to have given him the inside track. He got instead an early retirement with a pension of 3,413 francs a year, which the army soon found reason to reduce to 2,731 francs in 1874.

Stoffel's financial state, as the army had discovered when endeavoring to discern what other personal resources might be tapped, remains elusive. How did he finance the historical research and travel of his later years? It may be that his widowed mother provided him occasional sums from her inheritance. She would not die until 28 April 1886, in her ninety-third year. Stoffel proved to be her sole heir and received an estate valued at 49,600 francs.[1] Before that event, his means must have been limited. As officers' pay was notoriously low during the Second Empire, Stoffel cannot have saved anything substantial for his later years. In late 1877, he received an invitation to Camden Place to answer questions the prince imperial wished to ask him. Piétri assured him that a room would be provided, adding: "Do not worry about the expenses of the trip. I shall see that you are reimbursed, or can even advance you expenses if you are short."[2] Officers, Stoffel included, rather frequently remained single, giving the impression of being married to the service. It may be that their relative poverty often left them little choice.[3]

His good fortune was a legacy of a different sort. The events of 1866 had interrupted the emperor's historical work at a moment when the second volume of his *Histoire de Jules César* had been published. Even though Stoffel had been sent off to Berlin as military attaché, he was expected to prepare more reports for the completion of the imperial work. By the time the regime fell in 1870, he had assembled a substantial amount of material for a history of Caesar's wars with Pompey's faction. The emperor also left to Stoffel valuable documents he had collected for the completion of the work, including papers addressed to the emperor by Léon Heuzey, Georges Perrot, and Charles-Joseph Tissot. It appears that Stoffel did not fully commit himself to the task until about 1879, but he had let it be known that the materials were his to use as originally intended. Consequently, the scholars who had contributed papers to the emperor hastened to get their material into print before his could see the light of day—to his rather considerable irritation.[4]

It should not be inferred from this that Stoffel was entirely indebted to the work of others for the volumes he would publish in 1887 and 1890. He had already prepared the material on the fighting in Egypt and Spain by 1862 for the history of Caesar's civil wars. And, beginning in 1879, he spent an entire year traveling in Italy, Albania, Macedonia, Thessaly, and North Africa conducting research on the military campaigns.[5] The two volumes on the civil wars, covering the years from the crossing of the Rubicon until the death of Caesar, were published in 1887. The following year he was in Alsace attempting to locate the battlefield where Caesar had fought Ariovistus for a volume on that campaign which he would publish in 1890.

Having gone first to Switzerland on personal matters, he had belatedly decided to visit Alsace before returning to Paris and reached Strasburg without a proper passport. He obtained, nevertheless, authorization to pursue his research owing to the kindness of a local official. Several days later, after completing his research, he returned to Strasburg, expecting to take a train to Paris the following day. But a policeman called at his hotel and subjected him to a thorough interrogation. He was given to understand that Strasburg was a garrison city, and that he was suspected of being there for purposes of espionage. Instructed to leave on the next train, he was given two hours to prepare his departure and followed through the streets to the railway station as if he were a common crook.

In that period of Boulangism, and in the aftermath of the Schnaebelé affair, German authorities were supersensitive about Alsace; but Stoffel took the "humiliating proceedings" personally and addressed a wrathful letter to the German government. Beyond describing the incident in detail, he complained about the want of tact and courtesy he had met. What had annoyed him the most, he explained, was the apparent official indifference to his good will. He had been a moderate voice in France on the subject of Franco-German relations, exempt from the usual hatred or blind passion directed against Germany, and he declined to tolerate the treatment he had just received. Would the German government please recognize his moderation and not subject him further to such treatment![6] Perhaps the incident had jogged his memory of a similar expulsion from Berlin eighteen years earlier and the bitterness of that moment in his career. He had lived to be treated as a criminal by both the Germans and the French, when his fondest hope had been to see the two peoples reconciled.

While Stoffel sought to complete the historical work begun by Napoleon III, the inspiration for the later volumes was novel. Napoleon III had sought through the life of Caesar a rationale for a Napoleonic empire. Stoffel meant to demonstrate that the study of military history, far from being merely a respectable use of leisure time, was a necessary part of an officer's instruction. There was, in short, a tacit connection between his reports from Berlin and the later volumes on Caesar: a concern for the intellectual improvement of the French officer corps. The argument for military history had been made by that ultimate authority, Napoleon I, who had dictated his commentaries on Caesar when at St. Helena.

Stoffel had been a student of classical history since his days as a junior officer, and many a fellow officer had questioned the utility of studying ancient warfare on the grounds that the techniques of war had entirely changed. Stoffel, citing Napoleon I, argued that one critical aspect of war had remained unchanged: "Achilles was the son of a goddess and of a mortal man; The very image of the genius of war. The godlike part encompasses everything which derives from moral considerations, from character, from the talent of one's adversary, from judgment, from the very spirit of the soldier, who is either strong and victorious, or weak and defeated, according to what he believes himself to be. The worldly part includes the arms, the entrenchments, positions, battle array, everything which contributes to the material resources."[7]

The *worldly* part of war had indeed changed since Caesar's time, Stoffel commented, but the *divine* part of the art had remained the same, and so it would always be. It followed that one should seek these eternal lessons through the study of the great men of war. As Napoleon had put it, tactics, movements, engineering science, and gunnery can all be learned from textbooks, rather like geometry; but a knowledge of the higher aspects of war can only be acquired through the study of battles and wars fought by the great captains *and* through experience. Stoffel believed that the study of Caesar's campaigns provided that genre of instruction, as Napoleon had recognized. As examples he had noted Caesar's ability to keep his forces intact; his care to leave no part of his army vulnerable to attack; the rapidity with which he marched on important points; his reliance upon moral methods—on the reputation of his arms, on the fear that one inspires—as well as upon political means to guarantee the fidelity of allies and the obedience of conquered peoples; his attention to give himself every possible chance of victory on the battlefield by employing all available troops. But Napoleon had also seen in Caesar the personal qualities of the great warrior: the cool head; a mind that could be impressed by facts or events only according to their true degree of importance; a knowledge of the human heart; a character of such firmness as to dominate the most critical situations, and which could not be thrown off balance by either good or bad fortune, even at the most extreme limits.

Stoffel, writing after the Franco-Prussian War, saw an additional instructive feature in Caesar's campaigns: the frequency with which one army had been invested by another army. Stoffel believed that the enormous improvement in weapons in the 19th century would increasingly recommend investment rather than frontal attack, and that the outcome of wars would be decided by great investments such as those of Metz, Paris, and Plevna. Warfare would then acquire a striking analogy with Caesar's wars.[8]

During the editing of the two-volume work at the Imprimerie Nationale, a copy editor was dismayed to find a substantial passage on Marshal de MacMahon's conduct during the Franco-Prussian War intruded gratuitously into the text. Not only was the material extraneous, it was an expression of Stoffel's blunt candor, revealing that he had not forgotten for a moment the attempt to brand him a criminal in 1873. To the editor's suggestion that the material be removed, Stoffel responded with such abuse that the poor man gave way. One can understand his concern, as MacMahon was still living in retirement, and the publishing agency was backed by the state. The material appeared untouched, but word of the incident spread through the world of scholarship.

MacMahon's conduct of operations from beginning to end, Stoffel began, could only be explained by the most complete incapacity joined to an absolute want of character. Although critical of MacMahon's judgment at the outset of the war in Alsace, Stoffel focused his fire primarily on MacMahon's decision to move an army toward Metz, an army known to be unready to maneuver, to take such a force into the midst of three victorious enemy armies, finally allowing himself to be enveloped by two of them at Sedan. "Such profound mistakes confound the reason of anyone trying to explain them. What is to be said of a commander-in-chief who undertakes, on his own initiative, a military operation with the certainty—recognized by him—of leading his army to disaster?

"More than one general in history, following the order of a minister or a ruler, has put a plan into execution that he disapproved. So that Napoleon I said on that subject, in his *Commentaries*, that any general charged with executing a plan he found to be bad or disastrous must either insist that it be altered or tender his resignation rather than be the instrument of the ruination of his charges. To do otherwise is *criminal*. Referring to the degree of obedience he had owed his government when he had been commander of the Army of Italy, Napoleon wrote that he believed himself obliged to execute the orders of his government as long as he judged them to be reasonable and that success appeared to him to be probable. If he had carried out a plan he had found to be defective, it would have amounted to a criminal act. One must judge from this that he would have attributed MacMahon's operations to the realm of psychopathology."[9]

The volumes were further marred by Stoffel's failure to cite appropriately some of the material that had been prepared for Napoleon III, revealing the temper he had always shown when improperly crossed, at least in his opinion. He managed to insult Heuzey in the second volume; he failed to cite Tissot at all; and he referred only to Perrot's manuscript even though it had been in print since 1875. His major reviewer, Salomon Reinach in the *Revue historique*, criticized his unjust and distasteful tactics, but otherwise applauded Stoffel for his scholarship. He called the history a work of great worth, full of detailed discoveries, revealing at once the insights of the professional soldier and unexpected philological gifts, the latter perhaps reflecting his long friendship with Wilhelm Froehner.[10]

As in the volumes published in 1887, the book Stoffel published in 1890 provided remarks for contemporary readers which went beyond a simple interest in Caesar's campaigns. At a critical moment in the development of Caesar's plan of operation against Ariovistus, Stoffel noted that Caesar's plan had been dictated to him by the state of his army's morale, a factor which made his thought and action worthy of meditation. "For nothing is more instructive than to explain the conduct of great soldiers under difficult circumstances."[11] He then intruded a short essay into his text entitled "Etude de l'histoire des guerres. Conseils aux jeunes officiers," in which he again disputed a fashionable opinion in military circles that no profit could be drawn from the study of the wars of antiquity. References to the conduct of various

French commanders under duress in the Franco-Prussian War were this time more discreetly veiled, but still transparent.

He also made explicit his desire to contribute in some measure to the instruction of French officers, especially to those who might someday be called to exercise supreme command. While the references were again to Napoleon's commentaries dictated at St. Helena, the essay certainly reflected what he had learned about Moltke's system for the preparation of young officers during his years in Berlin, in particular the attention paid to instruction in history and geography. Beyond the technical fundamentals which are learned in school, and which every officer must have, one must ultimately acquire the instinct for war, that is, a sense of the art of war. Experience is one teacher, but the other is prolonged reflection upon the experiences of the great captains, whether ancient or modern.

Every young officer, he continued, ought to be preparing himself for the highest command, studying the function of the commander-in-chief in battle. The conduct of the French generals-in-chief in 1870 he also thought to have instructional value. "It will be seen that one of them remained at the rear during battle from where he could see nothing and direct nothing. Another confined his activity to galloping back and forth before his troops, in advance of the firing line, succeeding on one occasion in getting his staff officers killed for no good reason, on another occasion in getting himself wounded. Another charged sword in hand into the raging battle to kill an enemy soldier personally. Student-officers will seek to explain the cause of such evident aberrations and will find that they reside in the incapacity to exercise high command with all its difficulties."[12]

Stoffel, who had appreciated the technical superiority of the Prussians before 1870, had come to worry that the French, in the two decades after 1870, were devoting themselves too entirely to technical improvement, to war as a science. In contrast to the commentaries written by Caesar, Napoleon I, or the Archduke Charles, much that had been written in France since 1870 was by authors "who have not exercised high and independent commands, and by professors deprived of any personal knowledge of war, but who treat this great art scientifically, reasoning out all problems as in geometry." They had given birth to a new military jargon which Stoffel ridiculed: clef tactique, objectif, défensive-offensive, bataille offensive, bataille défensive, and so on, all unknown to the great warriors, who were also great writers.[13]

It would appear that Colonel Stoffel was among the earliest to perceive that, in the use of jargon, much of it invented in the quest for scientific legitimacy, the common culture was threatened. Was it not a symptom of the times that Caesar's *Commentarii de bello Gallico*, so long a fundamental text for the study of the geography and the early history of France, had come to be used chiefly to teach Latin to the young! The nation now had reason to return to that work with renewed interest, Stoffel concluded, but through the medium of the *Histoire de Jules César*, where the fruit of the research ordered by the emperor would be found.[14]

In 1888, meanwhile, Stoffel had sought relief from the 20% deduction which had been made from his pension since 1874. Although he had benefited from a recent improvement in the pension rates, raising him to 3,050 francs a year, the 20% deficit was still in effect. As he left no explanation why he believed exoneration by then to be possible, it may be that the appointment of Charles de Freycinet as minister of war, the first *civilian* to hold that post, was the key. Stoffel's petition to the minister was strikingly temperate. He provided a fair history of the financial settlement, did not pose as a victim of army injustice, and made his request not as a claim but as a personal favor. He offered four considerations in seeking a benevolent understanding:

> By including (in the monies that were paid to me on 2 September 1870 at Sedan) the campaign allowance that the emperor had granted me as his ordnance officer, I did not perceive that the political events which transpired two days later would put me in a position of being unable to accept the money from the civil list and of later being obliged to restore that sum to the treasury of the state.
>
> I did not regret the use I made of the monies taken in excess on 2 September; for, having succeeded in escaping from Sedan on the 8th, and reaching Paris on the 12th without uniform, without arms, and without horses, I was named there to be chief-of-staff for army artillery, which required me to buy four horses and all necessary equipment. The money taken at Sedan thus helped me to rejoin the ranks in better condition in order to continue to defend the fatherland.
>
> I am among the small number of officers who participated in the war of 1870-71 from the first day to the last.
>
> I am approaching 70 years of age [he was 67]; I count 31 years of service; I was put in retirement by an act of bitterness; and I have no other resource but my pension. [Was he concealing the recent legacy from his mother, or had it been consumed?][15]

As an exoneration had to be treated as a pardon, Freycinet proposed to the president of the Republic that Stoffel's petition be granted. This was accomplished by a presidential decree signed by Sadi Carnot on 16 March 1889. The order went down to notify Colonel Stoffel that no further deductions would be made from his pension.[16]

As a student of the ancient world, Stoffel had acquired a detailed knowledge of the historic conflicts between the Germanic and the Gallic peoples. In 1890, he made his final effort to terminate the traditional enmity, a campaign quite consistent with the attitudes of his earlier years; but he undertook it without any illusions of probable success. The immediate impulsion to be heard publicly on the subject was the evident probability of a Franco-Russian entente or alliance. In the two decades following the Treaty of Frankfurt, the European order had remained unstable, threatened repeatedly by dangerous crises. The idea of a Franco-Russian accord was especially obnoxious to Stoffel as it was inconsistent with the advice on foreign policy dictated from St. Helena: if Europe was to be republican rather than cossack, that is, civilized rather than barbaric, Europe would have to become united against Russia.

As the instability dated from the Treaty of Frankfurt, it made sense to Stoffel to push for a revision of that treaty. He quite understood that no French government, given the mood of popular opinion in France, could even dream of a reconciliation with Germany so long as the Germans did nothing to repair the "profound mistakes" made by her statesmen in 1871. France had lost not merely two provinces but, with them, her security. Paris had been left highly vulnerable to attack, while Berlin was protected in considerable depth. The situation was worse than humiliating for France: it was dangerous. In Stoffel's opinion, the Germans had committed the same mistake in 1871 that Napoleon had made in 1806: dictating harsh terms which could only breed deep resentment and desire for revenge.[17]

Stoffel apparently did not know that, at Sedan, Bismarck had thought it best to make peace immediately while the Germans were in control of Alsace and Lorraine, not merely to compel the payment of an enormous indemnity as the way of keeping the French weak; but that the Prussian military had prevailed upon the king to move at once upon Paris as a matter of revenge and to position the Germans to make territorial acquisitions as well.[18] Consequently, Stoffel simply believed that the peace terms, and the subsequent German foreign policy made necessary by the peace terms, had been "peculiar" in view of Bismarck's intelligence and political insight, especially given his treatment of Austria after 1866.

The harsh peace terms in 1871 had forced Bismarck to check a relatively defenseless France by forming close ties with Russia and Austria, both relatively powerful states, suspicious of each other and both jealous of the sudden rise in German power: surely an arrangement containing the seeds for future trouble. Once that league had broken down, Bismarck had tried to guarantee the peace through engagements with Austria and Italy, another arrangement inherently unstable. Bismarck's successors in 1890, Stoffel argued, would do well to contemplate a Franco-German reconciliation before the traditional policy gave birth to a Franco-Russian alliance.[19]

Was a voluntary retrocession of Alsace-Lorraine even possible? Stoffel admitted that such an action seemingly faced insurmountable barriers. The Germans would first have to recognize that it had been the dismemberment of France which had put Germany in such an uncomfortable international position. The retrocession would have to be a matter of self-interest. And the retrocession would only be feasible if the Germans insisted upon a lengthy defensive and offensive alliance with France. He believed that every Frenchman would accept that price for the recovery of the provinces. The Franco-German alliance, he concluded, would be the ultimate guarantee of indefinite international peace, and he predicted an eventual war between the two nations if the alliance did not come to fruition. Much depended upon whether the Germans understood that their real danger lay in the east, as the Russians would soon dominate the Danubian provinces, from whence they would push for the Adriatic.[20]

Le Figaro exposed the gist of Stoffel's views even before they were published. The newspaper received a wave of negative responses from readers, enabling Stoffel to acknowledge them in a supplement to his essay. The opinion that Germany would never agree to his proposal was the most temperate type of response. Most of them employed such words as *utopian*, *chimerical*, or *illusory*. An unnamed deputy wrote: "M. Stoffel quite simply forgets that, if France is still on her feet in the 19th century, she owes that fact to Russia," a remark Stoffel found incredible.[21] It might be thought that a man well-known for reliable prophecy should have commanded more intelligent attention.

But a prophet, quite simply, is never a man of his own time. He does not reflect current thought, nor does he say what the public wishes to hear. In Stoffel's case, what is more, the charge of a criminal act had been made against him in 1873. He had been formally absolved the following year as far as the public knew, but the sophisticated never take such matters at face value (except for Edmond de Goncourt who had thought Stoffel to have the appearance of a guilty man). Little was known or is remembered about his personal life during his years of retirement. His continuing research and publications, of course, made him known in the scholarly world, and there are occasional hints to indicate that he remained in the minds of the *cognoscenti* a personage too important to ignore but perhaps not quite trustworthy. Moreover, his persistent loyalty to the Bonapartism of his past could hardly recommend him to the ascendant republicans during the years of the Dreyfus controversy.

In November of 1897, at a time when the army labored to avoid a reopening of the Dreyfus case, General de Boisdeffre, chief of the general staff, told both Princesse Mathilde and Colonel Stoffel that Dreyfus had been mentioned in a note from William II to his ambassador in Paris, George Herbert, count von Münster-Ledenburg. The implication of the story was that the

Germans were well aware of Dreyfus' treachery. Stoffel had reported the discussion to a former Bonapartist deputy, Robert Mitchell, who repeated it to the radical Arthur Ranc. General Auguste Mercier would later testify that he had not seen the document but had been told about it by Colonel Stoffel. It became common talk that Stoffel had seen the damaging document with his own eyes; and Joseph Reinach, a leader in the campaign to have the Dreyfus verdict revised, believed that Stoffel had gossiped about the matter to give the appearance of being on the inside of events. As the document was one of the forgeries contrived by the infamous Major Henry, one can appreciate Reinach's outrage that it had been used, criminally or otherwise, to forestall a reopening of the case. On the other hand, had Stoffel known the whole truth about his own affair with military justice, he might not so readily have accepted the documentary evidence presented by the army against Dreyfus. The *authentic* German document which mentioned Dreyfus, and which was unknown at the time of the affair, was a report from Münster to William II, dated 9 November 1896, on the margin of which William II had written, "Dreyfus has been condemned in an illegal manner."[22]

Reinach, a former associate of Gambetta at *La République française* and Gambetta's secretary during his brief presidency of the cabinet, made no attempt to conceal the fact that he had never trusted Stoffel, calling him the author of a felony which had never been satisfactorily resolved and one of the least decipherable men of his time. Stoffel, eventually called to make a deposition on 23 April and 2 May 1904, was described as a robust man of 84 years. He denied having told anyone that he had actually seen a photograph of the annotated memorandum, saying he only knew that the document existed as he had been told about it by someone worthy of belief, but whom he felt obliged not to name. Depending upon the occasion, Reinach concluded, Stoffel had been as bold in the truth as in the lie: bold as the author of prophetic reports which would have saved the Empire had anyone heeded them, bold in his readiness to lie about the dispatch of 20 August 1870 if need be.[23]

For at least the final decade of his life, Stoffel worked on a major study of the campaign of 1815. As the son of a colonel who had served at Waterloo, who had known many of the survivors of that period, as a man experienced in war and in historical writing, he was expected to produce an extraordinarily valuable commentary on that inexhaustible topic. It is known that the manuscript was completed, the maps engraved ready for printing; but he died before the work could be published.[24] He died at his home, 12 rue Lamennais in the Eighth Arrondissement, 4 April 1907, at the age of 86. The funeral service was held three days later at the Eglise Saint-Philippe du Roule. As he died celibate and intestate, the entire succession was awarded to a second cousin, Cécil Veuillet, a Gelinek by birth. It would appear that Mme Veuillet had little reverence for Stoffel's work. The manuscript on Waterloo was sold on 12 July 1907 and never published under Stoffel's name. Not only did his manuscript disappear, but his correspondence and library as well.[25] The letters from Piétri survived only because Piétri had thought to ask for their return once Stoffel no longer had need of them.[26] The baronial title became extinct, as it could not be sold.

Stoffel would have had every reason to expect that the legend of his guilty act in 1870 would long survive him, no matter that he had been exonerated by the decree of non-suit. For, despite its issuance, popular and polemical histories of the war had long since been published, most of them meant to blacken the reputation of the entire imperial crew. In 1880, after the resignation of MacMahon from the presidency, Alfred Duquet, an attorney and a partisan of General Wimpffen, brought out a major example of the genre in which he claimed that it had been the empress-regent who had arranged for Stoffel to be attached to MacMahon's staff at Châlons. This interpretation disposed of the inconvenient problem of why the emperor should have ordered the suppression of a dispatch which might have recommended the retreat upon Paris he favored; it was well-known that the empress had opposed that retreat. Duquet, therefore, raised the possibility that Stoffel had followed the empress' instructions to intercept any information that might obstruct the movement toward Metz. As he had no evidence to document that connection, Duquet admitted the possibility that Stoffel had simply failed to communicate the document to the marshal having found no importance in it: a grave error of judgment.[27] But he had introduced a new dimension to the controversy which would reappear in the work of other writers. Arthur-Maxime Chuquet, an historian, wrote quite plainly in 1895 that Colonel Stoffel, a confidant of the empress, had received the dispatch of 20 August 1870 and concealed it from MacMahon.[28]

The following year, 1896, the memoirs of General Trochu appeared in two volumes, published immediately after his death. The first volume, written between 1878 and 1890, focused primarily on the siege of Paris. His discussion of the military reform movement in 1866-67 omitted any mention of Stoffel's reports from Berlin, Trochu asserting that *he* had been the one who had forewarned of the dangers from Prussia, and that the warnings had been poorly received by the Empire. Stoffel's name did not appear among those who had been distinguished in the attempted sortie from Paris beginning on 29 November 1870; the eventual necessity to abandon the Avron plateau was described in some detail without reference to Stoffel as the commander of the artillery.[29] Did Trochu mean to obscure the fact, made plain by the publication of Stoffel's reports in 1871, that Stoffel's impact upon the reform movement had been far greater than Trochu's? Or were the omissions retribution for Stoffel's spiteful words in the letter-preface to the published reports? In any case, the intent to ignore Stoffel spared him any comment on the dispatch of 20 August.

Between 1895 and 1899, the first substantial history of the Franco-Prussian War was published in six volumes with atlas. The author, Lt. Colonel Léonce Rousset, taught military history at the Ecole supérieure de guerre. Despite the extreme nationalist views he expressed during the Dreyfus affair, which could have inclined him to a blind defense of the army, his treatment of the Stoffel affair was markedly moderate and fair if not definitive. While he concluded that the controversy over the dispatch of 20 August was probably forever inexplicable, he took pains to illuminate the conflicting testimony by Miès and Abzac. And, by indicating that the emperor had sent successively two of his officers to point out to MacMahon that the telegrams from the minister of war did not constitute formal orders and must not prevent him from acting according to his own judgment, Rousset demolished the prosecutor's opinion that the imperial party had sought to force the march toward Bazaine through the interception of the dispatch. It would appear that Rousset had formed an opinion on the affair, but either lacked the evidence to justify a formal statement or shrank from an interpretation likely to embarrass the army.[30]

The historical section of the French general staff, in association with the *Revue d'histoire*, began the publication of source materials on the Franco-Prussian War in 1901. More than forty volumes of text and documents had been published by the time the series ended in 1913.[31] An official publication of critical documents, if useful for historical researchers, sooner or later raises questions about what has been withheld from exposure for personal or political reasons. With the status of Alsace-Lorraine to serve the French as a daily reminder of the humiliation of 1870-71, the passage of thirty years had done little to attenuate the bitterness of those grievances which had poisoned political life in the aftermath. The availability of new source material thus opened the road for new discourse, dispassionate and passionate, just as the death of a controversial figure from that era necessarily provoked comment about his part in the disaster.

In 1904, a former minister of war, General Emile-Auguste-François-Thomas Zurlinden, published his recollections of the Franco-Prussian War without thinking to mention Colonel Stoffel.[32] The death of Stoffel in April of 1907 aroused Zurlinden to second thoughts, especially after a necrology for Stoffel, written by Salomon Reinach, noted that the matter of the dispatch of 20 August had never been as simple as historians like Chuquet had implied, and that Stoffel's guilt had never been satisfactorily established. The Bazaine trial, Reinach continued, had brought "other responsibilities" to the surface which history would someday reveal.[33] The obituary itself revealed that the Reinach brothers had disagreed about the Stoffel affair.

General Zurlinden responded in a newspaper, providing a variation on a theme introduced by Alfred Duquet in 1880. Not accusing Stoffel of having concealed the dispatch, Zurlinden simply held him to have been negligent. That is, he criticized Stoffel, having found the deciphered dispatch on his table, for simply assuming that it had already been delivered to MacMahon. [Stoffel had written that he had been told by an officer on duty that the dispatch had been given to MacMahon.] Zurlinden took it for granted that the marshal had not seen the dispatch, but believed he would not have altered his decision to march toward Metz had he received it.[34]

Zurlinden's opinion proved to be influential, at least among those who made some serious effort to examine the facts. It also revealed that the hostility to Stoffel had not withered away no matter the facts. The immense history of the war published by Henri Welschinger in 1910 is a case in point. Welschinger, an Alsatian born in 1846, had been an official employed by the archives of the Corps législatif from 1868 to 1870, thereafter as secretary-archivist to the National Assembly from 1871 to 1876. In those capacities he had attended all parliamentary sessions and had had access to many state papers and political notables. (His greatest antipathy seems to have been reserved for Emile Ollivier.) A prolific historian, he postponed until his maturity the topic that touched him most deeply as a French patriot, perhaps because of his professional obligation to remain silent about official documents until they could be published.

His treatment of the Stoffel affair reflected the influence of General Zurlinden's opinion. But Welschinger had also discussed the issue with General de Vaulgrenant, the officer identified in Janicot's report (then a commandant) as having shared Lt. Marescalchi's room, but who had not given a deposition in 1874. Vaulgrenant now accused Stoffel of nothing more than serious neglect in not making an effort to be certain that Marshal de MacMahon had seen the dispatch. Consequently, Welschinger concluded that there had never been proof that Stoffel had deliberately concealed the dispatch out of subservience to the empress-regent or the minister of war.[35] Not guilty as charged, in sum, but still remiss.

Emile Ollivier waited for a quarter of a century after his fall from office in August of 1870 to begin the publication of his vast account of the liberal empire and its fall. While he sought to be fair in his interpretations, his history, like Welschinger's, was also memoirs. Even though polemical, the seventeen-volume work remains the most important history for its period by a contemporary: important not only for the record but for the splendid character studies which make it a literary monument.[36] His reading of the controversy over the dispatch of 20 August, cited earlier, has to be taken seriously. For Ollivier was one of those, before 1870, who had suspected that Stoffel had become too friendly with Bismarck. Ollivier had also had his differences with the empress and knew that she had been instrumental in his overthrow that August. Yet, as to the accusation that she had induced Stoffel to suppress a critical dispatch, he found such a "vile maneuver" entirely foreign to her character, beyond which she did not like Stoffel personally and had no association with him. He described Stoffel as an honest, decent man, who would not have lent himself to such tactics.[37] These views went into print in 1915.

The persistent silence of Marshal de MacMahon about the allegations, especially after the publication of Alfred Duquet's book in 1880, remains in several respects the most puzzling aspect of the Stoffel affair. Those who had studied the transcripts of the Bazaine court-martial had been left to speculate about whether MacMahon had accepted the army's version of Stoffel's guilt, whether his subordinates had not bothered him with a message they honestly believed contained nothing new, or whether he had seen the dispatch but had forgotten about it. His inability to recall his interview with Monsieur Hulme, while giving some credence to the third of those options, does not tell us whether MacMahon's powers of concentration had finally been overwhelmed by the appalling anxieties of his command; or whether, in the aftermath of crushing defeat, his mind had worked a merciful forgetfulness.

After abandoning the presidency of the Republic in 1879, MacMahon undertook to write his memoirs. Only fragments of it were ever published, insignificant in view of the magnitude of what he wrote before completion in 1890: five large manuscript volumes. It would appear that he never meant the material to be published, either writing down his recollections for the sole benefit of his family and heirs, or simply to occupy his hours. His most recent biographer, Jacques Silvestre de Sacy, having obtained the use of the manuscript through permission of the family, attributed the obvious inconsistencies and errors in the text to the evident fact that these were recollections long after the events. It is equally true that the advantage of hindsight permits an advantageous clarification of our actions. Forgetting the inconsistencies in his various earlier depositions about what he would have done had he received the dispatch of 20 August, MacMahon had reached the opinion in the eighteen-eighties that he probably would have abandoned his march toward Metz in order to retire upon Paris. As for the accusation made against Stoffel during Bazaine's trial, MacMahon wrote that neither the empress-regent nor Palikao were capable of ordering the suppression of a dispatch, and that Stoffel was too much a man of honor to have carried out such an order.[38]

Why, then, had he never spoken out publicly when the man's honor and career had been put in jeopardy!

As it was, an undercurrent of belief in Stoffel's guilt persisted in France despite the publication of histories in the twentieth century which acknowledged that no proof of that guilt had ever been established. While those historians were correct, they were unaware of Captain Janicot's report as it was a confidential document not then available to researchers. But *confidential* does not mean hidden from everyone, but reserved rather for the fortunate few authorized to see it, which too frequently is taken as the authority to gossip about it. The ultimate privilege seems to be the right to copy confidential material. How many copies of Janicot's report were distributed to interested but unauthorized people cannot now be determined. One copy did go to General Séré de Rivières, the author of the original charges made in his report in 1873, along with a copy of General de Ladmirault's letter recommending against prosecution despite Stoffel's guilt. Not only did Rivières not destroy the documents once he had been assured that his opinion had been sustained, he filed them for future reference. His son inherited his papers.

A few months after Stoffel's death, the son wrote to the minister of war, Georges Picquart, to protest the interpretation of the Stoffel affair in one of the recently-published volumes of the official history of the war. The passage he found objectionable read as follows: "As the report of General de Rivières accused Colonel Stoffel of having intercepted the telegram addressed to Marshal de MacMahon at least twice, Colonel Stoffel asked to be tried before a court-martial. On 13 July 1874, the minister issued an order of non-suit." Why, le Maître de Rivières inquired, had not the full report of the *instruction* been published? He enclosed with his letter two copies of the letters in his father's papers for the minister's edification. Because of the failure of the army to act upon Janicot's recommendation, Rivières added, Colonel Stoffel had been free to renew his attacks upon General de Rivières in the brochure published in 1874. Surely the head of the historical section could not have been ignorant of the documentary evidence. Why had he permitted erroneous interpretations to be published?[39]

General Picquart, while evidently unfamiliar with what had transpired in 1874, happened to have been the intelligence officer who in earlier years had discovered the false documents placed in the file of Captain Dreyfus. He at once asked his chef de cabinet to send the inquiry, with enclosures, to the historical section with a request to study the matter and to make a recommendation for a response that would give the complainant satisfaction "if there are justifiable grounds for his complaint."[40] The order was marked *confidential*, a hint that Picquart may have sensed the possibility of a new scandal arising from the mismanagement of military documents.

The task was quite appropriately assigned to the officer who, in 1902, had conducted the research on the history of the Army of Châlons for the official publications. Accordingly, he had obtained authorization from the minister of war on 30 October 1902 to examine the documents relative to the Stoffel case; and thus he knew that the initial charges, made by General Séré de Rivières, had been confirmed by the investigation of 1874. But he had also obtained a military legal opinion which held that it was not possible to reveal the results of his research, because an ordinance of non-suit had been issued, and because Colonel Stoffel was still alive. Consequently, when the material was published in the *Revue d'histoire* in July of 1905, even though the writers had been adequately informed, they were obliged to remain silent.

Since then, of course, Colonel Stoffel had died. But, meanwhile, the minister of war had ruled on 11 February 1907 that all publicists working on historical matters could conduct their research in the archives of military justice only for the years before 1814. Even before 1814, any case concluding with an ordinance of non-suit could not be communicated, that is, could not be examined. Without making an exception to the rules, *complete* satisfaction could not be given to M. Séré de Rivières. One could circumvent the rules to give him a *partial* satisfaction, the report concluded, by publishing the two documents the attorney had sent them in the *Revue d'histoire*, stating that they had come from the unpublished memoirs of his father. "The historical section will be pleased to take orders on this matter from M. le Ministre."[41]

Several weeks passed before General Picquart responded to Séré de Rivières. The file is silent, unfortunately, about what transpired during the interim, except that several rough drafts of an official response were rejected as unacceptable before the minister signed a final version. It appears that Picquart was seriously concerned to maintain propriety, and he rebuffed any idea of circumventing regulations. On the other hand, his ultimate letter to the complainant contained several sentences that were half-truths at best in his attempt to explain the interpretation published in the *Revue d'histoire*. Rivières was told the version published in 1905 had been based upon incomplete evidence, the archives not then possessing the documents Rivières had sent to the ministry. But even had the documents been known, he added, it would have been contrary to standard practice to use them given the likelihood of serious consequences. In that spirit, he himself had issued an order on 11 February 1907 to the archives of military justice limiting the communication of documents to matters before 1814, and even then on the condition that the cases had not terminated in an ordinance of non-suit. To his great regret, therefore, he could not give the complainant any satisfaction.[42] Rivières did not pursue the matter further.

We are the poorer for not knowing what Picquart may have discovered about the character of the Stoffel affair. His response to Rivières was limited to a defense of the army's procedures, but he had also rejected the opportunity to publish Janicot's report. If he suspected the integrity of that report, he did not say so. Yet, by 1908 he must have known that ranking officers and scholars of repute no longer gave credence to the charges made against Stoffel, and surely the Dreyfus affair had taught him to be suspicious about the alleged integrity of files. But the matter had become a sleeping dog thanks to the ordinance of non-suit. Except for Colonel Stoffel, whose guilt lay buried in the archives, the affair was closed.

At the end of his life, he returned to his beginnings. After the turn of the century, the excavation of the Alesia site had been reopened after nearly forty years of neglect. On 1 October 1906, he paid a visit to the site to indicate his continuing interest in the project. Victor Pernet, his collaborator of so many years ago, was on hand to greet him: an occasion of great cordiality, deeply touching those who were now in charge. There were reminiscences, first of the dig in the eighteen-sixties, then of various personages of the Second Empire. He called Napoleon III a great-hearted man surrounded by incompetence, as a result badly informed and advised, especially by the officers of the general staff. Bourbaki: a man of the most ordinary intelligence. Leboeuf: honest and loyal, but of limited capacity. Bazaine: no traitor, but incapacity coupled to great personal ambition, and a man too cynical to be an attractive person. No mention of MacMahon, but then he had disposed of MacMahon in a recent publication. An informal photograph of Stoffel being shown the site by Pernet was taken by a M. Fornerot fils and was thought to be the only photograph ever taken of Stoffel, for he had always refused to pose for the camera. When reproduced, the photograph was so small as to provide no detail; but it gave a clear suggestion of an upright and well-made man, still robust, wearing a moustache but no beard, well-turned out in black coat and hat, carrying a cane.[43] Six months later he was dead.

In 1911, the prolific English journalist Edward Legge, who had a long knowledge of French affairs dating from the Second Empire, and who had always remained favorably disposed to the fallen regime and its major figures, published a volume entitled *The Comedy and Tragedy of the Second Empire*. He had read both Stoffel's reports from Berlin and Piétri's letters to Stoffel, the latter having just been published in the *Revue de Paris*. He devoted a chapter in the book, "The Man Who Gave the Warning," to Stoffel as a tribute, calling him the most prescient of servants who had made as clear as daylight, not once, but again and again, the state of Prussian preparations. "When," he concluded, "will Paris 'do the right thing' by Stoffel? *When?*"[44]

Notes

1. Willy Schädler, *Les Barons Stoffel* 2: 181.
2. Piétri to Stoffel, 3 December 1877. Piétri, "Lettres au colonel Stoffel," 2: 138.
3. Richard Holmes, *The Road to Sedan*, pp. 106–10, treats other aspects of low officer-pay.
4. George Perrot, *Mémoires d'archéologie, d'épigraphie, et d'histoire* (1875); Charles-Joseph Tissot, *Recherches sur la campagne de César en Afrique* (1884), but initially read in three installments before the Académie des Inscriptions et Belles-Lettres in May, July, and September of 1881; Léon Heuzey, *Les Opérations militaires de Jules César* (1886).
5. Stoffel Histoire de *Jules César; guerre civile* 1: iii.
6. Stoffel to the Minister of State [the State Secretary in Berlin], 29 November 1888. Dossiers Stoffel (3rd dossier), no. 76381/2. Bibliothèque du service historique du ministère de la guerre, Vincennes.
7. Stoffel, *Histoire de Jules César* 1:239
8. Ibid. 1: v–vi.
9. Ibid. 1: 239.
10. Salomon Reinach, "Le Colonel Stoffel," *Revue archéologique* 9, sér. 4 (April 1907): 330–31.
11. Stoffel, *Guerre de César et d'Arioviste, premières opérations de César en l'an 702*, p. 108.
12. Ibid., p. 108.
13. Ibid., p. 109.
14. Ibid., p. 129.
15. Stoffel to the Minister of War [Charles de Freycinet], 2 November 1888. Dossiers Stoffel (3rd dossier).
16. Auguste Mercier [General Director of the Ministry of War] to the Governor of Paris, 24 March 1889. Ibid.
17. Stoffel, *De la possibilité d'une future alliance franco–allemande*, pp. 12–14, 32–34.
18. P. H. Sheridan, *Personal Memoirs of Philip Henry Sheridan* 2: 408–409.
19. Stoffel, *De la possibilité d'une future alliance franco-allemande*, pp. 23–24.
20. Ibid., pp. 26–32.
21. Ibid., pp. 35–43.
22. Jacques Chastenet, *La République triomphante*, p. 356.
23. Joseph Reinach, *Histoire de l'affaire Dreyfus* 1: 349; 3: 165; 6: 247.
24. Salomon Reinach, "Le Colonel Stoffel," 9: 331.
25. Willy Schädler, *Les Barons Stoffel* 2: 223–23.
26. Piétri to Stoffel, 14 July 1871. Piétri, "Lettres au colonel Stoffel," 2: 135.
27. Alfred Duquet, *Froeschwiller, Châlons, Sedan*, pp. 231–34.
28. Arthur-Maxime Chuquet, *La Guerre 1870–1871*, p. 83.
29. Louis-Jules Trochu, *Oeuvres posthumes* 1: 497, 501–504.
30. Léonce Rousset, *Le Second campagne de France. Histoire général de la guerre Franco-Allemande, 1870–1871* 2: 163–64, 210.

31. For the proper cataloguing note France, Armée, Etat-Major, Section Historique. *La Guerre de 1870/1*, publiée par *la Revue d'histoire*, rédigée à la Section historique de l'Etat-Major de l'Armée. Paris: 1901–13. See Michael Howard, *The Franco-Prussian War*, for a bibliography of primary sources.

32. Emile-Auguste-François-Thomas Zurlinden, *La Guerre de 1870–1871. Réflexions et souvenirs.*

33. Reinach, "Le Colonel Stoffel," 9, ser. 4: 329.

34. Zurlinden, "La Dépêche du 20 août 1870," *Le Gaulois*, 22 August 1907.

35. Henri Welschinger, *La Guerre de 1870, causes et responsabilitiés* 1: 279–81.

36. Theodore Zeldin, *Emile Ollivier and the Liberal Empire of Napoleon III*, pp. 202–207.

37. Emile Ollivier, *L'Empire libéral* 17: 335–37.

38. Jacques Silvestre de Sacy, *Le Maréchal de MacMahon, duc de Magenta (1808–1893)*, pp. 236–38.

39. Le Maître Séré de Rivières to the Minister of War [Georges Picquart], 2 February 1908. Dossiers Stoffel (dossier Lt20).

40. General Georges Toutée to the Historical Section of Army Headquarters, 10 February 1908. Ibid.

41. Major Picard to General Georges Toutée, 7 February 1908. Ibid.

42. General Georges Picquart to Le Maître Séré de Rivieres, 9 March 1908. Ibid.

43. Gaston Testart, "Stoffel," *Pro Alesia* 1, no. 12 (June 1907): 177–80.

44. Edward Legge, *The Comedy and Tragedy of the Second Empire*, p. 338.

Sources

Aubry-Vitet, Cécile, comtesse de Rohan-Chabot. *Souvenirs de Froehner.* Nogent-le-Rotrau: Daupeley-Gouverneur, 1931. The author was a friend of Froehner and took notes from him in his later years for this book.

Aumale, Henri-Eugène-Philippe-Louis d'Orléans, duc d'. *Correspondance du duc d'Aumale et de Cuvillier-Fleury.* 4 vols. Paris: Plon-Nourrit, 1910-1914. Alfred-Auguste Cuvillier-Fleury, a writer and a member of the Académie française, had been Aumale's tutor beginning in 1827 and his secretary during his command in Algeria.

———. *Les Institutions militaires de la France.* Brussels: C. Muquardt, 1867.

Bapst, Germain. Le *Maréchal* Canrobert: souvenirs *d'un siècle.* 4 vols. Bapst, reflecting Canrobert's views, was very hostile to General Trochu, believing him to be self-seeking and untrustworthy.

Bardoux, Jacques. *Les Origines du malheur européen: l'aide anglo-française à la domination prussienne, 1863-75.* Inspired by the many analogies between the defeats in 1870 and 1940.

Baumont, Maurice. *Bazaine, les secrets d'un maréchal (1811-1888).* Paris: Imprimerie nationale, 1978. A fuller volume than his 1971 book on Metz.

Bazancourt, César, baron de. *La Campagne d'Italie.* 2 vols. Paris: Amyot, 1859-1860. The army's view of the campaign.

Benedetti, Vincent, comte. "Déposition de." *Enquête Parlementaire sur les actes du Gouvernement de la Défense Nationale. Dépositions des témoins* 1: 83-92. Versailles: Cerf et fils, 1872. Session of 22 July 1871.

———. *Ma Mission en Prusse.* Paris: H. Plon, 1871.

Bertrand, Alexandre-Louis-Joseph. *Les Voies romaines en Gaule, voies des itinéraires.* Résumé du travail de la Commission de la topographie des Gaules. Paris: Aux bureaux de la Revue archéologique, 1864. Bertrand was an associate of Salomon Reinach for many years.

Bonnal, Guillaume-Auguste-Balthazar-Eugène-Henri, General. *Le Haut Commandement français au début de chacune des guerres de 1859 et 1870.* Paris: La Revue des Idées, 1905. An insightful study.

Bonnin, Georges. *Bismarck and the Hohenzollern Candidature for the Spanish Throne. The Documents in the German Diplomatic Archives.* London: Chatto and Windus, 1957. The material became available only after 1945.

Bury, J. P. T. *Gambetta and the National Defense.* London: Longmans, Green, 196. Good bibliography on the primary sources for the period and a judicious account of Gambetta's drastic administrative measures.

Busch, Moritz. *Bismarck in the Franco-German War 1870-1871.* 2 vols. New York: Charles Scribner's Sons, 1879. An advocate of German unity who entered the Prussian foreign ministry in 1870 and accompanied Bismarck on the campaign.

———. *Bismarck: Some Secret Pages of his History.* 2 vols. London: Macmillan, 1898.

Cambacérès, Marie-Jean-Pierre, duc de. *Funérailles de Napoléon III.* Paris: Librairie Générale, 1873. The proces-verbal by the grand master of the ceremonies, including an alphabetical list of those who signed the register at Camden House.

Carette, Mme A. (Mlle Bouvet). *Souvenirs intimes de la cour des Tuileries.* Paris: Paul Ollendorff, 1888-1891. The granddaughter of Admiral Pierre François-Henri-Etienne Bouvet (1775-1860) . She held the title reader to the empress. Froehner found her to be an outrageous snoop and had a low opinion of her character.

Case, Lynn M. *Edouard Thouvenel et la diplomatie du Second Empire.* Paris: A. Pedone, 1976. The best work on Thouvenel's career.

Casevitz, Jean. *Une Loi manquée: la loi Niel (1866-1868). L'armée française à la veille de la guerre de 1870.* Rennes: Oberthur, 1960.

Castellane, Esprit-Victor de. *Journal du maréchal de Castellane, 1804-1862.* 5 vols. Paris: Plon-Nourrit, 1895-1897.

Cazelles, Raymond. *Le Duc d'Aumale, prince aux dix visages.* Paris: Tallandier, 1984. Based upon the papers in the Musée de Condé at the Château de Chantilly where the author is conservateur.

Challener, Richard D. *The French Theory of the Nation in Arms 1866–1939.* New York: Columbia University Press, 1952. Contains good bibliography.

Charles-Roux, François J. *Alexandre II, Gortchakoff et Napoléon III.* Paris: Plon-Nourrit, 1913. Dated but still useful.

Chastenet, Jacques. *L'Enfance de la troisième, 1870-1879.* Paris: Hachette, 1952.

———. *La République triomphante, 1893-1906.* Paris: Hachette, 1955.

Chesney, Charles C., Lt. Col., and Henry Reeve. *The Military Resources of Prussia and France,* and *Recent Changes in the Art* of War. London: Longmans, Green, 1870. The book was a republication of four essays which had appeared in the *Edinburgh Review* between 1864 and 1867. The final essay shows the influence of General Trochu's book.

Chuquet, Arthur-Maxime. *La Guerre 1870-1871.* Paris: L. Chailley, 1895. One of the books which preserved the legend of Stoffel's guilt, as an associate of the empress, in suppressing the dispatch of 20 August 1870.

[Clappier] Dossier Alexandre-Victor-Edmond Clappier, no. 4075 GB 2ᵉ Div. Bibliothèque du service historique du ministère de la guerre, Vincennes.

Claretie, Arsène-Arnaud, called Jules. *Histoire de la Révolution de 1870 1871.* 2 vols. Paris: Librairie Illustrée, 2nd ed., 1877. A prolific journalist who also published under a variety of pseudonyms (Olivier de Jalin, Candide, and Perdican among others). Very hostile to the imperial regime and the emperor, a partisan of General de Wimpffen, and a supporter of Thiers, not Gambetta.

Coffinières de Nordeck, Grégoire-Gaspard-Félix, General. *Capitulation de Metz. Réponse du Général Coffinières de Nordeck à ses détracteurs.* Brussels: C. Muquardt, 1871. The commander of the post of Metz who had opposed the idea of breaking out of the fortress.

Coynart, Raymond, Lt. Col. *Etude historique, topographique et militaire sur la cité gauloise d'Alésia.* Paris: L. Martinet, 1856. A member of the commission for Alesia.

Creuly, Casimir, General. *Carte de la Gaule sous le proconsulat de César.* Paris: Aux bureaux de la Revue archéologique, 1864. A member of the commission for Alesia.

Dansette, Adrien. *Du 2 décembre au 4 septembre: le Second Empire.* Paris: Hachette, 1972. A reliable recent survey.

Du Barail, François-Charles, General. *Mes Souvenirs, 1820-1879.* 3 vols. Paris: Plon-Nourrit, 1894-1896. Conservative and Bonapartist but moderate in tone. Valuable memoirs.

Ducrot, Auguste-Alexandre, General. *La Journée de Sedan.* Paris: E. Dentu, 1871. The public response to Wimpffen's charges, which had been dated 1 August 1871. Ducrot's reply was dated 18 September 1871.

Duquet, Alfred. *Froeschwiller, Châlons, Sedan.* Paris: Charpentier, 1880. The author, an attorney, was a partisan of General Wimpffen. A polemical work unfavorable to Napoleon III, MacMahon, Ducrot, and Stoffel.

Faverot de Kerbrech, François-Nicolas-Guy-Napoléon, General baron. *Mes souvenirs, la guerre contre l'Allemagne.* Paris: Plon-Nourrit, 2nd ed., 1905. An equerry to the emperor at the outset of the campaign; later attached to General Ducrot as an ordnance officer.

Fletcher, Willard A. *The Mission of Vincent Benedetti to Berlin 1864-1870.* The Hague: Martinus Nijhoff, 1965. If not well written, the book contains valuable information and shows Benedetti's difficulties with the personal diplomacy of Napoleon III and Bismarck's deviousness.

Fleury, Emile-Félix, General comte. *Souvenirs.* 2 vols. Paris: Plon Nourrit, 1897-1898. One of the emperor's best friends. His account of the Italian campaign is valuable and explains why he favored army reform.

Forbes, Archibald. *Memories and Studies of War and Peace.* London, Paris: Cassell, 1895. A war correspondent for the London *Daily News*. He was present at Sedan.

Frère-Orban, Hubert-Joseph-Walther. "The Belgian question after 1866." *Le Temps*, 18 April 1892. A former Belgian foreign minister endeavoring to clarify the Belgian question after 1866. He knew that the acquisition of Belgium had not been a matter of French policy, but had been initiated by Bismarck.

Garçon, Maurice. *Histoire de la justice sous la IIIe république*. 3 vols. Paris: Arthème Fayard, 1957. A good survey of notable cases.

Girard, Georges-A.-M. *La Vie et les souvenirs du général de Castelnau, 1814-1890*. Paris: Calmann-Lévy, 1930. General Henri de Castelnau, an aide to Napoleon III. Despite the absence of bibliography and the presence of few footnotes, the sections on Mexico and 1870-71 were based on Castelnau's journal which had remained unpublished until a daughter-in law released it in 1927. A valuable, if limited, volume.

Giraudeau, Fernand. *La Mort et les funérailles de Napoleon III*. Paris: Amyot, 1873. A Bonapartist publicist and former officer in the ministry of the interior. A good account of the funeral.

Goncourt, Edmond and Jules. *Journal, mémoires de la vie littéraire*. 22 vols. Monaco: Les Editions de l'Imprimerie nationale de Monaco, 1956–1958.

Hastier, Louis. "L'Evasion de Bazaine." *Historia* 15 (February 1954): 25 44. Article based on new documents lent by Georges Bazaine, grand-nephew of the marshal. See Maurice Baumont for updated information.

Hauterive, Ernest d'. *Napoléon III et le Prince Napoléon: correspondance inédite*. Paris: Calmann-Levy, 1925.

Hérisson, Maurice d'Irisson d'Hérisson de Saulnier, Captain comte. *La Légende de Metz*. Paris: Paul Ollendorff, 4th ed., 1888. A prolific writer on military topics, much of it polemical, hostile in particular to MacMahon. A source on both General Trochu and Jules Favre.

Heuzey, Léon. *Les Opérations militaires de Jules César*. Paris: Hachette, 1886.

Hohenlohe-Ingelfingen, Kraft Karl, Prince zu. *Aus meinem Leben: Aufzeichnungen aus den Jahren 1848-1871*. 4 vols. Berlin: E. S. Mittler & Son, 1897-1907. Vol. 3 covers 1866, Vol. 4 the War of 1870-71.

———. *Letters on Strategy*. 2 vols. London: Trench, Trübner, 1897. Very valuable for comments on French leadership, notably on MacMahon's lack of resolve. Hohenlohe was so wedded to the Prussian autocracy that he could not conceive of successful warfare unless the sovereign commanded.

Holmes, Richard. *The Road to Sedan: The French Army 1866-70*. London: Royal Historical Society, 1984. The study is in two parts: on military structure and on doctrine. An excellent supplement to the good operational histories of the Franco-Prussian War by Palat and Howard.

Holt, Edgar. *Plon-Plon: The Life of Prince Napoleon, 1822-1891*. London: Michael Joseph, 1973. A popular work with a bibliography of secondary sources. The prince has not attracted scholars.

Howard, Michael. *The Franco-Prussian War: The German Invasion of France*. New York: Macmillan, 1961. A splendid achievement, the very model for what military history ought to be.

[Janicot] Dossier Paul-Joseph-Louis Janicot, no. 40868—3e Série. Bibliothèque du service historique du ministère de la guerre, Vincennes.

Jerrold, Blanchard. *The Life of Napoleon III*. 4 vols. London: Longmans, Green & Co., 1874-1882. Very dated, but useful for published letters.

Juste, Théodore. *Napoléon III et la Belgique, le traité secret*. Brussels: C. Muquardt,

1870. This eminent Belgian historian was suspicious of Bismarck and Benedetti in the business, but not of Napoleon III.

Kovacs, Arpad F. "French Military Institutions Before the Franco-Prussian War." *American Historical Review* 51, no. 1 (October 1945): 217-35. While he knew of Stoffel's reports, Kovacs' subject was what the French were actually doing—and why. Strong personal bias against Napoleon III.

Kranzberg, Melvin. "An Emperor Writes History." H. Stuart Hughes, *Teachers of History: Essays in Honor of Laurence* B. Packard. Ithaca: Cornell University Press, 1954. Amusing and well done.

La Chapelle, Alfred, comte de. *Oeuvres posthumes et autographes inédits de Napoléon* III *en exil.* Paris: E. Lachaud, 1873. Part I had originally been a brochure, "La Guerre de 1870," written by La Chapelle who had covered the war for the London *Standard.* He had not known the emperor before visiting him at Chistlehurst to show him a copy. The version republished here carries annotations in the emperor's very difficult hand. Part II was attributed to the emperor, but he had the collaboration of La Chapelle, by then a devoted courtier.

Laforge, Léon. *Histoire complète de MacMahon.* 3 vols. Paris: Lamulle & Poisson, 1898. Obviously partisan, but based on much documentary material.

La Gorce, Pierre de. *Histoire du Second Empire.* 7 vols. Paris: Plon Nourrit, 1894-1905. The classic history of the period, liberal Catholic in outlook.

La Motte-Rouge, Joseph-Edouard, General comte de. *Souvenirs et campagnes.* 3 vols. Nantes: V. Forest & E. Grimaud, 1888-89. Nobility of old extraction (1427). Although a friend of Trochu (they were both Bretons), he was bitterly hostile to the civilians who engineered the Revolution of 4 September.

[Laurens de Waru] Dossier Paul Laurens de Waru, no. 548 GB 3e Div. Bibliothèque du service historique du ministère de la guerre, Vincennes.

Leboeuf, Edmond, Marshal. "Déposition de." *Enquête parlementaire sur les actes du Gouvernement de la Defénse Nationale. Dépositions des témoins* 1: 41-66. Versailles: Cerf et fils, 1872. Session of 16 December 1871.

Lebrun, Barthelémy-Louis-Joseph, General. *Souvenirs militaires, 1866-1870. Préliminaires de la guerre*; *mes missions à Vienne et en Belgique.* Paris: E. Dentu, 1895.

———. *Guerre de 1870: Bazeilles-Sedan.* Paris: E. Dentu, 1884. The first volume of his memoirs was published later, because it contained controversial diplomatic material, recommending discretion until 1895.

Le Faure, Amédée. *Procès du Maréchal Bazaine. Rapport. Audiences du premier conseil de guerre. Compte rendu, rédigé avec l'adjonction de notes explicatives.* 2 vols. in 1. Paris: Garnier frères, 1874. The most complete and reliable published account of the court-martial.

Le Gall, Joël. *Alésia; archéologie et histoire.* Paris: Fayard, 1963. The most recent documented account.

Legge, Edward. *The Comedy and Tragedy of the Second Empire.* London & New York: Harper & Bros., 1911. A well-informed journalist, really an insider, who remained a partisan of the imperial regime.

Lehautcourt, Pierre (pseud. Palat, Barthélemy-Edmond). "La Réorganisation de l'armée avant 1870." *Revue de Paris* 4 (August 1901), 525-52. General Palat wrote many volumes on the history of the Franco-Prussian War under this pseudonym, but published a general bibliography of the war in 1896 under his own name. Fundamental for a detailed study of the war.

L'Huillier, Fernand, and Pierre Benaerts. *Nationalité et nationalisme (1860-1878).* Paris: Presses Universitaires de France, 1968.

MacMahon, Marie-Edme-Patrice-Maurice, Marshal comte de, duc de Magenta. "Déposition de." *Enquête parlementaire sur les actes du Gouvernement de la Défense Nationale*: *Dépositions des témoins* 1: 28-40. Session of 9 September 1871.

Manevy Raymond. *La Presse de la IIIe République*. Paris: J. Foret, 1955.

Marquiset, Robert, and Pierre Lorain. "Le Système 1866 dit 'Chassepot'." *Armes à feu françaises modèles réglementaires: 1858-1918, chargement culasse.* (Collection J. Boudriot, P. Lorain & R. Marquiset, Cahier no. 2.) Paris: L'Emancipatrice, n.d. The authoritative text accompanied by excellent drawings.

Moltke, Helmut Carl Bernhard, Graf von. *The Franco-Prussian War of 1870–71.* New York: Harper, 1907. The original German edition was 1891. Includes excellent map of the campaign and useful tables on the rival armies.

Monteilhet, Joseph. *Les Institutions militaires de la France 1814-1932.* Paris: Félix Alcan, 1932. A dated but useful survey.

Napoléon III. *Histoire de Jules César.* 2 vols. Paris: Henri Plon, 1865-1866.

———. *Oeuvres de Napoléon III.* 5 vols. Paris: Henri Plon, 1869.

Ollivier, Emile. *L'Empire libéral.* 17 vols. Paris: Garnier frères, 1895-1915. Tables and index were published in 1918 as Vol. 18.

———. *The Franco-Prussian* War and *its Hidden Causes.* Boston: Little, Brown, 1912. Extracts from Vols. 13-14 of *L'Empire libéral*, published in 1911 as *Philosophie d'une guerre.*

———. *Lettres de l'exil, 1870-1874.* Paris: Hachette, 1921.

[Oppermann] Dossier Auguste Oppermann, no. 383—2e Série. Bibliothèque du service historique du ministère de la guerre, Vincennes.

Pajol, Charles-Pierre-Victor, General comte. Lettre de M. le général [Eugène] *Pajol sur la capitulation de Sedan.* Lefebvre, 1871. Eugène Pajol was one of the emperor's aides during the campaign.

Palikao, Charles Cousin de Montauban, General comte de. *Un Ministère de la guerre de vingt-quatre jours, du 10 août au 4 septembre 1870.* Paris: Henri Plon, 1871. Published in October of 1871.

———. "Déposition de." *Enquête parlementaire sur les actes du Gouvernement de la Défense Nationale. Dépositions des témoins* 1: 164-84. Ver sailles: Cerf et fils, 1872. Session of 20 July 1871.

Perrot, Georges. *Mémoires d'archéologie, d'épigraphie, et d'histoire.* Paris: Didier, 1875.

Pflanze, Otto. *Bismarck and the Development of Germany: The Period of Unification 1815-1871.* Princeton: Princeton University Press, 1963. The first volume of a distinguished study of Bismarck's policies.

Piétri, Franceschini. "Lettres au colonel Stoffel." *Revue de Paris* 18th Year, 3 (15

June 1911): 718-38; 4 (1 July 1911): 121-38. Piétri was personal secretary to Napoleon III until the emperor's death, thereafter secretary to the empress.

Poulet-Malassis, Auguste, ed. *Papiers secrets et correspondance du Second Empire*. Paris: Auguste Ghio, 1873.

Procès Bazaine. Conseil de guerre du Grand Trianon. Compte-rendu sténographique quotidien. Paris: Bureau des Célébrités Contemporaines, 1873.

Procès du Général Trochu contre MM. Vitu et de Villemessant du Figaro. Paris: Journal la Petite Press, 1872.

Reinach, Joseph. *Histoire de l'affaire Dreyfus*. 7 vols. Paris: Charpentier and Fasquelle, 1903-11. The partisan but indispensable account.

Reinach, Salomon. "Le Colonel Stoffel." *Revue archéologique* 9, sér. 4 (April 1907): 329-32. An obituary.

Renan, Ernest. *Correspondance*. 2 vols. Paris: Calmann-Lévy, 1926-1928.

Révérend, Albert, vicomte. *Armorial du Premier Empire*. 4 vols. in 2. Paris: H. Champion, n. ed., 1974.

———. *Titres, anoblissements et pairies de la Restauration, 1814-1830*. 6 vols. in 3. Paris: Champion, n. ed., 1974.

———. *Titres et confirmations de titres: Monarchie de Juillet, 2ᵉ République, 2ᵉ Empire, 3ᵉ République, 1830-1908*. Paris: H. Champion, n. ed., 1974. The introduction to this reprinted classic is by Jean Tulard.

Richard, Jules (pseud. Maillot, Thomas-Jules-Richard). *Le Bonapartisme sous la République*. Paris: E. Rouveyre & G. Blond, 1883. Dated but still valuable for its personal insights.

Robert, Adolphe et al. Dictionnaire des parlementaires français (1 Mai 1789 *jusqu'au 1 mai 1889)*. 5 vols. Paris: Bourloton, 1891.

[Robert, Pierre-Joseph, Colonel]. *La Campagne de 1870 jusqu'au ler septembre, par un officier de l'armée du Rhin*. Brussels: J. Rozez, 1871. Brief, useful book, but often unjust in its embittered judgments. Favorable to Trochu, severely critical of MacMahon. The book had to remain anonymous as Robert, as a general, later served as a political partisan of MacMahon.

Rothan, Gustave. *Souvenirs diplomatiques. L'affaire du Luxembourg—le prélude de la guerre de 1870*. Paris: Calmann Lévy, 1882. The French representative in Frankfurt in 1867, who believed Stoffel was blind to what went on in Prussia.

Rothney, John. *Bonapartism after Sedan*. Ithaca: Cornell University Press, 1969. The last and best word on the topic.

Rousset, Léonce, Lt. Colonel. *Le Second Campagne de France. Histoire générale de la guerre Franco-Allemande, 1870-71*. 6 vols., atlas. Paris: Montgredien, rev. ed., 1900. Originally published 1895-99 by a specialist in military history at the Ecole supérieure de guerre.

Ruby, Edmond, and Jean Regnault, Generals. *Bazaine, coupable ou victime*. Paris: J. Peyronnet, 1960. Using new evidence from the archives of the German foreign ministry, they prove that the charge of treason was baseless.

Saulcy, Louis-Félicien-Joseph Caignart de. *Les Campagnes de Jules César dans les Gaules: études d'archéologie militaire*. Paris: Didier, 1862. A member of the commission for Alesia.

Schädler, Willy. *Les Barons Stoffel*. 2 vols. A typescript completed in 1979 and deposited in the Bibliothèque du service historique du ministère de la guerre, Vincennes. Cote 66.174. A native of Arbon, home of the Stoffel family, a small port on the Lake of Constance in the canton of Thurgau. While he visited the archives in Vincennes, he did not have the time to study all the relevant dossiers, nor did he read the main works on the campaigns of 1870-71. The genealogical material is very useful, but the typescript contains long quotations from published sources, especially from those by Stoffel himself.

Schnapper, Bernard. *Le Remplacement militaire en France: Quelques aspects politiques, économiques et sociaux du recrutement au XIXe siècle*. Paris: S.E.V.P.E.N., 1968. Detailed and important, more comprehensive on this topic than Challener's book.

Séré de Rivières, Raymond-Adolphe, General. "Déposition de." *Enquête parlementaire sur les actes du Gouvernement de la Défense Nationale: Dépositions des témoins* 5: 96-101. Versailles: Cerf et fils, 1875. Session of 1 June 1874.

———. *Rapport complet. Procès du Maréchal Bazaine*. Paris: Garnier frères, 1874. Appended to the Le Faure edition of the *Procès*.

Sereville, E. de, and F. de Saint Simon. *Dictionnaire de la noblesse française*. Paris: La Société Française au XXe Siècle, 1975. The nobility as of the end of the 19th century and evidently reliable.

Sheridan, Philip Henry, General. *Personal Memoirs of Philip Henry Sheridan*. 2 vols. New York: Charles L. Webster, 1888. Sheridan an observer with the German army and present at Sedan. His intense dislike of Napoleon III, as the destroyer of a republic, had been magnified by the French intervention in Mexico.

Silvestre de Sacy, Jacques. *Le Maréchal de MacMahon, duc de Magenta (1808-1893)*. Paris: Les Editions Inter-nationales, 1960. The latest and most judicious biography of MacMahon using the unpublished memoirs.

Simpson, F. A. *Louis Napoleon and the Recovery of France, 1848-1856*. London: Longmans, Green, 3rd ed., 1951. Originally published in 1923, the book describes the emperor's difficulties with his generals in the Crimea.

[Stoffel] Dossiers Eugène-Georges-Henri-Celeste Stoffel, baron, Cote 76381/2; Lt 20; and MR 2128. Bibliothèque du service historique du ministère de la guerre, Vincennes.

———. *Etude sur l'emplacement d'Alésia*. Paris: Imprimerie impériale, 1862. Originally written in 1860.

———. *Rapports militaires écrits de Berlin 1866-1870*. Paris: Garnier frères, 1871. The edition authorized by Stoffel. An English translation *Military Reorts, addressed to the French War Minister*, was published in London: H. M. Stationery Office, 1872. For an example of the snippets to which Stoffel objected, see "Rapports de M. le Bon. Stoffel sur les forces militaires de la Prusse, la garde nationale mobile de France, le mouvement politique de l'Allemagne, adressés au gouvernement français en 1868, 1869, et 1870." *Documents publics pour servir à l'histoire de la guerre de 1870-1871* 1: 1-106. Paris: A. Lacroix, Verboeckhoven, 1871.

———. *La Dépêche du 20 août 1870, du maréchal Bazaine au maréchal de MacMahon*. Paris: Lachaud & Burdin, 1874.

———. *Histoire de Jules César; guerre civil*. 2 vols. Paris: Imprimerie nationale, 1887.

———. *Guerre de César et d'Arioviste, premières opérations de César en l'an 702*. Paris: Imprimerie nationale, 1890.

———. *De la possibilité d'une future alliance franco-allemande*. Paris: Vormus, 1890.

Testart, Gaston. "Stoffel." *Pro Alesia; revue mensuelle des fouilles d'Alise et des questions relatives à Alesia* 1, no. 12 (June 1907): 177-80.

Thiers, Louis-Adolphe. Memoirs of M. Thiers 1870-1873. New York: Howard Fertig, 1973. An English translation of *Notes et souvenirs de M. Thiers, 1870-1873*, made in 1915.

Tissot, Charles-Joseph. *Recherches sur la campagne de César en Afrique*. Académie des Inscriptions et Belles-Lettres. *Mémoires*. 31, 2nd part (1884): 1-61.

Tombs, Robert. *The War Against Paris 1871*. Cambridge: Cambridge University Press, 1981. Particularly valuable for the role of the army in the suppression of the Commune.

Trochu, Louis-Jules, General. *L'Armée française en 1867*. Paris: Amyot, 1867.

———. *Oeuvres posthumes*. Tours: A. Mame, 1896. The first volume, on the siege of Paris, was written between 1878 and 1890. The second volume, subtitled "La Société, l'Etat, l'Armée," was written between 1874 and 1890.

Tulard, Jean. *Napoléon et la noblesse d'Empire*. Paris: Jules Tallandier, 1979. Supplements the volumes by Revérénd and Serreville.

Welschinger, Henri. *La Guerre de 1870, causes et responsabilités*. 2 vols. Paris: Plon-Nourrit, 1910. Openly partisan but valuable.

Wimpffen, Emmanuel-Félix, General de. *Sedan*. Paris: Librairie Internationale, 1871. He began the composition of the work while still a prisoner after Sedan; but the preface was dated 1 August 1871, by which time he had seen the published reports of Colonel Stoffel. Much partisan material in the book, some of it so poorly informed as to suggest a ready acceptance of gossip and rumor. Wimpffen remained embittered over his lack of command at the outset of the war, and a certain petty tone pervades the book. As the name suggests, he was Alsatian.

Zeldin, Theodore. *Emile Ollivier and the Liberal Empire of Napoleon III*. Oxford: Clarendon Press, 1963. Far and away the fairest treatment of Ollivier.

Zurlinden, Emile-Auguste-François-Thomas, General. *La Guerre de 1870-1871. Réflexions et souvenirs*. Paris: Hachette, 3rd ed., 1904. Taken prisoner at Metz, he escaped to serve again. A major figure in the Dreyfus case, resigning as minister of war rather than taking the initiative in the revision of the case. No mention of Stoffel.

———. "La Dépêche du 20 août 1870." *Le Gaulois*, 22 August 1907. His afterthoughts about the Stoffel affair.

Index

Abzac, marquis d', 131, 135–136, 142, 145–147, 155, 172–174, 179, 181–182, 196
Amigues, Jules, 115
Amiot, Jules-Armand-Gustave, 140–141
Andlau, Gaston, comte d', 51
Army, French, organization of, 11–15, 48–49, 54–55, 61–63, 75–77
Austro-Prussian War of 1860, 11, 19–22, 29, 61–63

Baraguay-d'Hilliers, Achille, comte, 123–125, 128
Barodet, Désiré, 115
Bazaine, François-Achille, 86–91, 100, 121–161, 165–182, 201
Bazelaire, 131, 132, 138–139
Benedek, Ludwig, Ritter von, 20, 23
Benedetti, Vincent, comte, 59–60, 70, 111
Berthaut, Jean-Auguste, 34, 87, 134
Bertrand, Alexandre-Louis-Joseph, 6
Bismarck, Otto, Prinz von, 59–60, 69–70, 73, 83, 105–106, 121, 192
Bleichröder, Gerson, 69–70
Bonaparte, Jérôme-Napoléon, Prince, 34–35, 41, 82, 87, 114, 134

Bourbaki (Charles-Denis Sauter), 71, 83, 201
Broyé, Louis de, 131, 135, 142–143

Caignart de Saulcy, Louis-Félicien-Joseph, 6, 8
Canrobert, François-Certain, 18, 40, 85, 86, 125
Castelnau, Henri, 18, 93, 114
Cavaignac, Louis-Eugéne, 12
Chabaud-Latour, François-Henri-Ernest, baron de, 152, 154, 162n
Challemel-Lacour, Paul-Armand, 129–130, 180
Changarnier, Nicolas-Anne-Théodule, 15, 39, 106
Chassepot, Antoine-Alphonse, 16
Chevalier, Michel, 64
Chuquet, Arthur-Maxime, 195
Cissey, Ernest-Louis-Octave Courtot de, 112–113, 124–126, 166, 169, 174, 176
Clappier, Alexandre-Victor-Edmond, 168–176, 179
Clermont-Tonnerre, Aynard-François-Antoine-Aymé, comte de, 11
Coffinières de Nordeck, Grégoire-Gaspard-Félix, 131, 139, 149, 150

215

Delacroix, Alphonse, 5
Desjardins, Ernest, 5
Dollfus, Charles, 64
Du Barail, François-Charles, 101, 106, 124, 127–128, 169, 174
Ducrot, Auguste-Alexandre, 36, 93–95, 99, 102–106, 114, 117
Duquet, Alfred, 195, 198

Failly, Pierre-Louis-Charles, 17, 92–93
Favre, Jules, 105–106, 111
Fleury, Emile-Félix, 34, 85
Forbes, Archibald, 165
Fould, Achille, 19, 33, 34
Franco-Prussian War, 81–105
Froehner, Wilhelm, 9–10, 99–100, 189

Gambetta, Léon, 100, 121, 127, 129, 166, 180
Gouvion, Saint-Cyr, Laurent, 11–12, 48
Gramont, Antoine-Alfred-Agénor, duc de, 110
Guiod, Adolphe-Simon, 18–19, 100–101, 162n
Guyard, Augustin, 131–132, 137–138, 139, 149

Hanoverian Question, 82
Heuzey, Léon, 186, 189
Hohenlohe-Ingelfingen, Kraft Karl, Prinz zu, 60, 81, 95, 105, 108
Hulme, 158–161

Janicot, Paul-Joseph-Louis, 168–176, 179, 199

Kératry, Emile de, 100
Krupp, Friedrich, 51

Lachaud, Charles-Alexandre, 129, 156, 157, 160–161
Ladmirault, Paul de, 175, 199
Lallemand, 162n
Lamorcière, Louis-Christophe-Léon Juchault de, 12–13, 74

La Motte-Rouge, Joseph-Edouard, comte de, 128, 162n
Leboeuf, Edmond, 53, 75, 84–86, 114, 125, 134, 201
Lebrun, Barthélemy-Louis-Joseph, 18–19, 41, 46–47, 49, 86, 114
Legge, Edward, 201
Luxembourg crisis (1867), 46, 59, 77

MacMahon, Marie-Edme-Petrice-Maurice de, duc de Magenta, 86–93, 114–115, 122, 123–161, 166–175, 180–182, 188–189, 196–199
Marescalchi, 147, 170, 172, 197
Martineau-Deschenez, Gaston-Philippe-Augustin, baron, 162n
Massaroli, 131, 134–135, 137–140, 145–146, 149, 152, 178
Maury, Louis-Ferdinand-Alfred, 6, 9–10
Mérimée, Prosper, 6, 7, 10
Miès, Frédéric, 88, 131, 134, 139, 144–150, 154–155, 157, 172, 173, 178–181, 196
Moltke, Helmuth Carl Bernhard, Graf von, 28, 62, 92, 100, 103

Nefftzer, Auguste, 64
Niel, Adolphe, 18–19, 33–34, 39, 41, 46–47, 49, 54–55, 66, 85
Niel Law, 54, 72–73

Ollivier, Emile, 77–78, 81, 86, 110, 171, 197–198
Oppermann, Auguste, 10
Orléans, Henri-Eugène-Philippe-Louis d', duc d'Aumale, 5, 124–160, 172, 181

Pajol, Eugène, 86
Palikao, Charles Cousin de Montauban, comte de, 19, 40, 88, 90–92, 198
Passy, Frédéric, 64
Peace movement, 63–64, 77–78
Pernet, Victor, 6, 8, 201
Perrot, Georges, 186, 189

216

Picquart, Georges, 199–200
Piétri, Franceschini, 22, 50–51, 55, 67–68, 78, 95, 108–109, 186, 195
Piétri, Joachim, 132, 135
Princeteau, 162n
Pourcet, Joseph-Auguste-Jean-Marie, 128–129, 138, 151–152, 156–157, 182
Prussian military system, 17–18, 22–29, 36–38, 50, 52, 61–72, 76–77

Quicherat, Jules, 5
Quinet, Edgar, 64

Rabasse, Achille-Napoléon, 88, 131, 134, 139–140, 144–150, 153–154, 157, 172–173, 178–179, 180–181
Randon, Jacques-Louis-César-Alexandre, 11, 34–35
Reinach, Joseph, 194, 197
Reinach, Salomon, 8, 189, 196–197
Rémusat, Charles de, 115, 133
Renan, Ernest, 64, 82
Renson, 112–113, 169
Resseyre, 162n
Rivières, Raymond-Adolphe,Séré de, 128–139, 150, 153, 155, 160, 170, 175, 180–182, 199
Robert, Pierre-Joseph, 95
Rossignol, Jean-Pierre, 5

Rouher, Eugène, 19, 33–34, 88
Rousset, Léonce, 196

Saisset, Théodore, 102, 103–104
Schmitz, Isidore-Pierre, 87, 102, 104
Sheridan, Philip Henry, 93–94
Simon, Jules, 100
Susleau de Malroy, 162n

Thiers, Louis-Adolphe, 13, 75, 106, 108, 111–112, 115, 122–126, 182
Tissot, Charles-Joseph, 186, 189
Tripier, Emile-Jules-Gustave, 162n
Trochu, Louis-Jules, 18–19, 34, 39≠47, 49, 82, 87, 99–107, 111, 114, 185, 195–196
Turnier, 131, 137–140, 158, 159

Vaillant, Jean-Baptiste-Philibert, 16, 19, 33–34, 36, 62–63
Vaulgrenant, 172, 179, 180, 197
Vuitry, Adolphe, 19, 33–34

War of 1859, 11, 52, 85
Waru, Paul Laurens de, 170, 177
Welschinger, Henri, 197
Wimpffen, Emanuel-Félix de, 92–94, 114

Zurlinden, Emil-Auguste, 196–197

The Author

Roger L. Williams is Distinguished Professor of History, Emeritus, University of Wyoming. He is the author of a number of books on French history, and of books and articles on the history of botany, among them *Gaslight and Shadow: The World of Napoleon III; Henri Rochefort: Prince of the Gutter Press; The French Revolution of 1870–1871; The Mortal Napoleon III; Manners and Murders in the World of Louis-Napoleon; The Horror of Life; Aven Nelson of Wyoming;* and co-author of *How Modernity Came to a Provençal Town: Citizens & Clergy of Grasse* and *Handbook of Rocky Mountain Plants.*